Howard Barker

PLAYS THREE

CLAW

URSULA

HE STUMBLED

THE LOVE OF A GOOD MAN

OBERON BOOKS

LONDON

First published in this collection in 2008
by Oberon Books Ltd
521 Caledonian Road, London N7 9RH
Tel: 020 7607 3637 / Fax: 020 7607 3629
e-mail: info@oberonbooks.com
www.oberonbooks.com

Claw first published in Great Britain by John Calder (Publishers)
Ltd in 1977; *Ursula* first published in Great Britain by John Calder
(Publishers) Ltd in 2001; *He Stumbled* first published in Great
Britain by John Calder (Publishers) Ltd in 1998; *The Love of a Good
Man* first published in Great Britain by John Calder (Publishers)
Ltd in 1980

A catalogue record for this book is available from the British
Library.

ISBN: 978 1 84002 676 4

Cover image and design: Dan Steward

Printed in Great Britain by Antony Rowe Ltd, Chippenham.

Contents

CLAW

An Odyssey

Characters

MRS BILEDEW
a Woman of London

BILEDEW
her Husband

NOEL BILEDEW
her Son

NORA
an Ally

POLICEMAN

CHRISTINE
a Waitress

FIRST ASSASSIN

SECOND ASSASSIN

CLAPCOTT
a Minister of State

ANGIE
his Wife

POLICE MOTORCYCLIST

SPECIAL BRANCH OFFICER

LILY
a Male Nurse

LUBSY
a Male Nurse

ACT ONE

SCENE 1

Widely scattered across the stage, bricks and rubble. Enter, scruffily dressed and holding a baby and a suitcase, MRS BILEDEW. The baby is crying. She picks her way over the bricks, looks around, bends down and extracts from the rubbish a framed wedding photograph. She blows the dust off it, stands it up against some masonry.

MRS BILEDEW: Shut up, miserable little bleeder! (*She looks at the child.*) Horrible yellow muck caked round your eyes… (*Pause.*) Makes you feel sick. (*She puts the baby down on the ground.*) Well, here we are. Unpack. Spread out your little treasures. Vera Biledew has come home. (*The baby cries.*) With a little nuisance picked up on the way. (*Pause.*) Well, was I supposed to go without for five whole years? Was he going without? Like hell he was. Got bastards all the way across the continent. (*Pause.*) Well, would have had, if he hadn't got captured at Dunkirk. (*She kneels down and begins unpacking the suitcase, spreading out little items along the ground, a hand mirror, lighter, clock, hairbrush.*) To start off with he'll want to bash my face in. I expect I'll lose a few teeth, maybe get my arm broken. Then he'll just get used to it. Or piss off altogether, I don't know. If he stays I'll have to have half a dozen kids of his, just to make up for it. And when he's lying on top of me I'll have to say, 'Oh, no, you're killing me!' For a few months, anyway. He always wanted to think I was dying. Pleased him. (*The child cries again.*) All right, we're home!
(*She carries on unpacking.*
Enter left, in battered army uniform, VICTOR BILEDEW. He keeps his hands in his pockets, kicks the floor resentfully. Then he watches her coldly for a few seconds.)
BILEDEW: I should kick your head in.
MRS BILEDEW: (*Looks up.*) You look well, Vic. (*Pause.*)
BILEDEW: You never wrote.

MRS BILEDEW: Nothing to say…

BILEDEW: Five years behind barbed wire! (*Pause.*)

MRS BILEDEW: You know what I'm like with letters…I started one…then I left it…I meant to pick it up again…it's here somewhere… (*She starts to look.*)

BILEDEW: Don't bother.

MRS BILEDEW: No… (*She smiles.*) Well, I'm here now…
(*Pause. BILEDEW looks at the baby.*)

BILEDEW: Whose is that? (*Pause.*)

MRS BILEDEW: Ours. (*Pause.*)

BILEDEW: Ours?

MRS BILEDEW: (*Aside.*) I could lie to him. I could say I found it in the ruins of a house, after a raid, clinging to its dead mother's tits… (*Pause. She turns back to him.*) Whose do you think?

BILEDEW: Jesus… (*Pause.*)

MRS BILEDEW: We'll get a prefab, I expect. On the edge of the common. The house was damp, if you remember. I'm not sorry it got blitzed. Apart from your mum, that was sad…
(*Pause.*)

BILEDEW: Oh, Christ…

MRS BILEDEW: (*Looks up at him.*) Victor… (*Pause.*) Come on, Victor…swallow your pride…
(*He sways slightly, eyes closed.*
She watches him, then goes back to her work, emptying the suitcase.)
Munitions work was horrible. But I saved a few quid. Put it in the post office.
(*BILEDEW walks over to where the child is lying, gazes down at it. Slowly, deliberately, he bends down and picks up a brick.*)
My skin went funny, and I was nearly in an accident. They reckoned twenty girls died in that blast. And hundreds without arms and legs.
(*BILEDEW is motionless, holding the brick, gazing at the child.*)
The boss went to the funeral. He was crying, I was surprised to see. But we got the day off. That was nice.

12

(*Suddenly* BILEDEW *throws the brick aside. She turns to him. He is weeping bitterly, silently. Pause.*)

You better go down for the ration books.

(*Pause and spotlight on* NOEL BILEDEW, *in a silver suit and thick-lensed spectacles.*)

NOEL: So I was saved, not for the first time, from a violent death, and the old man spared the guilt of child murder, which knowing him and his appetite for misery, would undoubtedly have led him to hang himself, or swallow glass, or something very loud and obvious. (*He goes out. Pause.*)

MRS BILEDEW: Victor never did hit me. But he never spoke to Noel.

BILEDEW: Why Noel?

MRS BILEDEW: *In Which We Serve.*

BILEDEW: What?

MRS BILEDEW: *In Which We Serve.*

BILEDEW: I've been behind barbed wire for five years.

MRS BILEDEW: Noël Coward. A week before he popped out I was taken to the flicks. And there was Noël. It just seemed obvious.

(*Pause.* BILEDEW *nods. She looks at him.*)

Some feller took me to the flicks.

BILEDEW: You said. (*Pause.*)

MRS BILEDEW: A bloke, Victor.

(*Long pause.* BILEDEW *doesn't react.*)

Be jealous, Victor! Knock me round the head. (*Pause.*) For your own good... (*Pause.*)

BILEDEW: On Tuesdays we played football in the yard. I was goalie. English and Poles versus Americans. The ball was made of rags tied up with string. Somebody kicked it very wide. It rolled, and stopped half across the white line where the guard patrolled. No prisoner was allowed across the line. It was a rule. But they all shouted at me, go on Victor, don't hang about. So I went up to the line and stood there and waited, just in case. But they all kept on at me, just pick it up! So I leant over and picked it up. (*Pause.*) And the guard came. And he kicked me in the privates. (*Pause. He starts to roll a cigarette.*

MRS BILEDEW shrugs, looks at the baby.)
We can't have kids.
(*Pause. She looks at him.*)
I can't. (*Long pause.*)

MRS BILEDEW: All right, Victor. We won't have kids. Now go and get the ration books. (*Pause, then he slowly walks out right.*)
(*An armchair, a paraffin heater, a fireplace, are brought on and assembled like a room. MRS BILEDEW attends to the paraffin heater.*
Enter NOEL, in shorts, school blazer, and thick-rimmed glasses.
He stands with his hand in his pockets.)

NOEL: Coronation just went by.

MRS BILEDEW: Did it?

NOEL: Loads of horses. Coppers with funny outfits on.

MRS BILEDEW: Pass us the paraffin.

NOEL: (*Handing her a can.*) When they'd gone there was horse-muck everywhere. People went and picked it up. Put it in their handkerchiefs…

MRS BILEDEW: Worth money that is. Find some matches.

NOEL: At school they gave us a pencil and a mug. They said always to treasure 'em, even when the lead ran out. They said I was to put the mug on the mantelpiece.

MRS BILEDEW: I'm not stopping you. (*Pause.*)

NOEL: I've got thirty of 'em.

MRS BILEDEW: Thirty mugs!

NOEL: I did a swap.

MRS BILEDEW: What for?

NOEL: A look.

MRS BILEDEW: At what?

NOEL: Joan Preston. Behind the lavatories.

MRS BILEDEW: You dirty little sod!

NOEL: I gave her half!

MRS BILEDEW: You give 'em back!

NOEL: I got you thirty mugs!

MRS BILEDEW: (*Grabbing him.*) You take 'em back!

NOEL: You always say we haven't got no china.

MRS BILEDEW: You heard me. Take 'em back.

NOEL: (*Pulling free.*) No. (*Long pause. They glare at one another.*)

MRS BILEDEW: No point in giving 'em back now, I s'pose…?

NOEL: Course not. I'll get 'em in. (*He goes out, returns with a cardboard box full of Coronation mugs, and begins lining them up on the mantelpiece.*) All right, aren't they?
(*As NOEL stands admiring them, enter BILEDEW, with a newspaper. He sits in the armchair, reads. Gradually his eyes travel to the mantelpiece. Pause.*)

BILEDEW: What's that?

MRS BILEDEW: What?

BILEDEW: Them.

MRS BILEDEW: Mugs. (*She turns to NOEL.*) Did you get them matches? Like an iceberg in this house.

BILEDEW: What mugs?

MRS BILEDEW: Never mind about the mugs. Have you got a job or not?

BILEDEW: I had offers.

MRS BILEDEW: And you accepted them?
(*Pause. BILEDEW is still staring at the mugs.*)

BILEDEW: Considering.

MRS BILEDEW: Blimey! Six months on the dole and you're –

BILEDEW: (*Angrily.*) Considering! (*Pause.*) No rush…

MRS BILEDEW: Give us three quid. No, make it four.

BILEDEW: What for?

MRS BILEDEW: Coal. Food. Electricity.

BILEDEW: I can't.

MRS BILEDEW: And you're considering! He goes out, he comes home with a tea service. You go out, you come home with nothing. He's nine. How old are you?

BILEDEW: Nicked!

MRS BILEDEW: Not nicked, so there! Fair deal!
(*Pause. BILEDEW looks back at his paper.*)

BILEDEW: I'm not a workhorse. I've got a life. (*Pause.*)

MRS BILEDEW: (*Aside.*) I should have stayed in Birmingham. I had offers. We might have had a car by now, me and whoever I was with. A Vauxhall with a sunroof, and them white wall tyres…matches!
(*NOEL runs out.*)

SCENE 2

Lights up on BILEDEW, *standing alone before the fireplace.*

BILEDEW: I met this feller. And he said had I read *Das Kapital.*
Das what? I said. About the oppression of the working
man, he said. No, I hadn't read it. Read it, he says. All
right, I start. I get the first line, and then the second line.
The third line I'm not so sure of, but I carry on. The fourth
line I skip. I know odd words, the sense I haven't got. I
skip the next two lines. I give up that paragraph. I carry
on. I can't get it – the second paragraph, that is. I turn over.
Now I'm angry. I skip that page, and start another, but I
don't know what it's all about, I'm lost now, I am fucking
angry, I am so fucking angry I throw it on the bloody floor!
(*Pause.*) It stays there. She doesn't move it. I don't move
it. Gets tea stains on the cover. Papers put on top of it. But
it's still there…niggling me. I'm sitting there, I look at it,
from a distance, then I get up, I pick it up, I open it, and
start again. I get the first line, and then the second line.
The third line I'm not sure of, and the fourth line – I'm so
bloody ignorant! (*Pause.*) So I go back to this feller. I cannot
read *Das Kapital,* I say. I'm ignorant. And he holds out the
Manifesto of the Communist Party. No thanks. It's short, he
says. I'll go through it with you. And for half an hour after
dinner he goes through it with me. Daily. In the canteen.
In all that racket. Karl Marx's words…
(*Enter MRS BILEDEW.*)

MRS BILEDEW: Noel's been expelled.

BILEDEW: (*Indifferently.*) Go on…

MRS BILEDEW: Chucked out of school!

BILEDEW: I saw it coming. It had to happen.

MRS BILEDEW: Get him a job.

BILEDEW: What as?

MRS BILEDEW: Apprentice him.

BILEDEW: I'm not the Personnel Manager.

MRS BILEDEW: You're in with the shop steward.

BILEDEW: We're friends.

MRS BILEDEW: Help him!

(*Enter NOEL, in a leather jacket, some sizes too large. He stands, hands in pockets.*
She turns to him.)

You silly sod. (*Pause.*) A week before your O-levels!

NOEL: No future in it. The accumulation of qualifications is a blind alley, as far as I can see.

MRS BILEDEW: On his expulsion form they called him deceitful. Said he hid behind his spectacles! Said he used his handicap as a means of challenging authority!

NOEL: Gym teacher confiscated my camera...

MRS BILEDEW: Apparently he took pictures of girls in the showers.

NOEL: They were flattered. They were queuing up to volunteer.

MRS BILEDEW: He was selling 'em to newsagents.

BILEDEW: Why tell me! I saw it coming.

(*They glare at one another.*)

MRS BILEDEW: Well, what are you going to do?

NOEL: I want some tea. And then I'll think about my future. Whether I shall make the effort to be a good citizen. Or drop coppers down manholes, rev my motorbike round village squares and prey on old men coming home from betting shops.

(*Pause. BILEDEW is looking at him as he relishes the image.*
MRS BILEDEW goes out to make tea.)

BILEDEW: To what end?

(*An astonished silence.*
Slowly NOEL turns to look at BILEDEW, mouth agape. Pause.)

NOEL: Blimey! (*Pause.*) He spoke! (*Pause.*) To me! (*Pause.*) He spoke! (*He rushes to the door.*) Phone a doctor! Get an ambulance! He's speaking to me!

(*Enter MRS BILEDEW.*)

Listen! (*He holds a finger to his lips, goes up to BILEDEW and cupping his ear, puts it up to BILEDEW's face. Pause, expectantly.*)

BILEDEW: Waste.

NOEL: Hear that!

MRS BILEDEW: (*Delighted.*) Victor, I'm so glad! (*She goes towards him, arms outstretched.*)

BILEDEW: Clear off!

MRS BILEDEW: (*Repulsed.*) Oh dear...

BILEDEW: Leave us alone.

(*Pause. Then she goes out, looking at NOEL.*
For some time NOEL and BILEDEW just look at one another.)

You're not my son.

NOEL: That had dawned on me.

BILEDEW: Even your mother doesn't know who your father was.

NOEL: I'm not bothered. Maybe I never had one. Maybe I'm immaculate.

BILEDEW: From the moment I set eyes on you I hated you. I wished you dead. When you had scarlet fever I went to the church and prayed. Not for you.

NOEL: No…

BILEDEW: Against you.

NOEL: Right.

BILEDEW: I hoped the devil would hear me and carry you off.

NOEL: I think he's rather fond of me.

BILEDEW: You ruined my happiness. For sixteen years I've looked at you and felt murder in my heart.

NOEL: Nice character…

BILEDEW: You felt it, did you? Scorching you across the breakfast table? Coming through the wall at nights from the bedroom where I was sweating in the dark?

NOEL: I'm used to being hated. From the first day I went to the infants school they had it in for me. Because of these. (*He touches his glasses.*) They never gave me a chance. They never said, Noel, what are you good at? What stamps do you collect? Will you be in our team, Noel? They hated me. Straight off. Like a disease.

BILEDEW: I pitied you.

NOEL: Don't strain yourself.

BILEDEW: Even while I hated you.

NOEL: Yeah, well – no surprises so far, then.

BILEDEW: I haven't come to my point yet.

NOEL: Oh… (*Pause.*)

BILEDEW: I am right, am I not, in believing you to be resentful?

(*NOEL shrugs.*)

You are angry, Noel. Correct me if I'm wrong.

(*He shrugs again.*)

Well, what I'm saying is, I don't think you should waste
your anger. Don't pour away your precious anger, Noel.
Use it. (*Pause.*) For the workers.

NOEL: (*Looks at him, curiously.*) Workers?

BILEDEW: Your people. Your own class.

NOEL: Come on –

BILEDEW: They need your anger –

NOEL: They can have it!

BILEDEW: Serve them!

NOEL: Serve who? The sods who hid my glasses so I wandered
round the playground with my hands outstretched, calling
out 'Boss-eyes' and 'Blind git' and making me fall on my
face? Help them! I was never Noel to them, just Four Eyes,
who always managed to step in their puke! (*Pause.*)

BILEDEW: All the more reason to assist in their improvement,
Noel. In an unjust society, the weak will always be the
persecuted. Just as they brutalised you, so they are
brutalised by the system. But when the system falls, so will
all forms of cruelty, and boys with bad eyesight will be
loved, even by their cuckolded stepfathers… (*Pause.*)

NOEL: Too late for me…

BILEDEW: Avenge yourself… (*Pause.*)

NOEL: (*Turning to the audience.*) So there I was, at sixteen,
thinking about the uprising of the proletariat, and
wondering, if the old man had a point, how I was to lead
them to the light, cast off their chains and so on, and
channel my hatred into the appropriate political response.
(*He has now taken off his jacket and extends his arms.*
Enter MRS BILEDEW, holding another jacket, which she slips
on him. As she does so, she notices a badge on the lapel.)

MRS BILEDEW: What's this!

NOEL: A badge.

MRS BILEDEW: Don't come it! What's it mean?

NOEL: Young Communists.

(*Pause. Then she rips it off.*)

My badge!

MRS BILEDEW: (*Tossing it across the stage.*) Don't let me catch you going near that lot again!

NOEL: Why not?

MRS BILEDEW: Join a youth club if you must go out.

NOEL: I like it there.

MRS BILEDEW: You like them? You like low characters who want to make the world as miserable as them?

NOEL: They like me there. They call me Trotsky. Because of these. (*He touches his glasses.*)

MRS BILEDEW: Noel…you could do well…get away from this…you've got brains, not like the old man…he's got nothing…he's dried up…in bed, lying beside him, it's like lying with a corpse… (*Pause.*) No need for you to be like that. You can get out of it. Don't waste yourself. Be free…
(*Enter NORA, a girl of seventeen.*)

NORA: 'ello.

NOEL: Nora…

NORA: Coming down the YCL?

NOEL: Dunno.

NORA: Haven't seen you.

NOEL: Haven't been.

NORA: Why not?
(*He shrugs.*
She looks at him, grinning.)
Trotsky!
(*She laughs.*
He laughs, feebly. Pause.)

MRS BILEDEW: Did you want something!

NORA: Not specially. (*Pause.*) Oh, well… (*She is about to go.*)

NOEL: I s'pose – (*He looks at his mother.*) Going out for a bit. Fresh air.
(*Without waiting for her response he goes out behind NORA.*
MRS BILEDEW watches ruefully. Pause.)

BILEDEW: Crushing him. (*Pause.*) What he has. (*Pause.*) Crushing him.

MRS BILEDEW: Saving him. For better things.

BILEDEW: You hope.

MRS BILEDEW: You can't have him. You've had me. You've parked your corpse on me for sixteen years, squeezing the joy out of me. But you're not having him. Oh, no.
(*Pause. BILEDEW looks at the oil heater.*)

BILEDEW: Needs some more paraffin. It's flickering.
(*MRS BILEDEW goes out.*)

SCENE 3

A bombsite. Enter NOEL and NORA. They stand around.

NOEL: Dismal. Our surroundings. Highly dismal.

NORA: Rather live here than in the flats.

NOEL: I like the flats. From the flats you see over the top of the power station. And beyond that, the little lights of Chelsea restaurants…

NORA: We'll burn down Chelsea.

NOEL: You will.

NORA: And you.

NOEL: The time's not ripe.

NORA: Maybe…

NOEL: So in the meantime, you exploit your opportunities.

NORA: But when the time's ripe –

NOEL: It's not ripe –

NORA: WHEN it is –

NOEL: We'll see. (*He walks up and down. She sits on a wall.*) What's your considered opinion on free love?

NORA: Favourable.

NOEL: I mean, the sanctity of marriage, for example? What's your view?

NORA: A capitalist convention, based on property.

NOEL: That's what I think. (*Pause.*) Fancy coming into business with me?

NORA: Business?

NOEL: Trade.

NORA: Dirty word.

NOEL: All right – exchange of goods or services. No exploitation of the masses.

NORA: How do you mean?

NOEL: Modelling. (*Pause.*)

NORA: How do you mean?

NOEL: Going with men.

NORA: (*Getting up.*) You filthy bastard.

NOEL: Well, you have.

NORA: Have I?

NOEL: The YCL.

NORA: Have I?

NOEL: Come on, been through the YCL – apart from me.

NORA: Have I?

NOEL: Money for jam!

(*Pause. NORA looks at him coldly.*)

NORA: You disgusting little parasite.

NOEL: Look, I don't want to die in this bloody hole, I don't want to be like my old man or like the silly bleeders in the YCL, all waiting, waiting, waiting till the time is ripe, I don't want to see the bright lights through the power station smoke if the wind should happen to be favourable, I want to be there, Nora, I want to be there squatting on their faces, spitting my acid in their eyes!

NORA: (*Just looks at him.*) Don't come to the YCL. We won't acknowledge you. (*She turns, starts to go out.*)

NOEL: This is a political action!

(*She stops, her back to him.*)

This isn't theory. This isn't arguing the toss for the millionth time in the Battersea cell of the world revolutionary party. This is action, this is carrying anthrax into their woolly nests!

(*Pause. NORA turns, looks at him for some seconds.*)

NORA: And what's my share?

NOEL: Halves.

NORA: No. (*Pause.*)

NOEL: All right. Sixty-forty.

NORA: (*Grinning.*) Rip their soiled knickers down!

NOEL: Hero of Labour!

NORA: How do we start?

NOEL: Right here. Tonight. Start small and local, then spread our wings.

NORA: There aren't any bourgeois in this street.

NOEL: Of course not. This is just for the experience.

NORA: (*Taking a deep breath.*) All right.

NOEL: First geezer comes along, I proposition him.

NORA: Suppose he's horrible?

NOEL: Got to start somewhere, haven't we? No point in alienating ourselves because of some aesthetic prejudice. This is an apprenticeship. (*NORA shrugs, unwilling.*) First geezer. And no chickening out. Now get behind that wall, all right?

NORA: (*Looking astonished.*) Can't do it in the street, can we? It's illegal.

(*Pause. Then she holds out her hand. He helps her over the wall.*)

NOEL: Comfortable?

NORA: It's filthy in here!

NOEL: Oh, Christ…

NORA: Suppose there's rats?

NOEL: (*Impatiently.*) No rats! (*Pause.*) Now just hold on.

NORA: It's dark.

NOEL: Shut up. (*He walks up and down, hands in pockets, whistling.*)

NORA: Maybe we should have gone up to town…

NOEL: There's someone coming. Get ready! (*There are measured footsteps offstage, then they stop and a torch flashes, finds NOEL.*) Hello?

NORA: Who, me?

(*Enter a POLICEMAN. He goes to within a couple of feet of NOEL, the torch still on him.*)

PC: What's your game?

NOEL: Nothing.

PC: Oh. Like bombsites, do you?

NOEL: They're all right.

(*Pause. Then they both start speaking at once and stop. Pause.*)

PC: I'm not keeping you.

NOEL: No… (*He doesn't move.*)

PC: (*Looking closer.*) What's the matter with your eyes?

NOEL: Nothing.

PC: (*Looking closer.*) Can you see?

NOEL: Yeah.

PC: (*Taking a step backward, then another.*) Tell me when I go out of focus.

NOEL: What's this –

PC: Just interested. (*He takes more steps.*) Now? (*Another step.*) Now? Don't tell me you can see me now!

NOEL: Look here –

PC: Don't get shirty. Just never seen lenses like them before. Terrible drawback. Eyes like fish in goldfish bowls…

NOEL: (*Under pressure.*) Do you like girls?

(*Pause. The POLICEMAN walks back, stands close to NOEL.*)

PC: What did you say?

NOEL: Do you like girls?

PC: (*Coldly.*) Don't be impertinent, Four Eyes.

NOEL: If you want one…she's yours for a quid… (*Long pause.*)

PC: Who is?

NOEL: Over there. (*Pause.*)

PC: Not your game, this, is it, son?

NOEL: Not really…

PC: New to it. Importuning me. Must be new to it.

NOEL: A quid. (*Pause.*)

PC: Your girlfriend, is it? (*He nods in the direction of the wall.*) Over the wall? (*NOEL nods.*) New to it, is she? (*NOEL nods.*) BRAND new?

(*NOEL nods again. Pause. The POLICEMAN reaches into his inside pockets, takes out his wallet and hands over a pound note. Then he surreptitiously goes to the wall, and looking either way quickly, hops over it. NOEL wipes his mouth nervously.*)

NOEL: So I did it. I had proved to myself I could do it. There was nothing could stop me going on. To bigger things. I was down for Chelsea. With my first pound note! (*He holds it up to the light, smiles, then takes out his own wallet and slips it in.*) Tell her it was ten bob. After all that risk.

(*He puts the wallet away.*

The POLICEMAN reappears, slowly climbing over the wall. NOEL looks up.)

All right?

(*The POLICEMAN approaches him, then suddenly punches him savagely in the stomach.*

NOEL collapses at once with a small groan and lies still on the ground.

The POLICEMAN removes NOEL's wallet and, taking the pound note, tosses the wallet on the ground.)

PC: Importuning me. Four Eyes.

NORA: How could you! Of all the people in the world, you had to pick that – lumpenproletariat! I froze. My flesh was creeping. I felt so degraded. How could you degrade me with a class enemy like that!

NOEL: (*Weakly.*) My glasses…

NORA: I'm contaminated…

NOEL: I'm hurt.

NORA: Good. And give me my cut.

NOEL: I can't.

NORA: All right, I'll take your jacket until you give me what you owe me. (*She strips off his jacket and starts walking away.*)

NOEL: I'll freeze!

NORA: Hooray!

(She goes out.

NOEL gradually sits up, feels around for his glasses, finds them, puts them on. He climbs to his feet, stands swaying a few moments.)

NOEL: He hit me! I was struck! I won't be struck! Never again will I be struck, I vow that! (*He sobs with anger, clenching his fists, then raises an arm to the sky.*) I'll tear their skin off first, I'll rip their faces off their skulls, I'll be a great claw ripping them, slitting their bellies like ripe fruits! Hear me, formerly Trotsky of the YCL, declare it on this night, note it in your calendars, I'll claw them first!

SCENE 4

The tea room of a department store. A table with silverware and stiff white tablecloth. Two cane chairs. As lights come on, MRS BILEDEW, dressed in an ill-fitting item of haute-couture, is waltzing around with an imaginary partner. She revolves for some moments, then as the tune comes to an end, she stops, claps, and returns to her seat, where she sits with a distinctly lonely and bored expression. She pours herself a cup of tea. Enter WAITRESS with a tray laden with pastries. MRS

*BILEDEW points to several, which are transferred to her plate. The
WAITRESS goes out.*

MRS BILEDEW: Every afternoon. At Fortnum's. Waited on.
Then at five, collected by taxi, and driven home, bursting
with pastries. Belching angelica and glacé cherries. Burping
double Devon cream. (*She bites into a cream puff. The voice of
BILEDEW is heard.*)

BILEDEW: Where's the money coming from, that's what I'd
like to know.

MRS BILEDEW: Here they treat you like you're someone. Pick
up your cream horn if you drop it. And give you another
one.

BILEDEW: Crime! Profits of crime!

MRS BILEDEW: Shut up, Biledew!

BILEDEW: Sordid gains of criminal activities!

MRS BILEDEW: I'll sort you out when I get home! (*Pause.*) Can't
say I've made that many friends, though I'm on nodding
terms with the other regulars. It's the surroundings, the
chandeliers, this lovely linen, and the music…it's like a
dream…
(*Enter NOEL, in a leather jacket emblazoned with a huge red
claw. He grabs a chair and sits back to front on it.*)

NOEL: Claw's here.

MRS BILEDEW: (*Shocked.*) Don't sit like that!

NOEL: Why not?

MRS BILEDEW: In here!

NOEL: S'all right.

MRS BILEDEW: I have to sit here every day.

NOEL: Go to Harrods. Go to Freebody's.

MRS BILEDEW: Please, Noel… (*Reluctantly he gets up, turns the
chair round, and sits facing the table, but begins tipping it back on
its back legs. She watches him.*) I don't think you should visit
me.

NOEL: Why not?

MRS BILEDEW: Uncouth. (*Pause.*) You'll break that chair… Your
father thinks you're in crime… (*Pause.*) Are you in crime?
(*NOEL looks at her.
The WAITRESS enters.*)

CHRISTINE: Yes, please?

NOEL: (*Looks her up and down. Pause.*) What's your name?

CHRISTINE: Christine.

NOEL: You could do better, Christine.

MRS BILEDEW: Take no notice of him.

CHRISTINE: Do you want tea?

NOEL: Show me your thighs.

(*CHRISTINE walks smartly away. He looks after her.*)

MRS BILEDEW: You disgusting beast! What are people going to think of me! I'm happy here, don't ruin it for me.

(*Pause. NOEL shrugs. Pause. He tips his chair back, taps a spoon on a plate.*)

NOEL: Don't expect I'll see much of you in the future.

MRS BILEDEW: (*Surprised.*) Why?

NOEL: Social mobility.

MRS BILEDEW: I'm your mother.

NOEL: I'm moving on.

MRS BILEDEW: You have moved on.

NOEL: Further.

MRS BILEDEW: (*Suddenly distraught.*) You're my boy…

NOEL: I'll send you hampers.

MRS BILEDEW: How could you –

NOEL: This table's yours – in perpetuity.

MRS BILEDEW: Noel, please –

(*Suddenly, angrily, NOEL thumps the table with his fist, making the crockery jump. There is a silence. The WAITRESS appears.*)

CHRISTINE: Yes, please?

NOEL: (*Looking at her.*) Christine, do you want to earn fabulous wages? Do you want to own more things? Eat out with celebrities?

(*She walks away again. Pause.*)

MRS BILEDEW: Don't leave me with the old man…please… I couldn't bear it…stuck with him…his dead face – the television droning on…I'm not young any more. Noel… (*Pause.*) I carried you down the A1 on my back.

NOEL: As an investment? As a maturing policy?

MRS BILEDEW: I'm human, Noel!

NOEL: Don't boast about it! (*Pause.*)

MRS BILEDEW: You don't…love me…at all, then. (*Pause.*) You
    don't feel anything…
    (*Suddenly, angrily, NOEL thumps the table with his fist again,
    shaking the crockery.*
    The WAITRESS enters.)

CHRISTINE: Yes!
    (*Pause. NOEL looks at her.*)

NOEL: Can you simulate an orgasm?

MRS BILEDEW: Here, what is this?

CHRISTINE: (*Looks at him, weighing him up.*) What's it worth?

NOEL: Prosperity. Draw up a chair.

MRS BILEDEW: What about me?

NOEL: In a minute.
    (*The WAITRESS drags a chair to the table.*
    MRS BILEDEW experiences a moment of clarity.)

MRS BILEDEW: You are mixed up with criminals!

BILEDEW: I told you so!

NOEL: This is purely a formality, Christine. I'm afraid I need
    to see your thighs.

MRS BILEDEW: You dirty minded little sod!

BILEDEW: This is where your cream horns come from!

CHRISTINE: (*As she pulls up her skirt.*) I take it this is high-class
    modelling. I don't want any of your common clientele.

NOEL: Nothing beneath a barrister.

CHRISTINE: How's that?

NOEL: All right.

CHRISTINE: Only all right?

NOEL: I don't expect you'll make Miss World.

CHRISTINE: I do not wish to be Miss World. I'm after a decent
    income like anybody else.

MRS BILEDEW: Noel are you living off…of girls? (*Distraught, she
    rises to her feet, speaks out to the audience.*) I could have ripped
    the clothes off me, I could have chucked my handbag,
    crocodile skin shoes and silk gloves in the gutter. I could
    have washed my mouth out with carbolic soap, I felt so
    sick and weary, so let down and dirty… (*Pause.*)

BILEDEW: I told you so…

MRS BILEDEW: And then I thought...what's done is done. There is no justice or I would have got my rewards long before now. What am I getting so high and mighty for, I had my little bit of happiness from his bad ways, this table in Fortnum and Mason's all due to him, not from the government or the charity of the rich, but by courtesy of Noel Biledew. You have to take what you can get, I'll pay for it at Judgement Day if I have to. I'm not young. I'll go along with it and what I don't like, shut my eyes to. Lifting my little finger doesn't shake the stars, does it? (*She sits down again.*) Noel –

NOEL: Claw. (*Pause.*)

MRS BILEDEW: What?...

NOEL: My name. Is Claw. (*Pause.*)

MRS BILEDEW: I'm sorry I got difficult.

NOEL: This is Christine. She's signed with me.

MRS BILEDEW: That's nice.

NOEL: Christine. My mum.

CHRISTINE: Pleased to meet you.

NOEL: I have found a niche for mum. She is going to take charge of wardrobes.

MRS BILEDEW: Oh, Noel – I'm so happy. Claw...

NOEL: Christine, order some cakes.

(*CHRISTINE clicks her fingers.*
Enter BILEDEW, holding a large, framed portrait of Karl Marx.
They all gaze at him. He is heaving with emotion. Pause.)
Who let you in?

MRS BILEDEW: This isn't any old tea bar, Biledew.

NOEL: Have you been walking down the streets with that? You must have looked a silly sod.

MRS BILEDEW: Wait for me outside. By the Number 68 bus stop. Quickly! Go on!

(*BILEDEW sways on his feet, as if intoxicated with grief.*)

BILEDEW: He weeps!

NOEL: (*To CHRISTINE.*) Cream slice?

BILEDEW: You betray him! You worms, crawling on the sweet carcass, you maggots in the watery filth!

CHRISTINE: Horrible old thing!

MRS BILEDEW: Biledew, you are embarrassing us in front of other people.

CHRISTINE: That's the idea. We get a lot of it in here. Show-offs, hippies, them bald-headed monks and that...

NOEL: Pull up a chair.

CHRISTINE: (*Shrinking.*) No thanks!

MRS BILEDEW: Biledew, go home!

BILEDEW: I have come here on a mission. To destroy degeneracy.

NOEL: Haven't you misread the texts?

BILEDEW: How would you know?

NOEL: I have had acquaintance with the works. It seems to me the point of old weirdbeard's diagnosis was to hasten the corruption, not run after it with a dustpan and broom. Which confers on me the status of a hero, so sit down and shut your gob.

MRS BILEDEW / CHRISTINE: Hear, hear.

BILEDEW: Oh, rancid worm, bred under my own roof –

NOEL: (*Rising to his feet.*) Not worm! Jaguar! Swift disemboweller of lazy herds! Red claw in the intestines of the overfed!

(*BILEDEW glares at him, trembling, then with a cry of 'Bastard!', he brings down the heavy portrait on NOEL's head. There are screams from MRS BILEDEW and CHRISTINE, the lights go out and the 'Internationale' erupts, then ceases.*)

SCENE 5

BILEDEW is alone on stage, hands hanging at his sides, under a spotlight.

BILEDEW: Watching him at breakfast, I couldn't force the food down me for thinking how he was conceived in some bedroom, some room in some street somewhere in Birmingham, some room which is still there with the same wallpaper for all I know, and how she lay there under him moaning all night or afternoon for all I know with her clothes across a chair, or chucked on the floor because of their hurry and how he had all he wanted from her, pushing her like some warm thing against the wall, that

30

same wallpaper still there in that room in the middle of that city somewhere where it happened on that night…
(*He dries.*
The voice of the MAGISTRATE *is heard.*)

MAGISTRATE: Had the attack occurred in some back street, in some low dive or public house, I would feel less disposed to allow my indignation to affect my judgement, but you calculatedly and deliberately chose to carry out this deed before the eyes of gentle and inoffensive persons taking tea, and I can only assume you did so in the furtherance of some misguided notion of class conflict, as the blunt instrument employed suggests. I am therefore withdrawing any influence of clemency that might have mollified my judgement. I sentence you to seven years.
(*Pause.*)

BILEDEW: I…I…my wife…during the war…in some bedroom with…the wallpaper…it's floral, I see it now…big roses with…

MAGISTRATE: Take him down.

BILEDEW: In Birmingham…I craved to know…what room it was…what window…was there running water in the room…

MAGISTRATE: Go down!
(*BILEDEW is silent for a moment, gathers himself together. Suddenly he bursts out singing the 'Red Flag' noisily and out of tune.*)
Go down! Take him down!

SCENE 6

The BILEDEW *home. Lying on a couch,* NOEL, *his head bandaged. A door slams off.*

MRS BILEDEW: (*Off.*) Claw! Claw!

NOEL: I'm kipping.

MRS BILEDEW: (*Entering, in coat.*) Biledew got seven years!

NOEL: Not bad.

MRS BILEDEW: Seven years!

NOEL: Not bad. For attempted filicide.

31

MRS BILEDEW: The poor old sod…my heart went out to him, he looked so frail beside the policeman, so hunched and undernourished. I expect people thought I never fed him properly. (*She takes her coat off.*) Seven years in some damp cell, with God knows who for company. He never had much comfort, never knew real luxury, always said no to an electric blanket or a bottle in the bed.

NOEL: He'll be in good condition for his deprivations, then.

MRS BILEDEW: I wept…I called out to him but he looked right through me…he looked so small… (*She sits in the chair, clasping her knees.*)

NOEL: He might like prison. Reading is encouraged, I believe!

MRS BILEDEW: I'll visit him. And meet him at the little door when he comes out. Can't do more than that, can I? (*She jumps up gaily.*)

NOEL: Scarcely. With your responsibilities.

MRS BILEDEW: I was wondering, what with the vast increase in our turnover, if maybe we weren't – over-extending?

NOEL: Big words for you.

MRS BILEDEW: I mean…you're doing very nicely.

NOEL: Quite adequate.

MRS BILEDEW: You're rich…

NOEL: Relatively.

MRS BILEDEW: You have a car.

NOEL: I have a car.

MRS BILEDEW: That's good going.

NOEL: Good going – That's good going, is it?

MRS BILEDEW: I'm happy, Claw…

NOEL: That's wonderful.

MRS BILEDEW: Be happy too.

NOEL: I will be. Happiness is before me, glowing like the sunset on a choppy sea, drawing me on…

MRS BILEDEW: What to?

NOEL: Chelsea. The love nests of HM Government.

MRS BILEDEW: Oh, Claw, what for?

NOEL: You wouldn't understand. Satisfaction is within arm's reach for you.

MRS BILEDEW: I'm glad.

NOEL: Of course.

MRS BILEDEW: I only thought…for a young man…you have so
little fun…that's all…

NOEL: I'm anticipating it.

MRS BILEDEW: But here…

NOEL: No, not here…just prowling here…

> (*MRS BILEDEW looks at him, pityingly, then turns to go.*)
>
> I have a dream.
>
> (*She stops, in the doorway.*)
>
> To be a sort of Cecil Beaton…in big hats…and white
> suits…with chiffon neckscarves blowing in the wind…on
> beaches in Jamaica…with women and celebrities and flash
> bulbs popping at me…and my memoirs in *The Sunday
> Times.*

MRS BILEDEW: That's nice…

NOEL: And then, in front of everybody…I would disembowel
myself…and chuck my innards in Mick Jagger's gob.

> (*Pause. MRS BILEDEW looks at him, lying there, lost in thought.*)

MRS BILEDEW: I'll put the kettle on. (*She goes out, returns at once
with a tray and puts it down.*) If anybody had told me that
Noel, or Claw, as he prefers to be called, wasn't absolutely
normal I'd have scratched their eyes out. But there is this
matter of that nasty blow, and who knows what effect that
might have on the brain. Still, I'm his mother, and I'll stick
by him.

> (*She goes out.*
>
> *Suddenly there is a sound of splintering glass.*
>
> *Enter right, two ASSASSINS. One holds a megaphone, the
> other a pistol. While one goes methodically through the room
> smashing everything in sight and grinding it under his feet, the
> other, taking up a convenient position, addresses the audience
> through the megaphone.*
>
> *NOEL instantly covers his face.*)

FIRST ASSASSIN: Into the peacefulness of a suburban street,
the rude interruption of a Mafia punishment squad,
hand picked for its ruthlessness and total lack of human
sympathy. No moral code restrains them, no pity glimmers
in their eyes, they are a punishment squad issuing in this

vivid way an unambiguous message: GET OFF OUR PATCH!

(*The FIRST ASSASSIN lowers his megaphone.*
NOEL remains perfectly still, hands over eyes.
Then the SECOND ASSASSIN goes into the kitchen, and drags in a terrified MRS BILEDEW.)

MRS BILEDEW: You've got the wrong house! What have we done?

FIRST ASSASSIN: (*Raising his megaphone.*) Typically the transgressor adopts a policy of injured innocence.

MRS BILEDEW: (*Forced to her knees.*) Don't hurt me! Don't kill me! Don't hurt me, please!

FIRST ASSASSIN: There follows a succession of appeals to the humanity of the assassins, the rejection of which inevitably evokes despair, or sometimes even loss of consciousness.

MRS BILEDEW: (*As the SECOND ASSASSIN levels his pistol.*) Oh, God…

FIRST ASSASSIN: A shot is fired, a signal for the car doors to be opened and the squad to make an orderly retirement to their vehicles.

(*The SECOND ASSASSIN fires one shot, into MRS BILEDEW's hand.*
She screams.
They withdraw.
Sound of car doors slamming and a vehicle roaring away.
MRS BILEDEW gets up, clutching her hand.
NOEL hasn't moved.)

MRS BILEDEW: Bastards! (*She walks about, picking up odd items, dropping them again.*) My home! My things! My little bits I scraped together, not worth nothing, no use to nobody, things I had to struggle for, not much, but my little things! (*She sobs for a few moments.*) Noel…

NOEL: Claw…

MRS BILEDEW: Noel to me!

(*He removes his hands from his eyes.*)

I'm not cleaning this lot up. You can do it. (*She picks up a chair, sits in it.*)

NOEL: I was afraid they'd smash my glasses. People always want to smash my glasses.

MRS BILEDEW: I've been shot!

NOEL: I know…

MRS BILEDEW: Well, do something!

NOEL: (*Getting up.*) I'll get one of the girls.

MRS BILEDEW: I want an ambulance!

NOEL: That's out of the question, you know that.

MRS BILEDEW: I'll bleed to death.

NOEL: Run it under the tap. I won't be long. (*He grabs his overcoat. She goes into the kitchen. He is about to go out when he stops.*) When I heard that shot, I thought – Claw, you are a dead man. Though of course rationally I knew all the time that a bullet travels faster than sound, and were the shot aimed at me I should have heard it only after the impact. But all the same I experienced a great peace, like all the seas had drained away… (*He ponders.*)

MRS BILEDEW: (*Off.*) It hurts!

NOEL: (*Snapping out of his mood, and buttoning his coat.*) This is a sign, of course. This is a clear warning.

(*Enter MRS BILEDEW, her hand wrapped in a tea towel. She sits on the sofa, rocks to and fro.*)

NOT to give in. NOT to scuttle away, but to go higher, use my long strides to bound into the exclusive areas where I belong…

(*Suddenly MRS BILEDEW collapses.*

NOEL looks at her, shocked. He lifts up her legs, laying her along the sofa, puts a cushion under her head and hurries out.

MRS BILEDEW, delirious, talks to herself.)

MRS BILEDEW: Biledew…what have we reared? To think I carried him, down the A1 in that awful winter, hitching lifts with blokes who stuck their hands up me…just to be shot in the hand…

(*Enter NOEL, followed by NORA, altogether more professional in style and manner than her previous appearance. Seeing the room she stops and gasps.*)

NORA: Blimey!

NOEL: She isn't dead.

NORA: What a shambles…

NOEL: See to her!

NORA: (*Gazes round.*) What a going over…

NOEL: Send 'em a postcard with your congratulations on, why don't you?

NORA: Sorry.

NOEL: My old mother has been shot and all you do is stand and gawp!

NORA: (*Quickly sitting beside her on the sofa.*) Sorry. (*She is quite helpless and squeamish.*) How are you? How do you feel?

NOEL: Jesus Christ! Bind up her hand! (*She flusters, looking round.*) Oh, the leadweight of their intellects…and me like lightning on the icecap…

NORA: Is there a bandage in the…?

NOEL: Tear up a sheet. Like they do it on the pictures. And tip some Dettol over it.

(*NORA rushes out.*

NOEL collapses in the chair.

NORA enters, dragging a sheet.)

NORA: Can't tear it.

(*NOEL is motionless.*)

Claw…

(*Pause. He looks at her.*)

Can't tear it.

(*He looks blankly at her for a moment, then gets up, takes the sheet and rips it.*)

Couldn't find the Dettol. Is bleach all right?

NOEL: Kills germs, don't it? That's all we want.

(*They go to MRS BILEDEW and sit beside her.*

NOEL douses her hand with the bleach, then NORA begins tying the bandage. NOEL watches her for some seconds. She ends with a knot.)

NORA: There. Done it.

NOEL: That was nice.

NORA: What?

NOEL: Watching you do that. Gave me funny feelings in my head. (*Pause.*)

NORA: Oh…

NOEL: I never felt that…warm tingling in my head. (*Pause.*)

NORA: Got a client at half past three…

(*Long pause. NOEL looks at her.*)

NOEL: Undress.

NORA: (*Incredulous.*) What?

NOEL: Please. Take your clothes off.

NORA: (*More so.*) What?

NOEL: I'm asking you.

NORA: That's very nice, but I've got a client coming here at –

NOEL: Take 'em off! (*Pause.*)

NORA: No. (*Pause.*)

NOEL: Why not?

NORA: I don't want to.

NOEL: Blimey, you're doing it all bloody day!

NORA: That's for money!

NOEL: All right, I'll pay.

NORA: I couldn't take it.

NOEL: Look, I'm your employer!

NORA: I think that's how it should be left – (*She gets up.*)

NOEL: (*On his feet too.*) Nora!
    (*She stops still. Pause.*)

NORA: I just…I really do not fancy you.
    (*Pause. Now it is he who looks incredulous.*)

NOEL: But you're a prostitute…

NORA: That's different. That's not personal. If you were
    a stranger, I might even do it as a favour, but I am
    acquainted with you, and that puts a different light on it.
    (*Pause.*)

NOEL: Look…I'm not ashamed to admit that I…for various
    reasons I'm not all that…I'm a virgin… (*Pause.*)

NORA: Christ…

NOEL: Funny, ain't it?

NORA: Jesus…

NOEL: So you see, I…if you would be so kind as to allow –

NORA: Oh, no, I couldn't possibly. Not now. It wouldn't be
    right. With me.

NOEL: It would.

NORA: No, not with me. With a nice girl –

NOEL: I don't know one.

NORA: I'm sure you will.

NOEL: Just then – watching you tie that bandage – I felt, I told
    you I felt warm, I never felt like that before, I felt so close
    to you.

NORA: Please, Claw…

NOEL: Call me Noel…

NORA: Out of the question.

NOEL: Look, don't turn me down, please –

NORA: I've got a client. I'm sorry –

NOEL: Please, Nora –

NORA: I'm sorry, no!

> (*She goes out, slams the door.*
> *NOEL staggers to the middle of the stage, his hands slowly*
> *extend in front of him, then in a paroxysm of despair:*)

NOEL: Oh give me wings, give me throttle, melting the tarmac to a sea of fire, the sleeve valves pissing carbon in the frosty air!

> (*There is a roar of a full-throttled motorbike.*
> *His teeth clenched, his eyes half-closed, NOEL mimes riding a*
> *powerful machine along a bumpy road. The roar accelerates*
> *into a climax, there is a sickening skid but instead of a crash,*
> *the thud of a heavy steel door.*
> *NOEL retains a pre-death posture, handlebars askew, jaw*
> *twisted.*
> *Enter, shuffling in prison clothes, BILEDEW. He looks at*
> *NOEL.*)

BILEDEW: Thinks he's T E Lawrence. Wants to rub out with the seedy panache of a hero of imperialism. No such luck. For you, the bitter, hard path of the class struggle, which you are twisting your intestines into knots to miss. You cannot miss! It is written. Your individualist daydreams lead only to the pit of self-disgust.

NOEL: Shut up.

BILEDEW: Wake up – 'Claw'.

NOEL: (*Still retaining posture.*) Shut up. I did not ask you to write to me on your snotty prison notepaper.

BILEDEW: Then read my thoughts.

NOEL: What for!

BILEDEW: Contentment.

NOEL: What's that?

BILEDEW: Contentment is to align yourself with the prevailing flow of history.

NOEL: Done you a lot of good, ain't it?

BILEDEW: I am happy.

NOEL: With your low expectations, happiness was a walkover.

BILEDEW: Must stop now, though I have much more to say.

NOEL: I wasn't going to read it anyway.

BILEDEW: Revolutionaries are the tallow in the candle of our dreams.

NOEL: What?

BILEDEW: I made that up.

NOEL: Who said you were a daft old git?

BILEDEW: (*Going out again, slowly.*) Have love, Noel, have love…

(*The steel door slams.*)

ACT TWO

SCENE 1

The drawing room of an expensive Chelsea residence. CLAPCOTT, a Home Secretary, is seated in an armchair. He is working through a paper, ticking off items. His patience is eroded. Suddenly, he throws back his head.

CLAPCOTT: Paroles, paroles, bloody paroles! Everybody's on parole! (*He looks back at the list, draws a thick line cruelly across a name.*) Well, no! Not you! You stay and rot! (*Pause. He reads on.*) Let you out, you go and murder somebody, makes me look a bloody fool. (*Pause.*) Social workers are in league with 'em. (*He works on.*) More convicts out than in, as far as I can see. (*He ticks, stops, draws a cruel line.*) Not you! Remember you. Swore to castrate the judge if I remember rightly. 'No gaol will hold me!' Loud-mouthed yob. Now crawling on your knees after parole. Loathsome specimen. (*He carries on, stops. He takes some whisky, looks at his watch, yawns, carries on.*) Yes…yes… (*He ticks names.*) Oh, yes…yes…yes…timid little embezzlers… yes…yes…yes… (*He stops.*) Child murderers! What's got into them?! I distinctly said no-one's crucifying me for some itchy-fingered child killer. (*He draws a line through it.*) Impertinence. (*He looks up.*) Wandering round commons with their doodles out, get carried away, impale some infant, costs a fortune finding them. (*Pause.*) My eyes are tired… (*He ticks away, squinting.*) Must get some drops… (*He ticks some more, then impatiently.*) The rest are noes. (*He draws a long, diagonal line through, then drops the file on the floor.*) No gratitude in any case. Don't even have the decency to send a note. Don't expect literacy, just a little gratitude. (*The front door slams.*)

ANGIE: (*Off.*) Oo – oo!

(*CLAPCOTT groans, takes a swig of whisky.*

Enter in long fur-trimmed coat, ANGIE. *She is forty-five,*
bright-eyed, energetic.)

CLAPCOTT: You weren't coming back tonight.

ANGIE: (*Slipping off her coat.*) His wife's in town. He said did I
want a hotel, I said no, let's do without the physicals, he
looked put out, like some schoolboy done out of his afters.
Anyway, I wasn't interested. He looked podgy, I felt sick
after the cassata, he got me a taxi, and here I am. (*She goes*
out with the coat, returns, sits down.)

CLAPCOTT: I was rather planning on being alone tonight.

ANGIE: I'll go to bed.

CLAPCOTT: If you would.

ANGIE: Or do you want it?

CLAPCOTT: The bed? No, I don't want the bed.

ANGIE: Didn't think you would. Never shit on your own
doorstep. That's what you learn at public school.

CLAPCOTT: (*Coldly.*) How would YOU know?

ANGIE: Well, isn't it?

CLAPCOTT: Did you go to public school?

ANGIE: You know bloody well I didn't.

CLAPCOTT: Shut up, then.

ANGIE: Oh, dear. A rotten evening with the prison files. Two
hours with the parole list and you're behaving like an
Eastbourne magistrate.

CLAPCOTT: (*Measured.*) I've been sitting here, quietly engaged
in work involving the hopes and happiness of several
hundred people, my eyes are tired, my mind is full of
doubts of the most serious nature, and you come in, quite
unexpectedly, gibbering like an inebriated whore and
expect me to be entertaining –

ANGIE: Never!

CLAPCOTT: You have been whoring, haven't you? As good as?

ANGIE: (*Icily.*) Never entertaining. Not from the first day that
we met. NEVER ENTERTAINING. (*Pause.*)

CLAPCOTT: You didn't have to marry me.

ANGIE: You pestered me.

CLAPCOTT: You didn't HAVE to marry me.

ANGIE: No…

CLAPCOTT: Well, then.

ANGIE: I was led on. By the insinuations of the press. The burst of flashbulbs blinded my discrimination. It was all too glamorous. And I was all too young, and innocent…

CLAPCOTT: Innocent! At twenty-six? A dancer in a chorus line, too innocent? You went into it wide-eyed with avarice. (*Pause.*)

ANGIE: You wouldn't leave me alone. You never have.

CLAPCOTT: That's my misfortune. It was one of those things.

ANGIE: A ghastly, everlasting, chemical attraction.

CLAPCOTT: I've paid the price.

ANGIE: (*Recollecting.*) The earnest, puppy politician, and the long-legged chorus-girl… (*Suddenly she sits forward.*) Shall we get the cuttings out?

CLAPCOTT: No.

ANGIE: Oh, go on!

CLAPCOTT: (*Glaring at her.*) No.

ANGIE: No… (*Pause.*)

CLAPCOTT: Look, why don't you go to bed?

ANGIE: Who's coming? (*He doesn't answer.*) An expert in ballistics? An authority on urban terrorism? A high-level conference lasting late into the morning… Oh, the bloody glamour of it all… (*With inspiration.*) Can I stay?

CLAPCOTT: No. You cannot.

ANGIE: I'm not tired…

CLAPCOTT: We did agree, I think –

ANGIE: Oh, yes. I don't embarrass you, and you give me a free hand in exchange…

CLAPCOTT: That's fair.

ANGIE: Oh, yes, appallingly. A real political deal.

CLAPCOTT: You've got the country cottage, jammed with second-hand car dealers, Hell's Angels, hippies, Christ knows what, go where you like with who you like, rubber-stamped moral disaster, but at least we keep it civil. All I ask is kindly do not fart around in my sphere. I don't think that's unreasonable.

ANGIE: Oh, no…

CLAPCOTT: You signed a bit of paper.

ANGIE: I know I did. We went together with it to the bank.

CLAPCOTT: Exactly. (*He looks at his watch.*) Now, if you don't mind – I have a visitor.

ANGIE: (*Getting up.*) I know all that, Gee-Gee, but I do sometimes get a little curious…the murmur of political voices in the drawing room, the hum of the conspiracy which keeps the lousy rotten show on the road… (*Pause.*) Can't I sit in?

CLAPCOTT: No.

ANGIE: I wouldn't speak.

CLAPCOTT: This is a top-level –

ANGIE: Well, of course it is!

CLAPCOTT: I don't ask to sit in on your seedy weekends.

ANGIE: No… I will say that for you. You're not a masochist.

CLAPCOTT: Go to bed…

ANGIE: Are you? (*Pause.*)

CLAPCOTT: My work. Above all things. The rest – is rubbish. (*Pause.*) Goodnight.

(*ANGIE starts to go out, stops, turns.*)

ANGIE: You know, you should have divorced me. When the PM told you to. When you were nobody.

(*She goes out.*

He reminisces.)

CLAPCOTT: Third from the end…in the chorus line of *Carousel*…with legs that never ended… I couldn't tear my eyes off her…and hair like copper…when the spotlights caught it…took my breath away…every movement seemed like an appeal to me… We married in St Martins… in February…it was snowing in the wind…newspaper photographers, wetting themselves with anticipation…and she came up the aisle and stood beside me…the organ was still playing and I whispered…what colour are your panties? No colour, she said…what…transparent, I gasped? No…none, she said… I was fainting at the thought of it… (*Pause.*) Prime Minister called me in his office. Old beaver glared at me…half spectacles catching the sunlight filtering through the Horseguards… Georgie, he said, keep a tight rein. I must have looked confused. Your actress, he said.

Got itchy hips… (*Pause.*) She was in the bath…shaving her legs, to be precise…and I went in and said…evidence has reached me, you are carrying on with somebody. Simply. Briefly. Like that. And then she abused me. Consistently abused me, for about half an hour…screaming…breaking things…and at the end of it I locked her in her room…and my nerves were like hot needles…and I went and drank myself silly in the summerhouse… (*Pause.*) And then it became regular. We went to a psychiatrist. She said I was inadequate, which isn't true. At least in my opinion… though I appreciate these things are relative. And then one day, the PM called me in…half spectacles catching the sunlight filtering through the Horseguards…and he said… Georgie, you've got a right one there…unstable marriages…terrible handicaps to promotion in the government. I'm afraid I can't give you the Treasury. I felt a prickling sensation in my eyes…the room was blurred… I was crying… I blinked, desperately blinked. He fobbed me off with Under-Secretary to the Colonial Office, as it was then. I wished to Christ I'd never set eyes on *Carousel*. I wished the whole damned chorus line to buggery. All I wanted was to get home and do the bitch an injury. There she was, shaving her legs. Your whoring, I said, has cost me the Treasury, I remember she just looked at me and one word escaped from her lips. 'Yippee…'
(*He recollects it bitterly for some moments, but his thoughts are interrupted by the door bell. He gets up, goes out.*
Suddenly, conspiratorially, ANGIE *enters in a dressing gown, and with a glance over her shoulder, secretes herself behind the thick velvet curtains.*
CLAPCOTT, *followed by* NOEL, *wearing a well-cut, dark suit and expensive, tinted lenses with gold frames. He is carrying a briefcase. He looks around him, taking everything in.*
CLAPCOTT *turns the key in the lock.*
NOEL *seems surprised.*)
Security. Somebody's always after maiming you, kidnapping you, torturing you. Can't mow the lawn

without some maniac wanting to blow your head off. These are rotten times. Whisky?

NOEL: Thank you.

CLAPCOTT: (*Goes to the bottles.*) Periodical. This loss of faith. Sort of moral vacuum. Just our bad luck to be stuck in the middle of an all-time low. Ice?

NOEL: Thank you.

CLAPCOTT: Took a ten-day course in unarmed combat. Bloody farce. Rolling about on coconut matting in the basement of the Home Office. (*He hands him a drink.*) Everywhere I went I had this police van trailing me, loaded with matting. They unrolled it and I snatched a lesson wherever I happened to be. Got bruises all along my spine. Try me.
(*NOEL looks surprised.*
CLAPCOTT, without waiting for his acquiescence, flings open the small drawer and removes a small pistol.)
Don't worry. Take the bullets out. (*He removes the magazine, throws it on the table. Then he hands the pistol to NOEL.*) Now. Threaten me!
(*NOEL holds it, unconvincingly.*)
Wave it about. Try to hate me. Be an Arab. Look violent.
(*NOEL adopts a stance.*)
Good. Now to start with I just play it cool. I lull you into a sense of false security. (*Pause.*) How does it go? Er…hang on… Yes, right. (*He quotes from memory.*) I want you to know, from the bottom of my heart, that the problems of your people – (*He stops.*) You are an Arab! If you're Irish I have a different text, you see…okay…that the problems of your people are forever uppermost in my thoughts, and I am at this moment – that's the bit, you see, imply some new development – in secret negotiations with the Liberation Front – (*He stops, goes to NOEL, pushes his hand down a little.*) By now your gunhand is supposed to drop a bit…that's it…you're lulled, you see… (*He goes back to his original position.*) – in secret negotiations with the Liberation Front for the immediate release of all those members who – (*Suddenly he makes a dive for NOEL'S gun but fails miserably*

45

to secure it. Instead he crashes headfirst into the armchair.) Don't shoot!

(*He covers his head with his hands.*
NOEL just aims the pistol at him.
CLAPCOTT slowly gets up.)

You were expecting it. The idea is to confuse them by implying that their action is superfluous. One assumes they speak good English, obviously. (*He holds out his hand for the gun.*) If we miss we have to cry 'Don't shoot!' as a sort of last appeal. (*He replaces the magazine, puts the gun away in the drawer.*) They don't hold out much hope for that. (*He rubs his back for a moment.*) Now then...in a word... (*He sits, expectantly.*) Long legs. (*He indicates the other chair. NOEL sits.*) I don't go for the dumpy stuff.

NOEL: You didn't go for Rosie, then?

CLAPCOTT: No legs. And dull as ditchwater.

NOEL: Really? She is a graduate.

CLAPCOTT: Of where?

NOEL: Essex, I think...

CLAPCOTT: I don't call those things universities. Anyway, she prattled too much. Thought she could help keep tabs on left-wing clients. Wanted to be a spy or something. Bored me stiff.

NOEL: (*Opening his briefcase with a snap.*) I'm sorry.

CLAPCOTT: Who was that one at party conference?

(*NOEL takes out a thick, glossy file of pictures.*)

NOEL: Stacey?

CLAPCOTT: I wouldn't know, but she had legs.

NOEL: I have a picture here, somewhere...

CLAPCOTT: Big mouth...black hair...the common touch...

NOEL: (*Finding the picture.*) Yes...her.

(*He holds up the picture.*
CLAPCOTT tips his head to one side.)

CLAPCOTT: Could be...

NOEL: I thought perhaps you'd care for something new.

CLAPCOTT: Well, yes, of course...

NOEL: I was thinking, maybe Lindsay...or Annabelle...

CLAPCOTT: (*Getting up.*) Show me. (*He takes the book.*) Red hair?

NOEL: Natural.

CLAPCOTT: Really?

NOEL: Can I get myself a drink?

CLAPCOTT: (*Gazing at the picture.*) Yes, of course…

    (*NOEL goes to the bottles.*)

    Any education?

NOEL: Swiss.

CLAPCOTT: (*Intrigued.*) Oh…foreign accent?

NOEL: No, just a finishing school. But she can do it if you want.

CLAPCOTT: I'd like that.

NOEL: I'll make a note of it.

CLAPCOTT: Yes, do. (*He flicks through.*)

NOEL: (*Returning with drink.*) That's settled, then.

CLAPCOTT: I think so… (*He stops at a picture.*) Who is this?

NOEL: (*Looking over his shoulder.*) Ahh…that's Nora.

CLAPCOTT: (*Disparagingly.*) Nora…

NOEL: Yes. We began as a team, and I've kept her ever since.

CLAPCOTT: Spoils the catalogue.

NOEL: Yes…a sentimental thing, that's all.

CLAPCOTT: Rubbish…body like a rabbit's arse…

NOEL: Mind you, there have been offers.

CLAPCOTT: Can't think why. Face like cat's spew.

    (*Suddenly, from behind the curtains, the loud, measured voice of ANGIE.*)

ANGIE: You vile pig…

    (*There is a startled pause.*

    CLAPCOTT instantly knows the situation.

    NOEL looks, with dismay, at the source of the voice.

    CLAPCOTT takes NOEL gently by the arm.)

CLAPCOTT: I'm very sorry. I must ask you to go.

ANGIE: Don't go!

    (*NOEL stares at the curtain.*)

CLAPCOTT: If you would please, Biledew –

ANGIE: Sod it, stick around!

CLAPCOTT: (*To NOEL.*) This must seem bizarre, but I really must insist – (*He begins pushing NOEL to the door.*)

ANGIE: Top level meeting! Gee-Gee, you are a shit!

CLAPCOTT: (*Turning angrily.*) Shut up, damn you!

(*At last* ANGIE *sweeps back the curtain and steps out.*)

ANGIE: (*To* NOEL.) I'm Angie. How d'you do?

(*She puts out her hand.*
NOEL *takes it, looking into her eyes.*
They freeze for a few bars of a musical routine.
She lets go of his hand.)

Gee-Gee keeps me hidden, don't you, dear? Like some shameful syphilitic relative, secreted in the attic. Actually I am his wife, as of the Fifteenth of February, 1952.

CLAPCOTT: I'm sorry you had to be subjected to this, Biledew, I'm sure you won't want to –

ANGIE: (*Pulling a face.*) Bile – dew? What an awful name!

NOEL: I inherited it.

ANGIE: Well, change it then. I was called Myrtle Ackroyd, but I changed it to Angie Diamond. Anyone can do it.

NOEL: I like my name.

CLAPCOTT: (*Staring at her.*) Lurking behind curtains, like a cheap thief…

ANGIE: I had a longing to experience the agony and tension of a major political decision. It's not my fault if I was tricked.

CLAPCOTT: You're drunk.

ANGIE: No. I have just had a blinding flash of insight. Into the tawdry circumstances of your life.

CLAPCOTT: Biledew, if you don't mind –

ANGIE: Oh, no, he can't go now! He might leave with completely the wrong impression. He might let it be known that we're not – compatible!

CLAPCOTT: You treacherous, insensitive bitch.

ANGIE: With his contacts there'd be a scandal strong enough to lift the fart-filled skirts of the Tory party and then where would poor Gee-Gee be?

CLAPCOTT: This disgusting, interminable squabbling…

ANGIE: Oh yes, the terrible squalor of domestic truths compared to your mutual – purity…he must be shocked. Can I look through the catalogue? (*Without waiting for permission, she grabs up the catalogue.*) Who was it now, Lindsay, or Annabelle… (*She flicks through.*) Long legs are mandatory… (*She stops.*) Oh, the monotony of his predilections. Hair – red. Bust – 36. (*She looks at NOEL.*) Has he asked for chorus costumes?

CLAPCOTT: Shut up.

ANGIE: He has a very stable chemistry, does Gee-Gee. Always bolts the same old dish. (*She tosses the book down on an armchair, looks at NOEL.*) You must find Gee-Gee and his cronies awfully pitiful. I mean, I knew he got his oats somewhere, but through a – what DO you call yourself?

NOEL: A pimp. (*Pause.*)

ANGIE: (*Impressed.*) Do you… (*Pause.*)

CLAPCOTT: All right, so you've made a great discovery. Congratulations. Your dirty little trick's paid off.

ANGIE: (*Sitting with deliberate poise.*) Don't worry. It's not possible for you to sink in my estimation.

CLAPCOTT: Don't imagine that bothers me!

ANGIE: Don't be silly. Of course it does. It's completely wrecked your miserable little edifice of moral superiority. I was rather led to believe you went without. Or had something awfully decent going on. But no. You're pure shit. (*She smiles, turns to NOEL.*) How old are you?

NOEL: Twenty-seven.

ANGIE: So young and so – (*Pause.*) How much do you make a year?

CLAPCOTT: Don't be impertinent!

ANGIE: In response to public pressure Gee-Gee's working on some legislation to eradicate your type. Aren't you, Gee-Gee?

CLAPCOTT: Go to bed… (*Pause.*)

ANGIE: Yes… I will… (*She gets up and goes to the door. She turns to NOEL.*) How much is Lindsay?
(*NOEL hesitates.*)
How much?

NOEL: Two hundred pounds.

ANGIE: Two hundred pounds. For his miserable little efforts! (*She unlocks the door, opens it.*) And there are people living on ten pounds a week…
(*She goes out, unhurriedly, closing the door behind her.
NOEL watches her, transfixed.*)

NOEL: I watched her… I watched her and I wanted – to bite her arse! (*Pause.*)

CLAPCOTT: Well, now you know, don't you?

(*NOEL looks at him.*)

The private burdens public figures have to bear. Imagine trying to smile with THAT behind you. Like swallowing elastic bands… (*He sits down, as if very tired.*) I don't deserve it. Christ knows I've done no wrong. Been ambitious, maybe. Couldn't see a ladder without wanting to climb up it. Not my fault, though… Don't know why I'm apologising, nothing wrong with getting on…what the Tory party's all about…my father was a self-made man. Came from nowhere. Built a factory. Are you interested?

NOEL: Fascinated.

CLAPCOTT: After the war, looked for a place to conquer, some field where the competition wasn't fierce, and there was the Conservative Party, flat on its back. I got myself a reputation for reliability. Not brilliance, but reliability. They go for that. And they bought me. I had smooth cheeks. And this way of looking people in the eyes. Always. Right in the eyes. I suppose you noticed that? And the handshake. Like a vice, not too prolonged, but very firm. You can read a handshake. Mine says – reliability. They never liked Rab Butler in this party. His handshake was like a dying fish. Heath's was the same, but he forced himself.

NOEL: I've never been in a politician's house before. Been in managing directors' houses, and lawyers' houses. They have a smell. Of endless squirming. Mind you, my nose is very sensitive, because my eyes are so weak. Nature's generous like that. My mother's house smelled of panic.

CLAPCOTT: And what does this place smell of?

NOEL: Contempt.

CLAPCOTT: (*Smiling.*) My wife's perfume lingering on the air…

NOEL: No, it comes from you.

CLAPCOTT: Really? You're dangerously outspoken for a pimp.

NOEL: I'm entitled to be a bit rude when I feel like it. I'm like a jester. I know a little something about everyone.

CLAPCOTT: Regale me.

NOEL: You'd like that, wouldn't you? Is the PM into bondage? Is the Employment Secretary a fetishist? (*He walks a little way, puts the catalogue back in his briefcase.*) People always want to know who else is swimming in the pitch.

CLAPCOTT: You needn't sound so damned censorious!

NOEL: Did I?

CLAPCOTT: You can't go peddling your wares and then get on your moral high horse when somebody purchases.

NOEL: Why not?

CLAPCOTT: Not fair practice, is it?

NOEL: Even the devil knows a sin.

CLAPCOTT: Sin! (*He laughs.*) A sin! Since when was laying whores a sin!

(*NOEL just looks at him.*)

A puritanical pimp. Good God... How you must suffer, as you cash your cheques...

NOEL: Pimping has its penalties. Until a very little while ago I felt sure my libido had done a bunk on me. (*He snaps the case shut.*)

CLAPCOTT: My heart bleeds for you. All that minge about. It must be hell. Now, if you don't mind, I have a couple of expulsion orders to confirm. Two Asians washed up on the Isle of Grain. (*He reaches for his files, drops them on his lap.*) Would you see yourself out, there's a good chap. (*He puts on his glasses, cranes forward over the files.*)

NOEL: (*Aside.*) So I left the white slug's drawing room, my heart full of malice, but my head buzzing with the sleek tart who was his wife. And in the hallway – very Clapcott, very Sandersons –

ANGIE: Rock me, baby...all night long...

NOEL: (*Transfixed.*) Cast a spell on me...

ANGIE: Shake, rattle and roll me...

NOEL: Why not, Chuck?

ANGIE: Highway child...

NOEL: Have hog, will travel...

ANGIE: Battersea Bridge. Hot dogs. At three...

NOEL: Burn me...

(A few bars of Elvis Presley's 'All Shook Up'.
CLAPCOTT looks up from his file.)

CLAPCOTT: Didn't like that specimen. Can't see his eyes.
Negotiate by phone in future. Never let the underworld
into your home. *(He looks back at the file.)* Well no, Mustafa!
(He draws across the name on his file.) Back to Karachi you
must go! Ee – ay, ee – ay, ee – ay – o!

SCENE 2

A layby on the Kingston Bypass. A motorbike stops.

ANGIE: I've done it quicker. On a Norton.

NOEL: Hold up at the Malden roundabout.

ANGIE: I counted that.

(He shrugs. Pause.
She takes out a chocolate bar, begins eating it.)
Last time I was here with a member of the Milwaukee
Chapter. He was half Apache. I was his squaw for nearly
a week. Then he was shot in Birmingham. Or was it
drowned in Brighton? We didn't have a lot to say. *(She
wanders aimlessly.)* Reaching one's destination is such an
anti-climax in this game. Want a bite?
(She extends the bar to him.
He takes a bite.
Sounds of cars passing.)
I hate the country. It bores me stiff.
(Pause. Then NOEL gets off the bike and heaves it onto its stand.)

NOEL: Did you want to marry him?

ANGIE: Gee-Gee? Yes, desperately.

NOEL: He's vile.

ANGIE: Oh, yes.

NOEL: I don't see it. He's ugly. He has horrible habits.

ANGIE: He didn't always look that hideous. Well...perhaps he
did...

NOEL: Why, then?

ANGIE: I was such a rotten dancer. That was the key to it. My
sense of timing was atrocious, and I never have been able
to touch my toes. They were about to chuck me out. Not

that he noticed. He was obsessed. Another week and I
would have got my cards. Then he proposed... And I did
so want to be a member of the upper class...

NOEL: (*Surprised.*) Weren't you?

ANGIE: Not then. I was born out of wedlock in the vicinity of
Aldershot.

NOEL: (*With delight.*) Bastard!

ANGIE: They did get married. He was a private in the
Engineers.

NOEL: (*Smiling with joy.*) Bastard! Beautiful bastard! You
common slut...

ANGIE: Most people are disappointed when they find that
out. They like to think I'm from the top drawer. You'd be
amazed at the things they say when they're having me. Or
perhaps you wouldn't, in your line... (*Pause.*)

NOEL: Climbing, slithering, clawing our way up the side of the
barrel, then – flip! Over the top, into the real pus, into the
real poison...

ANGIE: Well, now we're in it, we don't want to go back, do we?
(*Pause. NOEL sits.*)
My husband wouldn't like to think you're having an affair
with me. (*He looks up.*) You are going to have an affair with
me?

NOEL: It crossed my mind...

ANGIE: I signed a piece of paper saying I would desist from his
friends or business acquaintances.

NOEL: You'll have to renegotiate the contract. I'm an
unforeseen condition. (*Pause.*)

ANGIE: Well... (*She looks at him.*) Unzip a banana...
(*NOEL looks confused for a moment, then shocked.*)

NOEL: What...here?

ANGIE: Yes.

NOEL: The cars...

ANGIE: The audacity! (*She smiles, starts to unzip her jacket.*)

NOEL: Wait a minute. I don't think this environment appeals
to me. You know what an uncertain business this can be...
however much you might want to... People are watching!

ANGIE: Only on their way to Guildford. The merest glimpse, at sixty miles an hour. It's a Clearway, Noel…

(*Pause. He is hesitant.*)

NOEL: Angie…

(*Loud music from a musical dance routine.*

ANGIE adopts a chorus line posture, and high-kicks her way behind the shrubbery.

After a few moments NOEL tears off his jacket and follows after.

Sound of a distant motorbike approaching.

Laughter from behind the bushes.

The motorbike stops, the engine is switched off.

A POLICE MOTORCYCLIST enters. He looks at NOEL's bike with suspicion.

A burst of giggling diverts his attention. He lies on his belly and crawls towards the edge of the shrubbery.

NOEL bursts out in song, from South Pacific.)

I'm in love, I'm in love, I'm in love, I'm in love, I'm in love with a won – der – ful…guy!

ANGIE: Once you have found him, never let him go…

Once you have found him…

NOEL / ANGIE: Nev – er let him go!

(*They exclaim ecstatically.*

The POLICE MOTORCYCLIST carefully removes his notebook.)

NOEL: We'll murder him.

ANGIE: Pump him full of lead.

NOEL: You beautiful angel…

ANGIE: Blow his brains out.

NOEL: You beautiful sinner…

ANGIE: Rape him with chrome handlebars.

NOEL: Dismember him.

ANGIE: Cut off his little true blue penis.

NOEL: I love you. I am raging with love for you!

ANGIE: No, not again…

NOEL: It hurts…

(*The POLICE MOTORCYCLIST retreats and leans against the motorbike.*)

ANGIE: Take me to a restaurant. Some lousy, decrepit
restaurant with Pepsi-Cola stickers –
(*She appears, sees the POLICE MOTORCYCLIST, stops a second,
then continues with calculated indifference.*)
– and a plastic orange drifting round in urine coloured
orange juice.
(*She takes out a comb, and begins combing her hair.
Enter NOEL, zipping up his jacket.*)

PC: Is this your bike?

NOEL: Don't spoil everything.

PC: I asked you a question. Is this your bike?

NOEL: Don't spoil everything.
(*Pause.*)

PC: (*Observing his spectacles.*) Can you read a number plate at
twenty –

NOEL: You've been listening. You've been standing here
watching – and listening.

ANGIE: Noel…

NOEL: You filth.

ANGIE: Take me home, Noel, I feel – (*She chooses her word.*)
– shagged.

PC: (*Turning to her.*) Well, I'm afraid that isn't on. Just careering
home with a half-blind driver, following the uttering of
threats against an unknown party, following conspiracy to
murder. It's not on.

NOEL: Fuck off!
(*Violently, the POLICE MOTORCYCLIST turns to NOEL and
takes a step towards him, but impulsively NOEL trips him.
He stumbles.*)

ANGIE: Oh, God!
(*Grabbing a brick from the foot of a litterbin, NOEL hits the
POLICE MOTORCYCLIST on the helmet.*)

NOEL: Start it!
(*ANGIE attempts to kick start the bike.*)
Start it! Start it!

ANGIE: I can't!
(*The POLICE MOTORCYCLIST, sinking at NOEL's feet, grabs
him round the legs and clings on.*)

I can't!

(*NOEL hits the POLICE MOTORCYCLIST several more times before grabbing the waste bin and ramming it over his head. Then he pulls free and goes to the bike.*
ANGIE sits on the pillion and NOEL kick-starts it, revs up and pushes it off the stand.
The stunned POLICE MOTORCYCLIST grabs the bike by the rear number plate. There is a roar and NOEL slips into gear and drives away, leaving the POLICE MOTORCYCLIST holding the plate, stumbling round in a circle.)

SCENE 3

A café. Sitting at the table, holding hands above a crusty sugar bowl.
ANGIE and NOEL. Enter CHRISTINE, a slovenly and very pregnant waitress.

CHRISTINE: What?

NOEL: (*Not taking his eyes off ANGIE.*) Orange. Twice.
    (*CHRISTINE goes off.*)

ANGIE: Gee-Gee will be – apoplectic.

NOEL: Let him bleed.

ANGIE: He's very hot on protecting our policemen. He's
    chairman of the police widows' fund.

NOEL: He'll fix it.

ANGIE: Gee-Gee is a savage. He'll wound you, secretly.

NOEL: I've got all the cards…

ANGIE: Court jesters are dispensable.

NOEL: You'll save me. Or we'll all sink together. My claws are
    in him now. I'll drag him down.
    (*CHRISTINE returns with two orange squashes in paper cups.*
    She slams them down clumsily.)

CHRISTINE: Twenty P.
    (*NOEL reaches into his pocket.*
    With a flash of inspiration, CHRISTINE throws a cup of orange in NOEL's face.)
    I know you! You cheating swine!

ANGIE: (*Jumping to her feet.*) You stupid bitch.

CHRISTINE: Sit down! (*She shoves* ANGIE *in the chest, who falls back in her seat.*) Claw, is it? Big Claw, is it? You dirty little bleeder!

ANGIE: What are you on about?

CHRISTINE: He ruined my life, that's what! I had a decent job when I met him. High-class waitressing with great big tips! Fortnum and Mason's – I could have been the manageress! But no, he had to come and spoil it, the dirty ponce!

NOEL: (*Wiping his eyes.*) I know you...

CHRISTINE: Yeah, you know me, dropped me, didn't you? When I got pregnant by one of his dirty types, kicked me out I when I was four months gone and lost my fiancé –

ANGIE: I don't see why we need to stay –

CHRISTINE: Because this bastard ruined me, that's why! 'Claw', who was gonna get so big! And look at him, a dirty little rocker! You have got big!

NOEL: Christine, isn't it...?

CHRISTINE: He knows my name! How marvellous, after so long! What a memory for tarts! My legs aren't quite so lovely now, with three kids and another on the way. Do you wanna offer me a job? Nothing below a barrister!

NOEL: How are you, Christine?

CHRISTINE: How am I, Christine? You hypocrite! Seven years since I saw you, and I haven't forgotten your mug, Four Eyes, nor your old mother, you pair of swine.
(NOEL *gets up, reaches into his pocket and takes a wallet out. He holds out two five-pound notes.*)
You scum. Never show your face in here again. I'll set the Alsatians on yer. (*She takes the money.*)

SCENE 4

CLAPCOTT'S *Chelsea drawing-room. A door slams off.* CLAPCOTT *enters in overcoat and hat. He stops, sniffs the air.*

CLAPCOTT: I know that smell. That smell is cannabis. Thinly disguised beneath an aerosol. (*He goes to the ashtray, picks up a butt, sniffs it.*) Not that she likes the stuff. It gives her headaches. It's to spite me. She has a policy of pinpricks, which she assumes will eventually drain my veins. (*He removes his overcoat, goes out, hangs it up, returns.*) She is a dismal failure in this, as in everything.

(*Enter ANGIE, elegant.*)

ANGIE: How was the debate?

CLAPCOTT: (*Sitting down.*) Skilful. Some decent speeches all round. Opposition ragged, though, as usual.

ANGIE: Then you all had a drink in the Members' Bar.

CLAPCOTT: Of course.

ANGIE: The terrible bitterness of it all! (*She goes to the drinks, pours a whisky.*) Gee-Gee, I want you to block a prosecution. (*She takes the drink to him, holds it out.*

He doesn't take it.)

CLAPCOTT: Whose? (*Pause.*)

ANGIE: Biledew's.

(*He looks profoundly shocked.*)

Your pimp…is in a bit of bother with the fuzz.

(*He gawps at her.*)

I'm sorry, but you might as well know now. So you can nip it in the bud.

(*Pause. She thrusts the drink at him.*

He swallows.)

All you have to do is to pick up the phone and ring the Chief Commissioner and say – whatever you say – take the heat off, man – Official Secrets Act, or D Notice, or something, I could do it for you –

CLAPCOTT: Stop prattling!

(*She shrugs, sits in the other armchair, crosses her legs, taps her fingers. He wipes his mouth.*)

What do you know? What has he done?

ANGIE: Struck a copper.

CLAPCOTT: Oh, my God. What with?

ANGIE: A brick.

CLAPCOTT: Oh, Christ!

ANGIE: (*Impatiently.*) He had a helmet on!

CLAPCOTT: Why you? Why did he ring you? Why didn't he tell me? I'm the person he wants if he wants a cover up, not you. Why you?

ANGIE: Well…

CLAPCOTT: Well?

ANGIE: (*Gets up, walks a few paces.*) I was with him at the time.
(*He gawps again.*)
We were fifteen miles from Guildford. In a layby, when
this – zealous copper came along…
(*He looks her, she looks at him. Pause.*)

CLAPCOTT: I wish you dead. (*Pause.*) No more than that.
(*Pause.*) Just dead. And totally forgotten.

ANGIE: Yes, I understand that. We would have got away with
it but…you know what they're like…throwing themselves
on the bonnets of cars and so on…he riveted himself to the
back number plate…and it came off. So you see, it's only a
matter of time before they – swoop.

CLAPCOTT: (*Aside.*) And I went to the PM's office…and the
beaver glared at me…half spectacles catching the sunlight
filtering through the Horseguards…and he said, Gee-Gee,
that woman is out to ruin you. She'll have your balls off,
and carry your castration through the streets. Buy her a fast
car, he said. All you can hope for is an accident.

ANGIE: He can't go to court. (*Pause.*) Can he? (*Pause.*) The
Copper saw me, Gee-Gee!

CLAPCOTT: No…

ANGIE: Thank God. I thought for a moment you were
envisaging some – glorious kamikaze exit from the
government.

CLAPCOTT: Drowning, in all the sewage which came welling
up…

ANGIE: After all, it's not just you, is it?
(*He shakes his head.*)
Anyway, I'm sorry I broke our agreement. It was just…
Anyway, it happened…

CLAPCOTT: Yes…
(*ANGIE looks at him.*)

ANGIE: (*Aside.*) Sitting there, like some boiled lobster,
faintly blue around the ears…and in his belly, pasta and
liqueurs…churning slowly…while he plots some mean
revenge.

CLAPCOTT: (*Aside.*) One day, come in, burst in, kicking the
    door down like some Operation Motorman, catch them,
    throw acid on their writhing backs…
ANGIE: (*Aside.*) Static like beef…his podgy hands, made for
    fondling pens and the stems of glasses…
CLAPCOTT: (*Aside.*) Her bony fingers, the skin more mottled as
    she gets older, stained with endless fornication…
ANGIE: (*Aside.*) Little food stains on his tie…on his flies grubby
    marks…
CLAPCOTT: Tired sometimes, has to stay in bed with tonics…
    and her pubic hair is rather grey…
ANGIE: Short-breathed on staircases…forgets to change his
    underwear…
    (*A pause. They remain still. The music of the old ragtime tune,
    'I'm Happy, If You're Happy'. It stops.*)
CLAPCOTT: Finish with him. When I've cleared this. We can't
    have this. You know that.
ANGIE: Yes…
CLAPCOTT: Impossible.
    (*He gets up, goes to the telephone and dials a single digit.
    She watches him.*)
    Clapcott. This is a blue call. Yes. Thank you. (*Pause. He
    looks to* ANGIE.) I hate this! (*Pause, then into phone.*) Clapcott.
    Yes. I want a case rubbed out. (*Pause.*) Biledew. Yes. Bile.
    Dew. (*Pause.*) Assault against a policeman. Yes, I'm sorry
    too. I understand that very well, don't like it either. (*Pause.*)
    Near Guildford.
ANGIE: On the bypass.
CLAPCOTT: On the bypass.
ANGIE: Yesterday.
CLAPCOTT: Yesterday.
ANGIE: 'bout three.
CLAPCOTT: Three-ish. (*Pause.*) I'm very well, thank you. And
    you? Good. Bye bye. (*He puts the receiver down, then looks at
    her.*)
ANGIE: That was lovely. When it comes to protecting itself the
    government machine works like greased lightning.
CLAPCOTT: Never again.

ANGIE: Well, it was for you! You didn't want him bawling from the witness box, did you?

CLAPCOTT: Never again. Whatever the consequences, I make that clear.

ANGIE: (*Uneasily.*) I hope you don't mind, but as we weren't exactly positive how you'd react, I took the liberty of... I'm sorry Gee-Gee, I've asked him here... Noel, I mean...is on the premises...

(*Pause, then suddenly CLAPCOTT launches himself at the long curtains where ANGIE had hidden herself in Scene 1. He tears them back. There is nothing there.*)

Don't be silly.

CLAPCOTT: Bring him in.

ANGIE: Promise not to make a fool of yourself.

CLAPCOTT: Bring him in!

(*Pause. Then reluctantly, she goes to the door, opens it and calls.*)

ANGIE: Noel!

(*She returns, feigning casualness.*
CLAPCOTT fills his tumbler.
NOEL enters. He looks at her.)

NOEL: And I looked at her...and she was wonderful...

CLAPCOTT: There is a certain thing known as discretion. In the Tory Party, as in life, discretion is the difference between success and abject failure. If you have integrity, but no discretion, then you are nothing. If you have brilliance, but no discretion, then you are nothing. But if you have nothing else, but you have discretion...then you are like unto a god. (*He goes close to NOEL.*) You have nothing. And no discretion, either. You are pure shit.

(*They glare at one another for some seconds.*
ANGIE gets up nervously.)

ANGIE: Can I open a window? (*She goes to the windows, opens them slightly.*)

NOEL: (*Icily.*) I am your pimp.

CLAPCOTT: Not any more you're not.

NOEL: Always. And forever.

CLAPCOTT: Is that supposed to be some kind of threat?

NOEL: I have my teeth in your fat calf, and I won't let go.

CLAPCOTT: The police are dropping proceedings against you. Your nasty little assault is going unpunished. Scamper off with that and be grateful.

NOEL: Scamper off? Where to?

CLAPCOTT: The tenements you came from. The hovels they bred you in, you rodent. (*Pause.*)

NOEL: I'm one of you now. I'm your peer.

CLAPCOTT: It's a common fallacy that extravagance somehow confers a social status. The pennies you delved in the gutter for don't make you anyone.

NOEL: I am your pimp.

ANGIE: Is there any dry ginger?

NOEL: I am your pimp!

ANGIE: All right. Make do with ice. (*She fills her glass.*)

CLAPCOTT: Sink back into the murk, Biledew. You rose, your face saw daylight. You were privileged.

NOEL: To serve you? To dish out skin for your fat paws to fondle? Privileged to lay out women in your bed, you white cod?

CLAPCOTT: You are disgusted. Not by me. By yourself.

NOEL: Yes!

CLAPCOTT: I am not disgusted. I have whores. I accept that. It's a fact of life. I am not disgusted when I shit. That too's a fact of life. The disgust is all on your side. You are full of self-loathing.

NOEL: I won't let you go. My little rat teeth are locked on you.

CLAPCOTT: Don't try to take on the English ruling class.

NOEL: You! Son of a – what? A one-eyed sweatshop owner!

CLAPCOTT: What a peevish concern for origins. What a fastidious pimp.

NOEL: You phrase-maker. You trickling liar, spewing your poison out…

ANGIE: Does anybody want the television on?

NOEL: I'm not some shop steward who you can mock because he can't finish his sentences. I'm on the inside. The filth confronting the filth. I can destroy you, Clapcott.

ANGIE: (*Getting up, moving to go.*) I think I will.

(*As she passes him, NOEL takes her arm.*

She stops.)

NOEL: Give us a whisky, darling.

　(*She doesn't move.*

　NOEL is still glaring at CLAPCOTT.)

　Me and her. We've got you taped.

　(*Pause. CLAPCOTT looks at ANGIE.*)

　Angie…tell him we're burying him…

　(*Pause. She doesn't move.*)

　Tell him. (*Pause.*)

ANGIE: I'm sorry, Noel…

NOEL: What?

ANGIE: Well, it's not on, is it?

NOEL: What's not?

ANGIE: Well…the whole damned thing…

NOEL: Not on?

ANGIE: Not really, no. In practical terms. Really. Any more
　than my Apache…

NOEL: You hate his guts!

ANGIE: Yes.

NOEL: Well, then! (*He is desperate.*) Glorious bastards!

　(*ANGIE just looks at him, agonisingly.*)

CLAPCOTT: How touching…cops and robbers on the bypass,
　Easy Rider on the A23.

NOEL:… Angie…

ANGIE: I like it here…

　(*Pause. NOEL stares.*)

　Not like it here exactly…just…belong…

NOEL: You tricked me.

ANGIE: No, not deliberately…

NOEL: Liar.

ANGIE: No. I meant it. I need my moments of – delirium. I just
　– I can't shift now.

NOEL: Get out.

CLAPCOTT: Do no such thing.

NOEL: Get out.

CLAPCOTT: Stay where you are.

　(*Pause. ANGIE looks at NOEL, then goes out.*)

　Don't go!

　(*She is out of the room.*)

Don't go I said. (*Pause.*)

NOEL: (*Gritting his teeth, eyes shut.*) And I loved her, while she ripped me, my heart bled… I'm going straight to the newspapers. I'm laying everything before them. I'm kicking the shit out of you…

(*Pause. CLAPCOTT turns to him.*)

CLAPCOTT: Organised labour sends the Prime Minister lurching with diarrhoea. Union militants keep us up at night, sweating in secret conferences. But scandals, they're the bread and butter of the good society.

NOEL: Like hell. (*Pause.*)

CLAPCOTT: You strike me as someone who will shortly commit suicide.

(*NOEL stares at him. There is a great roll of drums, and when it stops, the voice of BILEDEW singing 'The Red Flag', alone and unaccompanied. The moment he stops, NOEL makes a dive for the drawer in which CLAPCOTT keeps his revolver. CLAPCOTT realises his intention too late, makes a move, but stops as NOEL aims the gun at him. Pause.*)

NOEL: I'm wiping you. For everyone. And then, maybe, I'll kill myself.

(*He lifts the gun to aim at CLAPCOTT's head. CLAPCOTT closes his eyes, then desperately.*)

CLAPCOTT: Before you do… (*There is a pause. He struggles to open his eyes.*) I think you should know…that Angie with reference to you, said if there was one thing she was certain of…it was that you had…absolutely no right to –

(*NOEL's gun hand has dropped an inch or two. CLAPCOTT makes a smart dive, seizing the weapon and aiming it at NOEL.*)

NOEL: Shoot me, then! Shoot me!

(*CLAPCOTT moves away, backing towards the telephone. ANGIE enters. She stands silently near the door. CLAPCOTT picks up the receiver.*)

CLAPCOTT: Clapcott. This is a red call.

(*Immediately the windows are flung open and a SPECIAL BRANCH OFFICER bursts in, clutching a machine gun. ANGIE and CLAPCOTT watch him with disdain.*)

OFFICER: All right, sir? All right, m'am?
> (*ANGIE walks to the drinks trolley and picks up a bottle.*)
> Him, is it?
> (*CLAPCOTT hands his pistol over to the OFFICER, who prods NOEL severely.*)
> Get moving.
> (*He nods in the direction of the window.*
> *NOEL looks at ANGIE.*)

NOEL: Claw loved you. And you pissed all over him. (*He looks at CLAPCOTT.*) You should have shot me. You'll be sorry, I'll gnaw through granite blocks to get to you. No gaol will hold me, Clapcott.

CLAPCOTT: No. No gaol…
> (*The OFFICER pushes NOEL out through the windows. Pause. ANGIE is pouring a drink.*)
> I was very scared…at one point I felt my bowels – the muscles in my bowels – sink down, like in the war, when they dive-bombed us out in Crete…but this time I stopped myself.

ANGIE: When he got the gun on you?

CLAPCOTT: When he said he'd tell the papers.

ANGIE: There'll be such a wicked lot of shit flying…

CLAPCOTT: I don't think so. The moment he grabbed the gun, I knew, assuming I survived, just what would happen to him. No publicity, no courts, no nothing. Not a squeak.
> (*ANGIE looks at him. Long pause.*)

ANGIE: Gee-Gee, after all the filth I've been with, no-one can twist my womb like you. You freeze my blood.

CLAPCOTT: (*Looking back at her for some seconds, turns.*) I'll book a table. (*Pause.*) Shall I? (*Pause.*) Shall I? (*Pause.*) Shall we eat?

ACT THREE

SCENE 1

A room in an institution. A table laid for one, and a chair. A trolley with covered dishes and crockery. After a pause of about ten seconds, LILY and LUBSY enter. They wear short white jackets, like waiters, and have napkins on their arms. They take up positions facing the audience. A silence.

LILY: And he said was it not the Abercorn where I first met you, sitting looking at the women who congregate there of a Saturday between their shopping, and girls drinking and smoking in short skirts, and I said as likely as not, I had a habit of haunting coffee bars, not being a drinking man but liking noisy places. Then that's the place, he said, I had several in mind, but your familiarity has decided me. The bag is in the basement. I said 'Goodbye, Captain' and he saluted smartly, being trained by the English army he gave great attention to these details as indeed we all did, liking to see ourselves as a crack regiment and not some round-shouldered university-trained amateurs. So in the sunshine of the morning I stepped out with my present whistling 'My Guy' by Mary Wells which had somehow got in my head and couldn't be shook off for nothing, and went up through the shopping precinct and I had to hand it to the Lord he had laid it on real proudly for my debut, as he always had done, my birthday having been fine my mother told me and my wedding so gorgeous you might have thought we were a blessed couple instead of as we were, a three weeks' wonder. The Abercorn was crowded, it seemed I could skip the formality of buying myself a coffee and just dump the bag down, who would notice in that hullabaloo, but I thought better of it, always sticking by instructions and remembering how I had to make a good impression and not cut corners, so I joined the queue, joggling my holdall with their stiff new carrier bags and thinking of this queue only the quickest drinkers, the gulpers to be accurate, would leave intact. Two tarts behind me took my eye, with skirts all up and giggling, to my regret bought steak and kidney and two veg so it was obvious they wouldn't leave complete, and it struck me as being wasteful of good cunt if they were hurt, but I was not in a position to be choosy who should die and who should live. I bought a raspberry milkshake because I knew how hot the tea was in this place. Half-finished beverages look suspicious – and picked a table well towards the back, the blast would have been dissipated if I'd set it near the window. I put the bag between my feet. An old bloke looked at me. I stared back. Two ladies joined me. They were going on about loose covers, whatever they may be. I drank my drink, with one eye on my watch and thinking Lily you are within ten minutes of eternity. That thought ran through my head. It moved me, in a funny way. I suddenly had the thought that the bomb's timing might not be that accurate, and having no wish to be disintegrated by my own hand, got up and pushed my chair in, hot and I thought conspicuous. Outside I broke into a sweat. I felt a prickling in my back. Supposing just as I stepped out, I was blown to buggery! But I walked stiff as a copper to the corner, and then I ran, oh did I run, the beauty of my running no Olympic athlete ever knew, my winged feet carried me across the pavements, past the concrete flower-boxes, human faces were like leaves whirling by me and I thought of all the beauty of the world and life and women and fresh air and it was like the whole world stretched her green hills out to me, Lily filling up his lungs with life and gasping with ecstasy! And then there was this wicked bang not four blocks away which shook the air, and I sat down and while the sirens wailed it came back to me – the tune, I mean, 'My Guy' by Mary Wells, and I thought why not buy the bloody thing, so got up and went into the record shop.

(*Pause of ten seconds. The two* NURSES *remain perfectly still.*

Enter from left, NOEL. He is wearing a battered grey suit,
plimsolls, and a creased white shirt undone at the neck. He
goes directly to the table and sits down.
After a moment LILY goes to the trolley, takes a jug of fruit
juice and pours NOEL a glass. He returns the jug and stands
near the table, ready to serve. Pause.)

LUBSY: And the guvnor said this kraut Podola weighed ten
stone eight pounds on arrival, did he not? Correct, I said,
therefore the drop will need to be five feet nine inches
according to the tables. The factor you have overlooked,
he said – he was a kind man, I never saw him angry, he
was like a father to me – the factor you have overlooked,
is weightloss. The chances of him putting on weight in the
death cell were hundreds to one against in his experience.
So he suggested an allowance of a stone for this kraut
Podola, which made the drop four feet ten inches, the
shortest in my brief experience.

(*NOEL finishes the fruit juice.*
LILY removes the glass, then takes a plate of bacon and eggs
from the trolley and lays it in front of him. He pours a cup of
tea, then delivers it and takes up his original position.)

When we fetched him I said I had this idea we were in
for bother, remembering how Bentley had struggled and
made such an issue of it, being dragged backwards down
the corridor and his heels had actually marked the floor
and screaming till you thought your eardrums would cave
in, and the guvnor in one of his rare angry moments had
said he couldn't think straight and nearly put the knot the
wrong side, everybody was on edge, but even so I never
could agree with sedatives as this would utterly destroy
the atmosphere and mystery of the ceremony, which is
after all of great importance to the client and worth doing
properly. Hello, Gunther, he said, I loved the way he
spoke, you'd think it was a doctor at a child's bedside,
being in a black suit, too, that image of the guvnor always
stays with me, and shook his hand, which was rather
flabby I remember, then he asked for an examination of
the neck in which I took part, stepping forward looking at

the haircut and the cleanliness. It looked a bit raw where the clippers had gone, but the smell of soap showed me he had made an effort, and then we waited outside while he relieved himself for the last time, the sound of his urine in the bucket I can hear it now... The guvnor wasn't keen on Wandsworth, the chamber being of very mean proportions and in the event of trouble very little room for manoeuvre. He liked Leeds best, he was always happy on the train to Leeds, had kippers in the restaurant car. As I suspected from his mien, Podola bucked at the threshold and had to be manhandled for the twenty yards, the prison governor walking stiff like he couldn't hear it going on. He was not a hard man, this kraut Podola, slight of build, and roped up very easily while bawling in his language some filth I expect, or more likely pleading, and my guvnor looked marvellous, unruffled as he drew the knot up to his ear, and then as if by the magic of his touch, the kraut was silent, and hung his head like he was ashamed to have made such a din in front of a man like the guvnor, who was very holy in his way, more holy than the priest in my opinion: there was a sort of faith there, in my guvnor's true talent. And then the priest stopped and stood back, and my hand was on the lever, and the guvnor inched him forward, gently, and I waited for the signal, my eyes fixed on the guvnor's eyes, he had exquisite timing and I was full of admiration for his good taste and dignity, and then at last with a slight nod he signalled me, a gentle dip of his head like some great archbishop blessing me, and I threw the lever, and the kraut went down four feet ten inches to his last erection. And afterwards as always, he shook my hand first, and I felt like kissing his fingers because I was in the presence of a master and I knew it wasn't ever in me to be like him...

(*Pause of ten seconds.*

NOEL finishes his breakfast and with a napkin wipes his mouth.

LILY takes a packet of cigarettes from his pocket and extends it to LUBSY, who takes one, at arm's length without moving. They light their own with lighters.

A pause of ten seconds.)

LILY: And it was closing time and I had drunk enough to ease
myself out of my misery and so felt like Popeye after the
spinach, sleek as a tomcat in my plimsolls, and no way
in the mood for kipping, or for fucking for that matter,
though there were women who would have had me in
with their husbands next to us if I'd have asked, being a
hero and not keeping it too close to my chest what I had
done for the brigade when they had cared to use me. It
was moonlight and a perfect evening for a bumping off, of
which there were no doubt a few in progress that moment
in back streets and lonely farmhouses, the thought of
which aroused in me a longing to be standing in some
doorway while the shadow of the dead man came towards
me in reply to my soft knock. And so in this frame of
mind I wandered with my right hand wrapped around
my pistol very eager to do something to somebody or I
would have an awful night tossing and turning, which I
didn't want, preferring almost anything to a bad night.
And so it happened I decided the next person – excepting
it should be a woman – should be the one to cop it. And
when I spied him some hundreds of yards away my heart
sang and I skipped to catch him up because he was in a
hurry to get home and tucked up in bed. He was by the
advertising hoardings in Dooley Street when I did it to
him, in the pale light of the council flats, beneath an advert
for Lamb's Navy Rum, if I remember, and I can say with
honesty I never clapped eyes on his face. And I turned
away from him, not waiting for the blood but light-hearted
as a sparrow, a great weight was off my shoulders and
skipped up Liffey Street, cutting through the alley behind
Woolworths, which was where they caught me with the
barrel still warm and the cordite sprinkled in my pocket,
and they threw me face down in the pig-van and took turns
sitting on me as we hurtled through the Creggan with my
nose bleeding and my fingers raw with the chafing of army
boots, and rifle butts…

(*Pause, then LILY and LUBSY clear NOEL's table, loading the crockery onto the trolley which LILY then removes.*
LUBSY remains smoking.
NOEL remains seated. After about ten seconds, NOEL rises to his feet, tense and desperate.)

NOEL: Ludovic Kennedy! I call to you across the spaces from this Christ-knows-where! Can you hear me, Ludovic?
(*He waits for an answer.*
LUBSY doesn't react.)
Thick, oily hair, with intellectual silver strands in it, sensitive fingers knotted for Hanratty on *Panorama*. A good man fighting for the underdog... Well, help me, Ludovic! Briefly I arrived here in the dead of night, in a van with sealed windows. The journey could have been an hour, maybe two – they took my watch – anyway that places me within a radius of fifty to a hundred miles of London, it should be relatively easy to find me if you looked! To be out of here, I would never grumble no matter what I went through. I'd have an amputation. I've always said I'd rather die than have a leg missing. Well, I hereby take that back. To be out of here I would lose a leg and an arm as well. No, two legs and an arm. I would be legless to be out of here. Because I have this feeling I never will be out of here. And no-one will hear me. And no-one is wondering where I am. And no questions are being asked. And I'm not missed. And my name is not on a newspaper that's blowing across the Common as I dreamed it was last night, and two kids playing football didn't pick it up and say 'It's him! Four Eyes!' because they'd seen me exercise my dog round there, my dog which has probably died of hunger in the flat. My home! My ordinary nothingness! I would fall down on the grass and kiss it no matter how many dogs had shit on it, I would lie there rolling in it and it could piss with rain and yobbos could beat me silly under the railway arch, and spit on me from passing trains I wouldn't care, my common, my scrubby little patch of grass!
(*Pause of ten seconds.*

Enter left, LILY carrying a newspaper and a light, upright chair. He sits down, starts reading. Pause.)

LUBSY: And it was four o'clock precisely, I knew because I heard Big Ben bashing it out above me, and the guvnor, who had been in the public gallery, smart as a solicitor in his pin-stripe suit, crossed the forecourt of the Houses of Parliament, grey-faced and slow of stride so that I knew before I opened the car door for him that things had gone against us. He sat there in silence for some moments, as the tourists wandered past, knocking the wing-mirrors with their cameras, and I felt the tears well up, first of pity for the guvnor, then of anger against the world doing this to him. The voting had been 200 for abolition, and 48 against. He took a small flask out of his pocket. 'Drive me home,' was all he said. We drove in silence over Vauxhall Bridge and into Lambeth, past the War Museum, into Kennington, and him so shattered, as if the world had flung dirty water in his face when he had carried out his tasks so beautifully, and me at the height of my apprenticeship left high and dry, and both of us somehow made to feel obscene. 'There's always the colonies,' he said at last. He always called the Commonwealth the colonies. I said it wasn't on for me. I loved England even though she spat on us.

(Pause of ten seconds.)

LILY: It's raining.

LUBSY: Want the light on?

(He goes out left, switching the light on as he goes. Pause.)

NOEL: I feel this is Berkshire. Don't ask me why. It feels like the country, because although the windows are too high – *(Pause.)* I was angry, but now I'm scared! Because it seems to me on balance there is no hullabaloo about me going on. That is a dreadful thought, but I must face it they have probably fixed it like they fixed it when I hit the copper, and there was no hullabaloo about that. There's no reason I can think of why I should ever leave here. Not that I would not willingly co-operate in every way including drugs or brain surgery to wipe out my memory, but this has not been offered. I would accept any conditions without hesitation. But they haven't offered me anything! (*Pause. Enter* LUBSY *with a newspaper and a light, upright chair. He sits and reads. Pause of ten seconds.*)

LILY: And then they took me to a small room which was hot and stuffy and above all silent and without saying anything to me they shut the door. And I thought this was all right and I sat down and only slowly did I realise it was not silent but there was a booming going on, I couldn't say from where but it got louder and it seemed inside me, in my ears and in my body and the more it frightened me the louder and quicker it boomed until I thought I'd lose my hearing and then I knew – it was my heart that I could hear, and the trickling of blood through the chambers of my heart was like a loud stream and my eyelids closing like a door slam and I shouted take me out I'll tell you every fucking thing you bastards and they opened the steel door and the world rushed in, and they dragged me to a table and I chattered like a monkey, telling them all the shootings I had done and all the things I could remember about the Brigade. And then, expecting to be taken to a long-term prison, I was asked into a special room and two Englishmen in ordinary suits said was I interested in a certain privilege. Go on, I said. I have an appetite for privilege. We're looking for men of your type, he said, who will be pardoned in exchange for certain services. My type, I said, and pray what is my type exactly? And they mentioned this post, in Hampshire, and I said yes, I would be pardoned by Her Majesty. (*Pause.*)

LUBSY: And we were packing our things together, taking the postcards off the wall, emptying the drawers, removing every trace of our existence from that little room in Wandsworth where we made the tea and looked out over the exercise yard, while the guvnor regaled me with stories about his family holidays, and we had taken looks at the condemned men walking down below. And our little room looked miserable, especially when I thought of all the laughter we'd had there. The guvnor was flying to South

Africa, taking his wife and kids with him, off to a new life
in a new country, but I had nowhere, no future and no
prospects, and was feeling right run down, when the old
black phone rang and a voice said would I care to step
along to room 711A, because some gentlemen would like
to see me there. And I knew at once, in my heart of hearts,
that HM Government wouldn't let a decent worker down,
not kick him in the street like some old lag because his
craft had suddenly become obscene, but they would find a
little niche for him because real loyalty is not that common
in this day and age. And there were two gentlemen in
burberries, who said they were recruiting a hand-picked
team to deal with a special category of criminals. I said
I would regard it as an honour to work in such a special
field on behalf of the best employers in the world. I only
had one regret, which was that at our parting I couldn't tell
my dear guvnor what a slice of luck I'd had, and as he and
his family went across the tarmac to their plane, I couldn't
help thinking he was feeling sorry for me, thinking I was as
good as on the dole.

(*Pause of fifteen seconds. LILY, still reading, bursts out singing,
the first line of the song, 'Hungry for Love' by Johnny Kidd
and the Pirates.*)

LILY: 'Hungry, so hungry for lo – o – o – o – ve!'

    (*A silence as they read. Pause.*)

LUBSY: See Lulu last night?

LILY: I did not.

LUBSY: Brilliant. (*Long pause.*)

LILY: Used to be a prostitute.

LUBSY: (*Looks up.*) How do you know?

LILY: Common knowledge.

LUBSY: First I've heard of it.

LILY: I can't help the vast gaps in your knowledge –

LUBSY: First I've heard of it.

    (*LILY doesn't look up.*

    LUBSY pauses, then goes back to his paper.)

LILY: So was Mick Jagger.

LUBSY: What?

LILY: A bumboy.

LUBSY: I can believe that. But not Lulu.

LILY: Please yerself. (*Long pause.* LILY *bursts out his one phrase.*) 'Hungry, so hungry for lo – o – o – o – ve!' (*Pause.*) All the Stones were queers. It was common knowledge.

LUBSY: I'm not denying that. (*Pause.*)

LILY: And drug addicts.

LUBSY: Anyone can see that.

LILY: Purple hearts. Hashish. Cocaine. Brian Jones died of heroin. (*Pause.*)

LUBSY: (*Looking up from paper.*) I thought he drowned.

LILY: That is the commonly accepted theory. In actual fact he died from an armful of Big H. During a homosexual orgy at his house. They dropped him in the swimming pool to divert attention from the sordid goings-on within.

LUBSY: You are a mine of information. (*Pause. They read.*)

LILY: Marianne Faithfull also was a prostitute.

LUBSY: That may be so.

LILY: It is so.

LUBSY: I don't think Lulu was that type. (*Pause. They read.*)

LILY: Tom Jones also has had considerable homosexual experience.

LUBSY: Is this a hobby of yours?

LILY: I wouldn't call it a hobby. I didn't go to any lengths to uncover this information. I came across it in the normal course of daily life.

LUBSY: I'm not a Lulu fan, but I think you may be wrong there. (*Long pause.*)

LILY: Cilla Black also was a street-walker.

(*Suddenly, under a strain he can no longer bear,* NOEL *cries out.*)

NOEL: Are you going to kill me! (*They ignore him.*) Because if you are, I want to know!

(*Pause. Then* LUBSY *walks out left.*)

LILY: Do you know how many illegitimate children the Beatles have between them?

NOEL: Tell me, please…

LILY: Eighteen.

NOEL: Tell me…please tell me…

LILY: You want to know everything.

(*LUBSY returns with coffee and biscuits on a tray. He places the tray on the table and begins pouring.*)

NOEL: Where am I then?

(*LUBSY returns to his chair. Picks up the paper.*)

LUBSY: To come back to Lulu. Why I don't think she is.

LILY: What you think is neither here nor there.

LUBSY: Let me finish…

LILY: In any case, I said she was, what she is now I could not say.

LUBSY: For one thing, her eyes. Whores do not have sparkling eyes.

LILY: What's your evidence for that?

LUBSY: Coroners' reports.

LILY: And have you not heard of contact lenses?

(*NOEL suddenly knocks the tray onto the floor.*)

NOEL: Help me, God!

(*Pause, then, putting his paper down, LILY goes off left.*)

LILY: 'Hungry, so hungry for lo – o – o – o – ve!'

(*He returns almost at once with a broom and begins sweeping up.*)

NOEL: Biledew! You knew the inside of a gaol! Guide me! You did nothing for me, help me now! (*Pause.*) Don't leave me! (*Pause.*) Dad!

(*Slowly, BILEDEW materialises in pyjamas and a dressing-gown, very old, very weary.*

NOEL stares at him.)

BILEDEW: I am in St Francis's Hospital, forty of us in the stench of urine and terminal flesh…and sometimes, over the sound of clattering pans…we hear children in the park.

NOEL: I'm scared…help me…

BILEDEW: Noel…they're going to murder you…

NOEL: I knew! I sensed it! Don't leave me!

BILEDEW: I'm dying, Noel…

NOEL: Advise me! Give me the benefit of your experience!

BILEDEW: Biledew's last testament…

NOEL: To his son… (*Pause.*)

BILEDEW: I was alone…always…all my life, alone and not expecting anything… (*Pause.*) No. Start again.

NOEL: I haven't got that long…

(*BILEDEW thinks, starts again.*)

BILEDEW: I was alone, in the prison of the world. I had endured the kicks and cuts of what I had assumed was Fate and followed the circumstances that what I thought was Fate imposed on me. And I was miserable, and a thing blowing in the wind, and thought that was the nature of the world, like all the others I was herded with. And after I had spent my prime, and suffered, and drifted at the calls of nations and prime ministers, being insulted and dealt blows, shrugging my shoulders like an Indian who felt out of favour with the gods, I took time to think, time when I could have worked and numbed myself. But I did not. I did nothing. And it dawned on me.

NOEL: What?

BILEDEW: The truth. Vaguely at first, in the form of restlessness, from which developed an inquisitiveness, and from that – a vision, shafting through the layers of my ignorance. And when I had that knowledge, the agonies of my past fell into place, and it was like I was the first man to see a skeleton, or like Harvey seeing the circulation of the blood, I saw it as a whole, I knew the way the world ran wasn't some divine miracle but was a machine, which came to pieces and was comprehensible. And I saw how I had been used, and shoved from place to place like scrap. And I wanted to tell you, but I hadn't got the language…

NOEL: What truth is this? Will it help me get out of here?

BILEDEW: The first truth is, there are no gods. That when a letter telling you to serve the government, to die for it or bow to it, lands on your doormat, it has not travelled from some distant galaxy but an individual, from a man, a human being who exists and is no more than you, and maybe less. And the second truth which follows from this is that what is, is not what has to be, but what we have allowed to be. And the consequence that flows from that is that we can change it. All this I have discovered through the miseries of my rotten life…

NOEL: I'd be scrap. I'd be happy to carry out the orders of the lowest reptile that just lets me crawl.

BILEDEW: They won't let you crawl. They will wipe you away, and it won't even leave a smudge.

NOEL: What, then!

BILEDEW: I tried to tell you, keep your anger for your class. They could not have murdered your whole class…

NOEL: Biledew…I want to die in bed…

BILEDEW: It's nothing marvellous…the stinking sheets laid on the rubber…it's no privilege.

NOEL: Tell me how to die then!

BILEDEW: I've only just begun myself.

NOEL: Well, I won't die!

BILEDEW: Win them, Noel. Win them with your common suffering. Find the eloquence of Lenin, lick their cruelty away.

NOEL: I'm not a speaker. I haven't got the vocabulary.

BILEDEW: Find it. Your brain will work overtime in your extremity.

NOEL: They're thick as shit!

BILEDEW: Don't despise them, win them, Noel!

NOEL: Give me a start…

BILEDEW: (*His light fading.*) Be cogent, earn their love –

NOEL: Don't go! Give me a phrase! Biledew!

> (*BILEDEW is extinguished.*
>
> *NOEL stares.*
>
> *Pause of ten seconds.*)

LILY: (*Who is still reading.*) I have nothing on Roy Orbison. Though his infatuation with leather entitles one to speculate…

> (*Pause. NOEL is in desperate thought.*
>
> *LILY looks up to LUBSY.*)

Do you remember some young men known as the Tornadoes?

LUBSY: No thank you.

LILY: (*Going back to his paper.*) As you wish.

> (*LILY continues reading.*
>
> *NOEL walks up and down, pondering his opening gambit.*

Suddenly, shattering the silence, LILY sings again.)
Hungry, so hungry for lo – o – o – o – ve!
(*LILY leans back in his chair, then, with a kind of weary
routine, slaps his thighs and is about to rise to his feet. At this
moment NOEL begins to speak. For a few moments LILY stands
suspended, then, slowly, sits down again.
NOEL's speech begins clumsily and brokenly. By the end, it is
eloquent and delivered with conviction.*)

NOEL: Claw. That was my nickname. I had it on my back,
in studs. Studs in a leather jacket. Like a rocker. But
not a rocker. Properly speaking. Just a lay-about, who
would have been a rocker if he could. But really nobody.
And Claw was just my way of saying here I am, Noel
Biledew, dragged up nowhere but flashy with it, king of
the pavement, Claw rules, OK? (*He runs his hand through
his hair, still walking up and down.*) Okay so I thought I was
somebody. Well, everybody has to think they're somebody.
All over England there were kids like me called Duke and
Tiger and Raven and Blade, all of us shouting it out with
our studs, you know, rubbing it in we didn't get off the
pavement but the grandmothers did, and we got shoved
around by coppers but we took that because after them
came us in the animal kingdom. (*Pause.*) You know all
that. But of all those kids only a handful went anywhere,
and the rest are stripping motor cars in breakers' yards
or delivering for Tip Top bakeries, going thin on top and
none of 'em wearing studs any more, but the names of
their employers on their overalls. McAlpine, Acres the
Bakers, Dunlop, Royal Engineers. And they don't know
it – what they've come down to, or they've stopped trying
and they keep their heads down and they have kids and
the kids are already calling themselves the Battersea Boot
Boys or the Streatham Park Crew, and they think they rule,
OK? (*Pause.*) You know all that. But Claw had set his heart
on something big, he had the Kings Road, Chelsea on his
mind, he dreamed of pigskin wallets crammed with credit
cards and because he would not lie down he squeezed in,
not by the entrance but by the greasy kitchen, so his hands
were dirty when he sat at their white tablecloths, but I was

there! And there were hardly any like me who had done what I had, who hadn't been washed out by Oxford and Cambridge so they had to scratch their heads to remember where they had been spewed up from. And I saw it all at spittle distance what you haven't dreamed of, I saw who ruled, OK! (*Pause.*) Who did I think I was, who had had to trade in filth to sniff their halitosis? I started hating in the dirty playgrounds when they pushed me on my knees and peed on me in the lavatories because some people like me invite punishment. I'm not an angel but I have seen things, and I've seen things that make the mugging of old ladies unstinted generosity! Because our little squabbles and our playground fights and little murders in the entrances of flats are hardly crimes compared to that crime they are working on us, all of us driven mad by their brutality and no coppers to protect us against their claws! Their great claw, slashing us, splitting our people up, their great claw ripping our faces and tearing up our streets, their jaguars feeding on our lazy herds! (*Pause.*) And we have nothing except each other. Our common nothingness. And our caring for each other. And our refusal to do each other down. Like a class of schoolboys we won't tell who is the thief. (*Pause.*) Defend me. Don't murder me.

(*NOEL is drained.*

There is a long silence, neither LILY nor LUBSY moving.
They have listened like jurors, still on their chairs, revealing
nothing. They are terrifying in their solidity and lack of
expression. Slowly, LILY's hand goes into his pocket. There
is a click. A transistor begins playing the tune 'Hungry for
Love'. For some seconds no-one moves, then LILY removes the
radio and places it on the floor. After some moments, a bath
is lowered slowly onto the stage. Above the music, slowly
drowning it out, the sound of running water which continues
until the end of the play. LILY and LUBSY rise to their feet and
roll up their sleeves.

After some time, NOEL begins slowly to undress. He goes
slowly to the bath and climbs in.

*With a single thrust LILY and LUBSY force his head beneath
the water.*
*Lights fade, and rise on CLAPCOTT, in a posture which
suggests he is speaking in Parliament.)*

CLAPCOTT: I am happy to be now in a position to reassure
the House that following the publication of the enquiry
set up to investigate the death of the patient Noel Biledew
at the Spencer Park Mental Institution, Hampshire, there
appears to be no question that death was accidental and
in no way reflects upon the capacities or dedication of the
staff. I would take this opportunity to remind the House
that accidental deaths in mental institutions are running
currently at slightly under twenty a year, and that what
at first sight may appear a high accidental death rate at
Spencer Park is not in any way exceptional, though I
would hasten to add that no-one in the Health Department
or Home Office is in any way complacent about these
figures or regards them as at all acceptable. I would,
however, stress that there are serious staff shortages in a
nursing field which quite properly not everyone regards as
the most congenial…

URSULA

Characters

PLACIDA
a Perfect Liar

PHYLLIS
a Virgin

LEONORA
a Vagrant

PERDITA
a Virgin

URSULA
a Virgin

JANET
a Virgin

LUCAS
a Temptation

CLARA
a Virgin

CYNTHIA
a Virgin

LAMENTINA
a Virgin

BENEDICTA
a Virgin

ANNE
a Virgin

ACT ONE

1

A nun runs in.

PLACIDA: Ursula is marrying…!
(She gnaws her hand. The sound of chairs dragged over flagstones. A class of young women enter, pulling wooden chairs behind them which they set in a semi-circle in a routine way. They stand behind the chairs. They are silent…)
Ursula…
Ursula…
Marrying…!
(They hang their heads…PLACIDA bites her lip…they look up, one after another…)
AND WHY NOT IS URSULA NOT BEAUTIFUL IS SHE NOT FECUND IS HER FATHER NOT RICH URSULA IS SO OH SO VERY IS SHE NOT THE VERY CORNUCOPIA OF MATRIMONY URSULA HER BELLY IS
(Pause…)
A fruit I always think
A fruit
He has a castle on the estuary wading birds reeds mudbanks rotting hulks extremely isolated and quite primitive I think I've never been there I shudder to think of the solitude of the estuary and she is companionable Ursula imagine the sunsets on an afternoon in winter lapping water and one solitary curlew crying I never go near estuaries they oppress the spirit but she must marry someone it appears and –
PHYLLIS: Shh…
PLACIDA: If not him another if not the estuary some other God-forsaken place possibly a mountain which is worse –
PHYLLIS: Shh…
PLACIDA: I don't know a mudbank or a crag with –
PHYLLIS: Shh…

PLACIDA: Vile crows perched on the –
PHYLLIS: Shh, oh, shh –
PLACIDA: I'M SO I'M SO –
PHYLLIS: Yes –
> (*Pause…PLACIDA struggles…*)
PLACIDA: DELIGHTED FOR HER IF THAT'S WHAT SHE
> (*Pause…they stare at PLACIDA…*)
> It isn't however, is it…?
> What she wants…?
> (*Pause…on the slightest signal from PLACIDA the class sits. They adopt various postures of concentration…PLACIDA drifts among them, supervising their concentration…*)
> I see a blind girl
> Ugly
> And unclean
> How unlike Ursula she is
> Clumsy
> Stubborn
> And she sulks
> I say stubborn because whilst it is obvious even to her the gate is locked still she
> And sulking yes you'd think the gate had uttered some abuse of her
> SHE'S CLIMBING IT
> Don't look I'll look for you
> AND NOW SHE'S FALLEN
> DO NOT MOVE
> Not badly
> Not badly fallen
> And she sulks again
> She looks upon the gate as if it were her mortal enemy
> How unlike Ursula she is
> The very opposite of Ursula
> Who would I think without doubt charm it off its hinges
> Yes…!
> (*She laughs…she turns away from the spectacle.*)
> Let us contemplate Ursula
> Ursula yes

How disingenuous I should be if I proposed another
subject
I should be quite
STIFF
WITH
HYPOCRISY
No
We are sometimes obliged to confess that for all our
aspirations towards tranquillity and evenness of temper a
single rumour can
AND THIS IS NO RUMOUR I HAVE IT ON AUTHORITY
Can blow us horribly off course
MARRIED…!
What is that exactly
MARRIAGE
A beautiful word
Soft in every syllable
MARRIAGE
You say it
(*They look up uneasily and one mutters…*)
No
All together
(*They hesitate…*)
Silly…! Say it…!
(*They obey…*)
Yes
The word is like a prayer
ONCE MORE
(*Again they dither…*)
Yes…!
Yes…!
(*They obey…PLACIDA laughs…*)
Your reluctance…! Your recalcitrance…! Have I ever
poisoned your minds against this word, you utter it as if OR
ANY WORD as if it might shrivel your tongues
NO WORD SURELY…?
(*A figure has appeared in the doorway…*)
LEONORA: I'll be Ursula.

(*They turn to look at the blind girl…a pause of surprise…one of the class stands…*)

PERDITA: You may not enter here, we are in private –

LEONORA: Is her room free…?

(*Pause…*)

PERDITA: (*Casting a glance to PLACIDA.*) Private discussion and –

LEONORA: I'll go up –

PERDITA: PRIVATE I SAID…

(*Pause…*)

LEONORA: (*Coolly.*) And dump my bag…

(*They are bewildered…*)

Coming along there I – along the corridor – I heard the most beautiful voice in the world – I trod so carefully I trod as if on eggs for horror I would obliterate one note…

(*They look at PLACIDA…*)

Speak then, owner of the voice…

(*PLACIDA is cool, silent…*)

I'll discover you, shall I…?

PERDITA: I THINK YOU SHOULD NOT TROUBLE OUR –

LEONORA: She's there…

(*She correctly identifies the direction in which PLACIDA stands in relation to herself…*)

It's perfectly true that her hair is yellow

Ursula's

Yellow as the plumage of

The petals of

The ripening

And so on

Yellow

Yellow

Whereas mine is black

And she is blue-eyed as the glacier

The sky

Slow moving veins

Blue

Blue

Ursula's eyes

Whereas mine are grey

All the same

I shall be Ursula
So very Ursula you will exclaim how little the first Ursula
became herself…
(*Pause…*)
PLACIDA: You are wrong…
(*Pause…*)
Ursula reveals her excellence…
At all times…
And in every way…
(*Pause…*)
You are filthy from the road from scaling fences and so on
from trespassing and inching along corridors there is no
room here nor any kind of vacancy as I'm sure you know I
hope your journey is a safe one…
LEONORA: It's ended, I assure you –
PLACIDA: Interrupted –
LEONORA: No, I'm here –
(*With the slightest suggestion of exasperation PLACIDA signals one
of the class…*)
PITY MY BLINDNESS, MOTHER…!
(*Pause…*)
Don't send for a man…
(*Pause…*)
PLACIDA: I pity where I choose –
LEONORA: EVERYTHING YOU SAY IS PERFECT…!
I was trying to coerce you
EVERYTHING PERFECT AND THIS VOICE
She might utter sentence of death on me and I should
yes oh yes a foolish smile would steal across my face yes
anything yes…
(*Pause…*)
What about under the steps, there is a small hole there…?
(*A suppressed giggle comes from the class…*)
I am not ambitious…!
(*They laugh.*)
MOTHER
MOTHER
(*They are silenced by her vehemence.*)

House me in your syllables cloak me in your breath I have heard the voice of Heaven and your odour washes me the odour of your flesh you are a garden do not drive me from your garden say yes to me say yes I have nothing more to plead with the proof of my passion must be the torment of my lips I cannot wring another word from them look oh look bruised lips…

(*The room is silent…*)

All beggars are liars

(*Pause…*)

From this moment I have ceased to beg

(*The class looks from* PLACIDA *to* LEONORA *and back again…*)

PLACIDA: Get beneath the steps…

(*LEONORA plucks up her ragged dresses and goes to leave…*)

And like a hound lie out when it's sunny and draw your head in when it rains…

(*LEONORA is still…*)

Bark

And

Bite

Your

Fleas…

(*She is still…*)

Scratch

Yawn

And

Sometimes

Howl…

(*Pause…*)

Bitch…

(*LEONORA goes out…the class is uncomfortable… PLACIDA is still…then she laughs…*)

Ursula has made me cruel…! I blame Ursula…!

(*She laughs again…*)

Run after her, say hot water's on the stove and towels, be nice –

NOT ALL OF YOU…!

(*They laugh with relief. Some hurry out...PLACIDA calls after them.*)

AND DINNER, SAY, THERE'S DINNER, BREAD AND STEW,
Oh, you know what to do...!
(*She waves her hand idly...*)

How clever she was, how ingratiating, and all that about my voice, the beauty of it and so on, does she think I can be flattered, as for being blind she isn't –
(*The class gasps...*)

NO, NOT A BIT...!
(*They giggle...*)

I've seen it before, oh, I have seen the entire repertoire of indigence, its masks, its mimicry, plaintive one moment, threatening the next...

PHYLLIS: All the same, it's true...
(*Pause...*)

Your voice...
(*Pause...*)

It's God's...
(*She shifts uncomfortably...*)

Isn't it...?
(*She looks around to the others...*)

We know it is...!
(*Pause...she sits to end the discomfort...*)

I think marriage is a state. A state, and not a desire.
(*She bites her lip with concentration. The others sit also...*)

The state is guarded. Locked. Inside it things happen which... I haven't been inside it I don't know but from the outside it –

PLACIDA: Ursula's here...!
(*She is pale...her hand goes involuntarily to her mouth...*)

Forgive me, do carry on, I –

PHYLLIS: No, I –

PLACIDA: Please, finish – I was –

PHYLLIS: I wasn't saying anything of profound importance, only –

PLACIDA: She's coming in...! Continue, please –

PHYLLIS: It wasn't very –

PLACIDA: I INSIST, CONTINUE WITH YOUR STATEMENT.

(Pause…)

PHYLLIS: From the outside, this state appears to be a place of mirrors…

PLACIDA: *(Not looking at PHYLLIS.)* Mirrors? How mirrors?

PHYLLIS: Mirrors because the gaze of marriage is forever back and back again, a permanent reflection of the self and therefore –

(She stops, as URSULA enters.)

PLACIDA: *(Avoiding looking at URSULA.)* Yes…? Does anyone agree with this…? Janet, do you see what Phyllis sees?

JANET: I –

PLACIDA: Mirrors?

(Pause. JANET is confused.)

JANET: I –

PLACIDA: When you contemplate the state of matrimony, is it mirrors that you see…?

JANET: I don't think I –

PLACIDA: Perhaps God intends it to be mirrors? Perhaps this endless mirroring is how God describes the perfect boundary of love?

(To URSULA without a glance.)

You're late…

URSULA: Forgive me, Mother –

PLACIDA: It doesn't matter – perhaps He discerns – in His absolute discernment – that this little state – as Phyllis has characterised the matrimonial condition – can be sustained by one thing only – which is vanity – yes – the mirroring of self in self – which is the nature of all acts of conjugality – not love therefore – not love at all – but temper – yes – frailty and temper – and that forlorn hope which echoes from the depths of Hell that in another's flesh might be discovered that refuge from solitude which in reality pertains only to God – is God's alone – and cannot be imitated in any other place – perhaps that is the awesome secret of the state of matrimony – perhaps that is what Phyllis intended to describe when she told us of the mirrors?

PHYLLIS: I wasn't certain what it was I –

PLACIDA: You were not certain, no –

PHYLLIS: I only wanted to articulate some sense of –

PLACIDA: And you did…! Wonderfully articulated it…! For me…! For everyone…! Let us stop there, let us take away the idea of the mirrors and separately contemplate its meaning – you have said such interesting things – all of you – mirrors – yes – thank you – thank you for the mirrors – Ursula stay behind, please…

(*The class rises and departs, dragging the chairs over the floor. As the sound fades, the small, half suppressed laugh of URSULA…she smothers it…she looks at PLACIDA, who stares out of a window… the laugh begins again…*)

URSULA: Your silences…

Your silences are bricks…

Sharp edges these bricks have…

AND WHEN THE WALL IS BUILT I SHAN'T LOOK OVER

NO

I SHAN'T GO RUNNING FOR A STOOL

(*PLACIDA yields nothing…*)

Please say lovely things

Please be adorable

Please

Please

(*PLACIDA ignores URSULA. URSULA goes silently to PLACIDA and shoves her playfully. PLACIDA winces but remains silent…*)

YOU ARE SUCH A FALSE BITCH SUCH A

(*She shoves PLACIDA again…*)

PLACIDA: Stop

Stop

Stop pushing me I

URSULA: ALL RIGHT I WON'T MARRY

(*A pause. PLACIDA turns at last. URSULA pulls a painted panel from her clothes, swiftly, deftly. She presents it to PLACIDA, holding it by its sides…*)

The body of a god.

(*PLACIDA lets her eyes rest on the panel…*)

The body of a god and sad eyes…

(*Pause…*)

These sad eyes made me certain…

(*Pause…*)

SAD EYES AND TWENTY-SEVEN CASTLES
(*She laughs…*)
I SHALL SHOVE YOU AGAIN THAT FACE
(*PLACIDA turns away…*)
I don't care for castles who wants his castles
YOU DO ENRAGE ME WITH THAT FACE
He seems perfectly acceptable to me please look at me
these portraits are fatuous of course not even approximate
utter fictions balderdash the artist waited on him fifteen
sittings so he says fifteen believe that if you wish to please
look at me
(*She flings the panel over the floor. The shock causes PLACIDA to
turn…*)
Thank you…
(*They exchange a long look…*)

PLACIDA: Ursula…
Oh, Ursula…
You are so…
LUMINOUS WITH INTELLIGENCE…
(*She bites her lip…*)

URSULA: They open your legs…
(*Pause…URSULA sits clumsily on a chair…*)
Don't they? Open your legs and
I saw it once
Funny posture
In a field
Cows nearby
Her heels went up
Higher and higher her shoes dropped off
One then the other
Such high heels
Ugly
Ugly
Oh God ugly
But ugly for the reason only for the reason that the thing is
rarely seen
Or not
Perhaps it is authentically ugly
Ugly because it's loathed by God

I CANNOT SAY FOR SURE THESE CASTLES DO NOT
CONSTITUTE AN ELEMENT OF HIS ATTRACTION I SIMPLY
CAN'T

(*She tips her chair…she looks at* PLACIDA…)

PLACIDA: Your wonderful intelligence…

URSULA: Yes…!

(*She laughs…*)

Lonely, all the same…

PLACIDA: Lonely? Lonely when I am here?

YOU WILL SCREAM WITH LONELINESS

YOUR LONELINESS WILL HOWL ACROSS THE SWAMP

URSULA: It's not a swamp it's an estuary –

PLACIDA: ALL RIGHT IT IS AN ESTUARY –

URSULA: Why must you call an estuary a swamp? Have you
been there?

PLACIDA: Never and nor shall I –

URSULA: Never been there and yet you presume to describe it
as a swamp –

PLACIDA: I do, I do presume –

URSULA: YOU SPOIL YOURSELF WITH YOUR PRESUMPTIONS

(*Pause…*)

Mother…

(*She suddenly flings herself forward, head in hands…*)

Tell me the beauty of virginity and I will tell you the
beauty of a man

(*Pause…*)

Please

Here

Now

THE PICTURE'S NOTHING

AND THE CASTLES NOTHING EITHER

He exists

I do not know him

He exists

And is a man

NAKED AND A MAN

(*Pause…* PLACIDA *looks at* URSULA…*who looks up at last…*)

Silence

Your silences are bricks

And when the wall is built I shan't look over
No…
(*She gets up, goes to retrieve the portrait…*)
Tell me can you why men sigh
You know the sigh
When they are near you
Near you especially
They sigh
(*She picks up the portrait…looks at* PLACIDA.)
PLACIDA: It's murder, Ursula…
URSULA: Murder? Why?
(*Pause…*URSULA *flings herself into* PLACIDA'*s arms…*)
I so so so
(*She sobs…*)
Require your blessing
GIVE IT TO ME GIVE YOUR BLESSING
(PLACIDA *is silent. At last* URSULA *frees herself from her arms…*)
No, that would be
How false and obviously demeaning that would be
A desecration of our
A smearing and a smudging of our
As I sat at the window
SEWING
And peering at the sunset on the swamp how
MY CHILD CRYING
The castle's slimy corridors
HOW I WOULD SQUIRM TO RECOLLECT A BLESSING OF
THAT SORT
No
Thank you
No
(*She extends the portrait before her.*)
He has brown eyes
My man…
(*She goes out.* PLACIDA *is still. She draws herself up…she
writhes…she calls.*)
PLACIDA: THE BLIND GIRL…! WHERE IS SHE…!

2

A man, naked, wet, staggers up a bank.

LUCAS: How hot is a bride
CHUCK US A BRIDE I'M FROZEN
That was silly oh so silly half-way over Death grabbed hold
of me look by the ankle marked me
WRAP ME IN HER
FLING HER OVER ME
THE HOT TAPS OF HER WOMB GUSH PLEASE
That was of all the infantile and ill-judged inspirations of
my life thus far the most oh certainly the most
SWIM THE ESTUARY IT'S WINTER
God
God
What caused me to even to
AND MY CLOTHES ON THE OPPOSITE BANK
Lucas
(*He smothers his nakedness in his arms.*)
Lucas
Lucas loved one
LET THAT CONCLUDE A PASSAGE OF YOUR LIFE
Slam the gates on such and brick the arch
Time surely to emerge from these
Riding horses up the vertical
Lying out all night in trees
Time to emerge
Ursula
Ursula, please…
(*He laughs a little…the cold causes him to shudder…*)
BLANKETS…!
(*LUCAS is surprised to see peasant women emerge anxiously from
the trees. They stare at him…*)
I
My clothes are on the other side I
Swam I
(*His shoulders rise and fall…*)
Swam the river God knows why

DON'T GAWP I AM NOT STUPID JUST A LITTLE

(*They stare…*)

Possibly I am

Yes

Very stupid possibly

But not for long oh no this stupidity has ceased a line is drawn under it Lucas was stupid certainly impulsive yes and oh intoxicated with himself but then a line was drawn under this

(*He looks intently at them…*)

Ursula held the chalk…

(*He laughs…only a little…*)

She has yellow hair I've seen the likeness very good I don't employ bad painters yellow as the plumage of

NOT THAT YELLOW I PROTESTED NO ONE HAS HAIR OF SUCH EXTRAORDINARY

Yes he says I gasped myself

The painter

GASPED HIMSELF

(*One of the women flings a gown at him…he catches it…*)

Thank you

He had to mix new colours yes new pigments isn't that the word

PIGMENT

(*He slips the gown over his shoulders…*)

I saw it

Half way across the –

(*He looks back at the estuary…*)

DID I SWIM THAT…?

OH, LUCAS-BEFORE-URSULA…

He was insane…

(*He bites his lip…*)

This yellow hair yes saw it as I swam and

(*Pause…*)

Who among you is

BOYS LIKE GIRLS' HAIR

WE DO

Have any of you yellow

(*Pause…*)

I can't testify as to her character obviously enquiries have been made but nothing detrimental yet reported and I must say were she bad-tempered melancholic spiteful even
TAKE OFF YOUR SCARVES NOW ALL OF YOU
It would not count against her because
SHAKE DOWN YOUR HAIR
Quite simply I have given my heart to her yes given my little heart to Ursula's hair
(*He gesticulates crossly.*)
SHOW
SHOW
(*They back away a little, and then tear off their headscarves…*)
Not one
Not one yellow-haired…
(*Pause…he seems gratified…they look at him…suddenly, on an impulse, one of the women launches herself at LUCAS and kisses him on the mouth. The kiss is long and desperate. The woman backs away, as if shocked at her own audacity. But she is instantly imitated by a second woman, and she by a third until LUCAS finds himself clustered by all the women at once. He sinks beneath the weight of their passions. A desperate encounter ensues, at the end of which the women flee, dragging with them the gown which had briefly covered LUCAS' nakedness. He lies in the snow, perfectly still.*)

3

The riverbank, upstream.

URSULA: You follow me.
    (*Pause…*)
    You follow me but I don't mind.
    (*Pause…*)
    Such bad manners trailing someone and without permission being blind is hardly an excuse is it for the neglect of simple courtesies come nearer keeping that distance seems superfluous COME NEARER SILLY
    (*LEONORA approaches…*)

LOOK…!

(*URSULA swiftly reveals the portrait of LUCAS from under her clothes…*)

YOU DID…!

You did…!

Look…

Liar…

(*URSULA smiles…*)

LEONORA: Look at what…?

(*URSULA laughs…*)

How beautiful he is the Lord of the Estuary and the painter in this instance quite unable to improve upon the subject rather his craft has been severely tested merely to describe what stood before him –

URSULA: Likewise me –

LEONORA: You likewise –

URSULA: Beautiful we both are and a destiny perhaps his sadness balanced by my joy his contemplation by my spontaneity our infants will in their perfection by the very oh the absolute

LISTEN I AM NOT SHALLOW OR ABSURD

YOU NEVER COULD BE ME BLIND GIRL

NEVER KNOW MY DESPERATION OR REPLACE ME IN THE MOTHER'S LOVE

I threaten you

Do you feel my breath scald you

I threaten you

(*Pause…*)

LEONORA: Show me the way back, then –

URSULA: Never –

LEONORA: (*Gesturing vaguely.*) Was it –

URSULA: Fall in ditches –

LEONORA: I've lost my bearings –

URSULA: Drown –

LEONORA: I shall if you refuse to –

URSULA: LISTEN…!

(*Pause…*)

The river…which if you plunge in…will carry your corpse
to my betrothed…the eyes gone…but the bones butting
the pier…a hollow drumming to his dawn…

(*LEONORA goes to leave and stops, her hand before her suggestive
of blindness, groping, an error…*

*Then she continues her way. URSULA remains. Her hands still
grasp the panel. A voice comes from the still body of LUCAS.*)

CHRIST: Throw the panel in the river.

(*Pause…*)

URSULA: Throw it in the river, why…?

(*Pause…*)

CHRIST: Are you Ursula…?

URSULA: I am Ursula, but –

CHRIST: Then do as I say…

(*Pause…*)

URSULA: Because I'm Ursula…I must do as you say…?

(*Pause…*)

And if I were not Ursula –

CHRIST: Shh…

URSULA: Don't shh me, I hate to be shh'd –

CHRIST: Your violence sometimes puzzles me –

URSULA: Is that so? It very rarely puzzles me, I always know
what lies behind my violence –

(*She flings the panel far away, into the river.*)

WHY DID I DO THAT

WHY DID I DO THAT

WHY

WHY

YOU'RE CHRIST

AND I AM URSULA

You see, I am not idolatrous and beauty is frankly of
very little interest to me it interests others and because it
interests them they will ascribe the selfsame interest to me
they're wrong however

(*Pause…*)

I did what you asked, but the reason for your asking was
poor…

(*Pause…*)

CHRIST ENVIES LUCAS

IS THAT NOT THE CASE
ENVIES HIM HIS BRIDE?
(*Pause…*)
Anyway it floats someone will discover it lying in the reeds
and
I AM A VIRGIN AND IT APPEARS IMPERFECT TO ME
Some herdsman watering his stock
Some boy fishing
YOU INSIST ON MY VIRGINITY THEN WHY WAS I MADE
YELLOW-HAIRED LIKE THIS
To pick out a single attribute
AND IF I MUST BE YELLOW-HAIRED WHY THESE BLUE EYES
And if blue eyes
THESE LIPS
I must tell you I have not encountered one man yet since I
became a woman who succeeded in concealing
INCLUDING PRIESTS
OH YES THEM ALSO
His fascination
IT'S THE SAME WITH MOTHER PLACIDA
The same you should walk with her down a street her
movements are so
MEN DART ABOUT LIKE BIRDS
Any excuse to perch alongside her and when she speaks
they
(*URSULA is silent…*)
Oh, and that –
Oh, that –
THAT IS
EXACTLY THAT IS OUR ORDEAL…
(*Pause…she shakes her head…*)
Easy to be a virgin when no man's eyes are ferreting in
us…
(*She laughs with recognition.*)
AND THEIRS ALSO…!
THEIR ORDEAL TO YEARN FOR WHAT BELONGS TO CHRIST
AND TO CHRIST ONLY…
(*She pouts, she presses her fingers to her lips.*)

I'll cut it off

This blazing banner of my sensuality

CHRIST: No –

URSULA: No, why not?

CHRIST: Keep your yellow hair –

URSULA: KEEP IT BUT IT'S PERMANENT TEMPTATION

(A fractional pause. She laughs a short laugh.)

I am so slow to catch your calculation

You are a streamer flying in the wind

I go to grasp you and

THE CHRISTMIND WHAT A

(She gasps…)

And I believed that I was clever…

(A girl runs on…)

CLARA: Ursula…!

URSULA: SH…!

CLARA: Ursula…!

URSULA: *(Violently.)* I AM WITH CHRIST…

(Pause…CLARA is holding the panel…a second girl appears, tentatively…)

CLARA: We –

(She looks at the second girl.)

Didn't we –

CYNTHIA: Found this…

(URSULA does not reply. The girls begin to withdraw, as tactfully as possible…)

URSULA: Found what…?

(CLARA turns to show the panel…)

CLARA: Floating…

PLACIDA: *(Entering.)* You have wounded Leonora –

URSULA: Shh –

PLACIDA: Leonora who is blind you have –

URSULA: I'VE GOT CHRIST HERE…

(CLARA and CYNTHIA exchange nervous glances…PLACIDA is infinitely patient…)

PLACIDA: You have Christ –

URSULA: WITH ME YES SO HUSH…

(She glares at PLACIDA. She makes an agonised gesture with her hands...)

Gone...!

Oh, gone...!

(She writhes, sobs, recovers...)

What do you expect, this forlorn place suddenly becomes a cross-roads, the wilderness swarms with teems with seethes in swirling

IT WAS IN THE RIVER FOR THE REASON THAT I PLACED IT THERE

NOT ALL THINGS THAT APPEAR INCONGRUOUS ARE SO

A PORTRAIT IN A RIVER SO WHAT

DOGS ON DINNER TABLES

GIRLS IN SWAMPS

(CLARA backs away, alarmed by URSULA's vehemence.)

PLACIDA: You are being coarse and violent –

URSULA: SOME GIRLS BELONG IN SWAMPS –

PLACIDA: Coarse and violent, Ursula –

URSULA: Yes –

PLACIDA: First you wish the blind girl drowned and now –

URSULA: SHE IS NOT BLIND AND I HATE HER YES...

(Pause...)

PLACIDA: Perhaps encountering Christ in certain individuals is not propitious –

URSULA: Oh, shut up...

PLACIDA: No, I shan't shut up –

URSULA: You will because –

PLACIDA: No –

URSULA: I CANNOT TOLERATE ANOTHER HOUR OF YOUR INFINITE TRANQUILLITY...!

IT DROWNS

IT SUFFOCATES

IT STIFLES ME

(She glares at PLACIDA. CYNTHIA and CLARA, unable to tolerate the tension, throw down the panel and run away. URSULA weeps through her rage...)

THE BLIND GIRL IS NOT BLIND

(Her gaze falters...)

Oh...
Do not replace me with the blind girl...
(*She shakes her head...she ceases to sob...*)
Christ says my beauty must be my ordeal...
(*She lifts her eyes to* PLACIDA.)
Help me, Mother...
(*Pause...*)
Teach me the sex that is not one...
TEACH ME TO LOVE THE ACT THAT IS NOT EVER DONE
(*Pause...*)

PLACIDA: Christ knows you.

URSULA: Does He...?

PLACIDA: He knows your excellence.

URSULA: My excellence, yes...

PLACIDA: This excellence He knows will never find its equal.

URSULA: No...

PLACIDA: Therefore He spares you.

URSULA: Spares me, yes –

PLACIDA: Oh, the solitude and melancholy He spares you,
    Ursula...!

URSULA: Yes –

PLACIDA: Because the act is false.

URSULA: False...?

PLACIDA: False, yes. An ecstasy, but false.
    (*URSULA struggles...*)

URSULA: Yes...

PLACIDA: False because it lies even as it promises.

URSULA: And what it promises is –

PLACIDA: The single thing which for all our desperate longing
    never can be
    NEVER
    NEVER
    Can be taken or conferred...
    (*Pause...*)

URSULA: And that –
    (*She gropes for words...*)
    That is –

PLACIDA: The –

URSULA: Shh…!

(She is herself placid…)

The annihilation of the self…

(PLACIDA is still…)

Self…

Self…

It fills my mouth like vomit…

(She is uncoiled…)

PLACIDA: Do pick up his picture and if you want it, keep it by you and –

URSULA: I don't want it –

PLACIDA: When you are ready to discard it –

URSULA: I'm ready now –

PLACIDA: *(Retrieving the panel herself.)* It can be returned to its –

URSULA: CHRIST SAID TO CHUCK IT IN THE RIVER.

(Pause…)

PLACIDA: Did he…?

URSULA: So I did.

(PLACIDA looks at the panel.)

PLACIDA: You did and yet –

(She wipes it with her sleeve.)

You did and still it –

URSULA: BLOODY WELL CAME BACK AGAIN…!

(She laughs wildly, and stops…)

I'm going to the estuary

The reeds

The mudbanks

The rotting hulks

PLACIDA: Going to the –

URSULA: Going to the estuary to say –

(Pause…)

Sorry…

(Pause…)

Which is a heavy word to carry

Take one end of it

(PLACIDA looks at URSULA…)

TAKE ONE END OF SORRY PLEASE

(As PLACIDA contemplates what has been proposed by URSULA, the figure of LUCAS rises from its prone position. PLACIDA senses

this. Her head slowly turns from URSULA *to observe him. He is
still for a moment before* LEONORA *rushes to him, clasping him
in her arms…she shudders…she sobs…he by contrast is still as a
monument…)*

PLACIDA: (*To* URSULA.) But he'll murder you…

URSULA: (*Bemused.*) Murder…? Why…?

PLACIDA: It's obvious…

URSULA: Why murder me when –

PLACIDA: LOOK

LOOK AT HIS FACE

(*PLACIDA extends the panel to* URSULA…*pause…*URSULA*'s eyes
strain at the portrait…)*

URSULA: Throw it in the river…!

PLACIDA: In the river…!

IN THE RIVER, YES…!

(*Laughing, she hurries to the riverbank…she lifts her arm…she
hesitates…)*

Or not…?

(*Pause…)*

No…

(*She looks earnestly at* URSULA…)

Let us overcome it, rather…

Let us pacify him…

LET US LEAD HIM TO CHRIST…

(URSULA *stares at* PLACIDA…PLACIDA *playfully throws the panel
to her…she catches it…she laughs…she tosses it back…*PLACIDA
laughs…she glances at the panel…)

Not so angry now…

Look…

(*She shows it to* URSULA…)

URSULA: Hmm….

PLACIDA: (*Turning it back to examine it.*) Oh, certainly…

Certainly not as angry now…

(*Biting her lip, she flings it back to* URSULA…*they laugh
simultaneously. They hurry off…)*

4

LEONORA: They don't know if I'm blind or not…

(*Pause…*)

NO MORE DO I

(*Pause…*)

What is seeing, Lucas…?

IT IS SEEING YOU AND IF I DON'T SEE YOU I DON'T SEE

(*He frowns at her…*)

Oh, I lean on your soul…!

I stack my passion on your soul which sags which groans under the weight of it I am so unkind to your soul it is no oak is it it is no elm thrusting its roots deep down to clays and rivers no it is a tender little sapling fixed to sticks I must not lean on it Ursula she will tend it with such a such a pretty water can

NOT TOO MUCH WATER HOWEVER

I MUST TELL HER

NOT TOO MUCH ANYTHING

I have almost killed her Ursula crept up behind her and so on almost but I like her

PLEASE DON'T FROWN IT SCALDS ME

She's very

Oh, I like Ursula…

(*She twitches, shifts, is still…*)

LUCAS: Good.

(*She lifts her eyes to him…*)

LEONORA: What is?

(*Pause…*)

I hate you like this this avoiding of my eyes this standing at a proper distance if you so shudder to recall our intimacy have me killed dropped down a shaft someone could scrape a little grave for me or in the river you know how fast it flows I'd be flotsam on a foreign beach before –

LUCAS: I HAVE CONSIDERED IT –

LEONORA: Good –

LUCAS: GOOD WHY –

LEONORA: At least it shows some –

LUCAS: PRECISELY –

LEONORA: Yes –

LUCAS: ALL YOU WANT IS FEELING FROM ME FEELING FEELING
ANY FEELING –

LEONORA: Yes –

LUCAS: LOATHING VIOLENCE OR CONTEMPT –

LEONORA: Yes –

LUCAS: I'VE NONE I'VE NONE OF THOSE.
(*Pause...*)

LEONORA: I'm so glad...
(*She weeps...*)
I'm so glad you don't hold me in contempt...
(*She laughs also...her head shakes...she sniffs...*)
The Mother is a
Oh, she has this studied possibly artificial I don't know
each syllable is grave and measured oh and this reflects
her whole appearance she is in every aspect not young still
beautiful even the way she lifts a hand closing her eyes
crossing one leg on the other all utterly
I LIKE HER ALSO
False you'd find it comical whereas
(*Pause...*)
Ursula is natural. This naturalness flows up against the
Mother's falseness...and erodes it...
(*She looks at LUCAS...*)
They are virgins...

LUCAS: Yes...

LEONORA: Virgins, Lucas...

LUCAS: Obviously...!
(*Pause...*)
I like virginity...

LEONORA: You liked mine...

LUCAS: On the contrary, it did not bother me if you were
sealed or used, fresh, rancid, healthy or diseased –
(*She laughs...*)
I HAD TO HAVE YOU...!
(*They both laugh...*)
Death might have peered out of your cunt and beckoned
me still I'd have gone...
(*LEONORA laughs with pleasure...*)

111

But I require virginity in Ursula...
(*She frowns...*)
What I will find with her...and what she finds in me...can
have been forecast by no other...
(*Pause...*)
And to tell the truth I certainly will howl and wail if
I discover some youth put fingers in her on a sunny
afternoon somewhere –
(*She snorts...*)
Yes...! That is how IMMACULATE I FEEL...
(*He shrugs, turns to LEONORA...*)
Poor woman, I shall interrogate her
I shall
Sifting her hair
On long agonies of moonshine
PROSECUTE HER FOR HER VERY THOUGHTS...
(*He smiles...*)
I'm like that
I'm
SO IMPERIAL...
(*He bites his lip...LEONORA endures...*)

LEONORA: And yet...
(*Pause...*)
She is a virgin...

LUCAS: So you say...and I say good...! Tell me, her body is it
straight, and hips...I like deep hips, I like an arse...yours
was a palace to me...yes...better than yours or worse?
(*Pause...*)

LEONORA: I've never seen her arse...

LUCAS: Oh...and I thought you all slept naked...but tall...?
TALL IS SHE, LEONORA...!

LEONORA: Tall, yes –

LUCAS: But not a freak? Not a shuddering shaft of timber, I
plastered questions on the painter but they lie, all painters
lie, they cannot help themselves,
YOUR HEIGHT OR MORE?
(*Pause...he detects the discomfort of LEONORA.*)
What...!
What...!

LEONORA: SHE IS A VIRGIN

LUCAS: YES

YES

I SAID YES DIDN'T I

LEONORA: AND INTENDS TO STAY ONE

(*Pause…*)

LUCAS: Stay one…? But of course, until I meet with her she must stay one, she is betrothed how can she not stay one…?

(*LEONORA is silent…*)

Stay one married or not…?

(*He laughs a bitter, short laugh…*)

Stay one

Funny phrase to stay one

I shall call her stay one

STAY ONE

BY CHRIST SHE WON'T STAY ONE MY DARLING STAY – ONE

NOT FOR LONG

LEONORA: It's Christ who says so –

LUCAS: WHAT CHRIST –

LEONORA: CHRIST THE LORD APPEARED TO HER –

LUCAS: DID HE CHRIST WHAT LORD I'M THE LORD OF HERE –

(*LEONORA turns a little away…*)

No –

I'm –

(*He is instantly cooled. He walks a few paces and returns again…*)

And said what?

(*Pause…*)

Christ…?

(*Pause…*)

His words…?

(*Pause…*)

What…?

(*Pause…*)

Lots…?

(*Pause…*)

Or little…?

(*Pause…*)

How verbose is Christ…?

LEONORA: Shh –

LUCAS: I'M TRYING TO BE –

LEONORA: Shh –

LUCAS: Leonora, I'm –

LEONORA: I know you are, yes –

LUCAS: TRYING TO BE SENSIBLE.

(Pause. He stares into her eyes…)

You see I am.

(Pause…)

God knows it.

LEONORA: Yes.

(Pause…)

LUCAS: Said what, then?

(Pause…)

LEONORA: To throw your picture in the river.

(Pause…)

LUCAS: And did she?

LEONORA: Yes.

(Pause…)

LUCAS: What – went and –

LEONORA: She was beside the river –

LUCAS: Beside the river? With my picture?

LEONORA: Yes. She carried it.

LUCAS: Carried my picture? All the time?

LEONORA: I think so –

LUCAS: You think so –

LEONORA: ALWAYS YES SHE KEPT IT IN HER CLOTHES…!

(She turns away…LUCAS shrugs…)

LUCAS: Hmm…

(He shakes his head…)

LEONORA: And then it got fished out again.

LUCAS: *(Turning.)* Ha…!

FISHED OUT AGAIN…?

LEONORA: Yes –

LUCAS: EXTRAORDINARY THE POWER OF HER LOVE –

LEONORA: Two girls were walking and –

LUCAS: CHRIST OVERRULED…!

(He stares with intensity and joy.)

CHRIST IN ERROR...!

(*Pause...*)

Surely...?

LEONORA: Lucas, Ursula is coming here. But not to be your bride.

(*He stares...a long pause elapses...*)

I have been so oh so passionately loyal to you to place myself in such a –

LUCAS: Never mind you –

LEONORA: Such a pitiful and painful –

LUCAS: Never mind you now –

LEONORA: I SLEEP UNDER THE STEPS, LUCAS –

LUCAS: WE CANNOT MIND YOU AND ME AT THE SAME TIME...!

(*Pause...*)

Can we...?

(*Pause...*)

We must attend to me now.

(*Pause...*)

Obviously...

(*Bitter tears rise in LEONORA's eyes...LUCAS extends a hand...she does not accept it...*)

LEONORA: Take me, Lucas...

(*Pause...he chews anxiously...he withdraws his hands...*)

CHRIST COULD NOT STOP MY LOVE I WOULD SLAP CHRIST ACROSS HIS JAW AND FLING CLODS AFTER HIM AS HE WENT RUNNING FROM MY WRATH BRUISED CHRIST CHRIST WITH FIVE CLAW MARKS IF ANYTHING GOES IN THE RIVER LORD IT'S YOU

(*LUCAS cannot prevent himself laughing...*)

I would

I would say that

I'd be so

Oh, Lucas, you know me

Christ could not kill my love so I must

(*Pause...*)

Mustn't I...?

(*She shuts her eyes...*)

Blind again...

(*She goes off...*)

ACT TWO

1

Two young women enter a boat.

BENEDICTA: No bags, she says...!

ANNE: No bags because our whole wealth is our person.

BENEDICTA: Soap, however...?

ANNE: Soap yes, but only soap, no powders, shadows, scents, gems, or crucifixes either.

BENEDICTA: But when we sleep, we –

ANNE: Sleep.

(*Pause...*)

BENEDICTA: Sleep...?

ANNE: On the ground...!

(*Two more young women enter.*)

BENEDICTA: (*Turning to them.*) We're sleeping on the ground...!

(*She points.*)

That's not allowed...!

CYNTHIA: What?

BENEDICTA: That bag –

CYNTHIA: It's a basket –

BENEDICTA: Baskets aren't allowed –

CYNTHIA: It's empty –

BENEDICTA: So what, it's not allowed – what do you want an empty basket for – Anne, she cannot have a basket, can she...?

CYNTHIA: Your hair's not loose –

BENEDICTA: What –

CYNTHIA: Your hair must look like Ursula's –

BENEDICTA: Don't change the subject –

LAMENTINA: Everybody's hair must look the same –

BENEDICTA: It will look the same, I have put it up because –

(*PERDITA and PHYLLIS enter...*)

HERS IS NOT LOOSE, EITHER...!

ANNE: I don't know about empty baskets, Benedicta –

PHYLLIS: Oh, are we supposed to keep our hair down?

116

ANNE: What do you want it for?

LAMENTINA: Everybody's hair must look the same –

CYNTHIA: My mother's given me a shopping list –

LAMENTINA: And no one is to wear a ring, or slides, or even bands –

ANNE: (*To CYNTHIA.*) But we are not shopping…
> (*PLACIDA enters, followed by URSULA and LEONORA, LEONORA assisted by JANET. The girls are swiftly silent…*)

PLACIDA: Shopping…?
> (*She smiles…*)

Who said shopping?
> (*Pause…CYNTHIA's head hangs…*)

CYNTHIA: My mother is…
> (*She shrugs with embarassment.*)

My mother is…incredibly…stupid…

PLACIDA: Of course she is not stupid…! She perhaps misunderstood the purpose of our voyage. She thought perhaps, it was a holiday…
> (*CYNTHIA shifts uncomfortably.*)

Perhaps you did…

CYNTHIA: No, Placida, I did not.
> (*CYNTHIA bites her lip…*)

My mother is not stupid. I should not have called my mother stupid. I apologise to my mother.
> (*A silence fills the deck…*)

PERDITA: BUT IS IT NOT A HOLIDAY IN SOME WAYS…!
> (*Laughter erupts on all sides. PLACIDA smiles…*)

Are you not rejoicing? Are we not so glad to have our yellow-haired and splendid Ursula confirmed in our companionship that –
> (*She stops…*)

That's odd…did you hear that…?
> (*They listen, puzzled.*)

The word, I used the word, oh, how peculiar, I said oh, how strange and miraculous, I said –

COMPANION-SHIP…
> (*They are suddenly serious. PLACIDA kisses PERDITA on the cheek…*)

And Ursula is –
I never saw Ursula more –
Did anyone –
More perfect than she is today…
(*Pause…*)

PLACIDA: No, never more perfect…
(*URSULA discreetly inclines her head…*)
How well it suits you all to wear no colour, shadow, gems,
or anything that was not granted you by God. We wear the
perfume of our own virginity…
(*They are moved…*)

LEONORA: I can't see Ursula…
I should so love to glimpse once only, Ursula…
Instead I hear Placida's voice
WHY DID GOD GRANT THAT VOICE TO PLACIDA
(*Pause…*)
If not to break our hearts with it…?
(*She laughs…CLARA appears swiftly.*)

CLARA: The river's high…! We have to sail, the men say…!

PLACIDA: (*To all of them.*) Wave, then…! Wave to your fathers
and your mothers… Hurry…go on deck…!
(*They surge out…only LEONORA remains…*)
You have no father…

LEONORA: No…
(*Pause…*)

PLACIDA: Neither eyes nor parents…

LEONORA: Only you…
(*Pause…PLACIDA watches her…then turns to go.*)
I love your scent…
(*Pause…*)
And your hair – I've enquired about your hair –
your hair is short –

PLACIDA: I also must wave from the deck –

LEONORA: Wave, yes…
(*PLACIDA starts to go up…stops…*)

PLACIDA: It is not easy, surely, for a vagrant to remain a
virgin…?
(*LEONORA is silent…*)
A vagrant has no treasure, has she…?

(*Pause…*)

Any treasure that she had the world would certainly have robbed her of…

(*Pause…*)

I daresay…

(*Pause…*)

I think you are not blind…and not a virgin, either…

(*LEONORA lifts her face to PLACIDA…*)

LEONORA: Don't throw me off this ship…

(*PLACIDA frowns…*)

I LOVE YOU DO NOT THROW ME OFF THIS SHIP

(*PLACIDA is agitated. She swiftly draws out from under her coats the panel. She shows it to LEONORA.*)

PLACIDA: WHO IS THIS…!

(*Pause…*)

LEONORA: It is Lucas…a man…

(*Pause…the sounds of the virgins on deck…*)

PLACIDA: And Lucas…is he sad?

LEONORA: He is sad, yes…

PLACIDA: Why? What makes him so?

(*LEONORA hesitates…*)

He is a prince, is he not?

WHAT MAKES HIM SAD…!

(*The descent of the virgins abruptly curtails PLACIDA's questions. She flings the panel, with a deliberate gesture, across the deck…*)

Lucas…!

Someone suspend him from a hook…or nail him…

(*The virgins stare…*)

I must wave, mustn't I…

(*She starts to go up.*)

Or stand…

Perhaps, just stand…

(*She hurries up to the deck…the virgins are briefly silent…chilled by an anxiety…*)

PHYLLIS: (*Going to retrieve the panel.*) I do think it's peculiar
    – going to a man – where shall we hang this – going to a
    man who –

ANNE: There's a nail here –

PHYLLIS: Who full of ardour and anticipation – we assume –

(*She hangs up the panel.*)

ANNE: That's not straight –

PHYLLIS: Fully expecting to throw his arms wide open to his
    bride – we assume –

ANNE: No –

PHYLLIS: Finds instead a boat loaded with virgins who –

ANNE: Still not straight –

PHYLLIS: (*Abandoning the nail.*) Declare not only is the bride no
    bride at all but –

CYNTHIA: (*As ANNE adjusts the picture.*) That's it –

PHYLLIS: But she is marrying elsewhere –

URSULA: To Christ –

PHYLLIS: To Christ, yes, but all the same I think we can
    assume most men would –

URSULA: You know most men, do you –

PHYLLIS: I don't know men at all, but most I think would be
    inclined to give way to a terrible –

URSULA: HE WON'T GIVE WAY TO ANYTHING.
    (*PHYLLIS is silenced…*)
    We thought of this. We thought of Lucas. Looking at his
    picture we wondered what lay concealed in such a sad
    expression. Anger, possibly. Or just as likely, shame, some
    act for which he cannot yet forgive himself.

CLARA: (*Looking at the panel.*) Murder…?

URSULA: Who knows, but in announcing how Christ claimed
    me –

CLARA: Murder, yes, he is a murderer –

BENEDICTA: Oh, Clara, please –

CLARA: Look at it, that is the face of someone who has
    murdered –

PERDITA: Rubbish –

CLARA: OR INTENDS TO.
    (*Pause…*)

URSULA: How could I have come alone?
    (*Pause…*)
    You would not have let me…!
    (*They are uncomfortable…*)

This dark river…these terrible trees…you would have
thrown your arms around me and insisted that I stayed…
but Christ…

(*She bites her lip thoughtfully…*)

It is the thing with Christ, is it not…?

CHRIST MUST BE TOLD…

(*They look at her…a chill atmosphere suffuses them…*)

LEONORA: The current…can you feel the current plucking us
along…? The river's impatience for the sea… It thinks the
sea is kind. It has heard rumours of the sea. Its strength.
Its moods. Its masculinity. What a surge of waters in the
estuary…! A turbulence. A passion. And then the river
vanishes. Perhaps it dies…

(*Pause…*)

And so shall we…

(*Pause…*)

Die…

(*Pause. She laughs…*)

I don't rule it out…! These princes…! They love swords…!
Short blades…! Long blades…! Double-handed…! Two-
edged…! Even three…! Three-edged long swords…!
You should see the armouries…! And halberds…! The
ingenuity…! I won't go on…! Fifteen cutting surfaces…and
that's not counting spikes…! Think of that in the entrails…!
Think of that in the womb…! I won't go on…

(*She laughs, shaking her head…*)

URSULA: You are not blind…

LEONORA: Everyone says I'm not blind…

URSULA: It's obvious…

LEONORA: Not to me, alas –

URSULA: But lie, lie if you want to, Christ will be the judge
of all our actions and our thoughts, and what may be
concealed from us is not –

LEONORA: No –

URSULA: And cannot be –

LEONORA: No, indeed –

URSULA: Concealed from him –

LEONORA: Oh, you are so –

LAMENTINA: Shh –

LEONORA: So very –

LAMENTINA: Shh –

LEONORA: Yes, but she is so – I like Ursula but – oh –

LAMENTINA: Please, this journey is so –

LEONORA: All right –

LAMENTINA: So very –

JANET: (*To LAMENTINA.*) Shh –

LAMENTINA: Difficult and actually quite –

JANET: Shh –

LAMENTINA: Quite frightening – I don't mind saying so – it frightens me and –

JANET: Shh –

LEONORA: Oh, everyone is shhshhing –

BENEDICTA: (*To LEONORA.*) You should not frighten people with talk of swords –

LEONORA: No, no, I shouldn't –

BENEDICTA: Halberds and so on –

LEONORA: I shouldn't no, but Ursula is so – has become so –

PERDITA: Shh –

LEONORA: Since meeting Christ –

URSULA: What? What have I become?

LEONORA: And I like Christ, I don't concede to anyone a greater love of Christ than I myself –

URSULA: WHAT –

LEONORA: DEATHLY...

  (*Pause...*)

  Oh, I've said death again...I've frightened everyone...

  (*Pause...*)

  I'll go on deck...

  (*Pause...*)

  Look –

  (*She walks...*)

  Straight to the ladder...how can I be blind...?

2

The deck at night.

URSULA: I do not like this landscape.

  (*Pause.*)

The trees are thin, and when a wind blows through them, all the leaves are stricken with a panic…
(*Pause.*)
The water's turbid…
(*Pause.*)
Even the air is heavy and turns my hair peculiar, look, it's dead as string and shrivelled…
(*She draws it through her fingers.*)
Yours is so short, perhaps you haven't noticed…

PLACIDA: I hadn't…

URSULA: Short hair must be the fashion round the estuary YOU MUST TALK WITH THEM THEY ARE IN A TERROR
(*Pause.*)
Perhaps you haven't noticed.
You separate yourself
Always you drift to one end or the other
Whichever end we're at you're not
Below deck when we're up
Up when we're down
They are convinced they will be murdered why don't you reassure them always they look to you they always have and you are nowhere to be seen

PLACIDA: Pray with them…
(*She looks at URSULA for the first time…*)
Pray with them, Ursula…
(*Pause.*)
Christ said did He not
THROW THE PICTURE IN THE RIVER
It is in the river, Ursula
We have done His will
(*Pause.*)

URSULA: You believe it…
You believe it yourself…
YOU BELIEVE WE WILL BE KILLED BY LUCAS
(*Pause…she stares at PLACIDA…*)
TURN THE BOAT ROUND…!
(*PLACIDA only looks into URSULA…the duration and profundity of this stare are interrupted by the appearance of four of the virgins.*)

PHYLLIS: There's been an election –

BENEDICTA: We were elected –

PHYLLIS: Everybody voted and –

PERDITA: The outcome was that we –

JANET: Everybody voted –

PERDITA: Except Leonora –

JANET: Leonora didn't –

PHYLLIS: Everybody voted except Leonora and it's us who –

> (*Pause…*)
>
> It's we who have the –
>
> (*Pause…*)
>
> We have to speak…
>
> (*A long pause…PLACIDA looks at them…URSULA at the deck…*)

PLACIDA: (*Rising to her feet…*) How wonderful these nights are…as if some blanket had been flung over the earth… and we were quite alone…we ten…alone with God…

> (*Pause…*)

PHYLLIS: We want to –

PLACIDA: Shh…!

> (*Pause…*)
>
> How dense this silence is…it sits in our ears…

BENEDICTA: Ten…?

PLACIDA: It occupies us…have you ever known a silence which took you in its hands like this…? It is the love of Christ…

> (*Pause…PLACIDA's expression has a radiance…*)

BENEDICTA: Ten…?

JANET: We –

> We –

PHYLLIS: Some of us think –

PLACIDA: Hold my hand…

> (*PHYLLIS extends her hand. PLACIDA takes it in hers…*)
>
> My hand is small…
>
> My hand is hardly bigger than a child's…
>
> And really, it touches rather few things…
>
> (*PHYLLIS looks at PLACIDA…*)
>
> Go to them and say not only were you four elected but we all were
>
> All ten of us

Elected by God
To carry Christ into the estuary
ALSO LET THEM BRUSH THEIR HAIR
The climate is not kind to it
(*PHYLLIS is hesitant, but overcome. She withdraws, followed by
the rest, except BENEDICTA, who hangs back...*)
BENEDICTA: Mother...we are not ten...
(*PLACIDA looks at her...*)
You said ten...
(*She goes swiftly...PLACIDA is suddenly seized by a sobbing which
is also a laughter, a kind of repressed triumph. URSULA takes
her in her arms. They breathe in gulps, holding one another. The
daylight rises on a solitary man...*)

3

LUCAS, naked with a sword of tremendous breadth, wrapped...

LUCAS: I'm not less beautiful than Christ
(*Pause...*)
Nor less lonely
Christ asked nothing never once did He ask of another
mortal any favour any kindness any
EXCEPT ONCE
I'm wrong
ONCE
DON'T LET THEM TEST ME ON THE GOSPELS I AM AN
AUTHORITY
This once the same night He was taken
In the garden
Watch with me He said
THE SOLITARY OCCASION OF HIS LIFE
And they fell asleep
They did
They fell asleep
THE WORST NIGHT OF HIS WRETCHED LIFE
They fell asleep
People
Humans

Oh
BEGGED THEM
NOT ONCE
NOT TWICE
THREE TIMES
Watch with me
They fell asleep
They fell asleep
Humans
Oh
I shan't be making that mistake
Others possibly
Not that
I'm not immune to error
NOT THAT HOWEVER
THAT PARTICULAR FAILURE OF
What
Judgement I suppose
His last night
Really
A catastrophe
Begging
Pleading
Squirming to avoid
His nerve went
Sad in many ways
Unedifying
SOLITUDE MUST BE VOCATIONAL
Surely
A desire
Surely
Solitude?
I'll flirt
Outrageously
He did
Oh yes
Christ flirted
Boys

Girls
Romans
Jews
That stillness
Never running
Never drunk
That ever-still
That ever-serious
FLIRTATION
Eleven unloved women
Virgins
I dislike the word
Virgin
Dislike it
Shan't say it again
The word has dropped from my vocabulary
Fell
Slipped
A playing card between the floorboards
Gone
Oh
Never mind
And if they use it I shall say
What's that
A what
A
Oh you mean unloved
(*Pause…*)
And having flirted
Having emptied every drawer and cupboard of my
personality
Littered
Scattered
Heaped
A mess of charm and temper
Ursula
I'll have your cunt now I will say
CUNT

CUNT
The word's okay
Imperfect but okay
A little coarse
A little brusque
Spoiled
Sullied
Ursula
YOU HAVE COME AND YOU MUST STAY
The others
Oh
Oh
Them
(*He lifts his shoulders in a prolonged shrug…*)
Let Christ have them to play with
(*He folds his arms over the hilt…*)

4

The virgins are drawn up on deck. One is bound in ropes and blindfolded. The rest scan the horizon. Suddenly, URSULA points.

URSULA: Three spires…! Three spires, look…!
    (*CYNTHIA lets out a moan…*)
    Be quiet…!
LEONORA: HIS CITY…
    (*The moan goes on…*)
    HIS CITY CLINGING TO THE RIVERBANK…
URSULA: (*To CYNTHIA.*) If you do not be quiet you will be
    gagged –
LEONORA: HIS CITY CLIMBING OUT THE MARSH –
URSULA: (*To CYNTHIA.*) Do you wish to be gagged, Cynthia –
LEONORA: AND TOPPLING IN THE SEA –
PHYLLIS: Three spires…! Yes…!
LAMENTINA: Three…?
ANNE: Fetch the Mother…!
    (*Several call PLACIDA's name…*)
CYNTHIA: (*With a groan.*) I AM NOT A VIRGIN –
URSULA: All right, I'm gagging you –
CYNTHIA: I'm not a virgin, Ursula…

URSULA: IT DOES NOT MATTER NOW –

CYNTHIA: I slept with the mad boy in the fallow field –

SEVERAL: OH, SHH...! SHH...!

CYNTHIA: I did...! I did...!

(*URSULA tips her head back. They gag her. She is subdued. In the silence, PLACIDA appears from the lower deck. She is wearing a small, neat hat...*)

PLACIDA: Yes...

The three spires, yes...

(*The virgins are awed, puzzled, and watch PLACIDA, who turns to them at last...*)

LEONORA: How perfect you are today...

(*Pause...*)

How perfect you are every day...

(*Pause...PLACIDA turns to look at the city...*)

PLACIDA: And each spire a different colour...

URSULA: The hat –

LEONORA: The first is slate –

URSULA: The hat –

LEONORA: The second shingle –

URSULA: WHAT IS THE HAT...?

LEONORA: And the third brick, from the clays of the estuary

THE HAT IS PERFECT, MOTHER...

(*Pause...*)

And reveals your mouth...

URSULA: As I am near to Christ, I tell you Christ abhors that hat...

BENEDICTA: Ursula –

URSULA: I speak Christ's anger –

BENEDICTA: Ursula –

URSULA: I speak Christ's injury –

PERDITA: I see him...!

CLARA: Where...?

PERDITA: Lucas...!

Alone...!

Lucas on the jetty...!

(*Pause...as the boat edges nearer to mooring, the virgins prepare themselves...their eyes fall...LUCAS walks the length*

of a gangway…he stops…in the silence, the gagged and bound
CYNTHIA emits strange and eerie sounds…)

LUCAS: My bride
My yellow haired
I had a speech prepared but where the speech was there is
a white and empty chamber
The flowers they can speak
(He offers two dense bouquets of flowers to URSULA…)
They are the dull blooms of the estuary but if you want
more dazzling then some slave can ride to Holland my
thought was Ursula will love what grows here what
flourishes in the country of her lover's birth they are quite
heavy do accept
(URSULA is immobile…)
Do
Do or I'll think she despises the poor flora of my
Do
(She is still…)
Forgive me I will send for greater blooms these local things
are quite without an odour unfragrant weeds of
(PLACIDA steps forward.)

PLACIDA: I can accept what Ursula may not accept what is
impossible for Ursula I'll
(CYNTHIA lets out a strange subdued cry…PLACIDA takes the
bouquets…)

LUCAS: And these are my bride's maids…!
(He walks along the line, inspecting them with a gentle
manner…)

PLACIDA: No…

LUCAS: *(Passing LEONORA without acknowledging her.)* No…?
Not bride's maids…
What, then…?

PLACIDA: Not bride's maids because there is no bride…
(LUCAS looks at PLACIDA…)

LUCAS: How terrible that might be if it were spoken in any
other voice…!
(He smiles…)
And one's mad…!
(He looks at CYNTHIA but addresses URSULA.)

Ursula, do greet me
Your beauty is vastly in excess of that poor painter's ability
to suggest I hardly can I really fear to look at you that is a
husband's compliment surely let us hope in twenty years I
still tremble with this disbelief unlikely but –

URSULA: I do greet you –

LUCAS: Thank you –

URSULA: But never as –

LUCAS: Oh, never mind the buts –

URSULA: I must –

LUCAS: No we've a life to but in –

URSULA: NEVER AS A HUSBAND –

(*He is still. He looks at the deck…a long pause elapses…he smiles
suddenly…*)

LUCAS: It's draughty here…!

I never was a sailor and no wonder…!
Welcome to each one of you
The sane
The blind
And the demented
Put the flowers in water
I own a castle
Invisible from here
Where preparations are oh FEVERISH
I came alone to look at you
The soldiers money-makers and the priests they'll glimpse
you later –

URSULA: Christ said –

(*She gathers her words…*)

Throw Lucas in the river…

(*LUCAS smiles uncomfortably…*)

His image…
Fling it in…

LUCAS: (*Disingenuously.*) And did you…?

URSULA: I did…

LUCAS: You did…!

PLACIDA: She did but –

CLARA: We discovered it…!

(*She bites her lip…*)

PLACIDA: Ursula did as Christ instructed her. But then it came ashore again. Some tide. Some current. His will however, has been done…

LUCAS: (*Looking at PLACIDA.*) Christ is all-powerful…

PLACIDA: He is. It's here.

(*As arranged, PHYLLIS shows the panel, which she has kept behind her…LUCAS affects a short laugh.*)

LUCAS: That is me, certainly…

And in this instance I think we must admit the painter did achieve a certain similarity –

Less of a challenge to his skills –

PHYLLIS: Oh, I don't think so, it's a –

LUCAS: Yes, yes –

(*PHYLLIS is tight-lipped.*)

My grimness, easy to

My sadness, any fool could

But Ursula she

(*He inclines his head…*)

WE CAN'T STAND ON THE DECK ALL DAY…!

(*He turns violently and walks off. The women are uncertain and linger, looking to each other…CYNTHIA emits a further sound of fear and anxiety…URSULA looks to PLACIDA…*)

LEONORA: (*Following LUCAS.*) A little castle, low, behind the roofs…

(*She stops. She extends a hand to PLACIDA.*)

Mother…

(*The virgins dither…look to one another…*)

URSULA: (*As PLACIDA goes to follow LUCAS.*) She can't…!

(*PLACIDA stops, shocked by URSULA's cry…*)

She cannot…

She can't like that…!

(*URSULA laughs…PLACIDA, suddenly self-aware, also laughs…*)

PLACIDA: I'm holding the flowers…!

URSULA: Holding the flowers…and in that little hat…!

(*PLACIDA shakes her head, confused, as the virgins also laugh… with a gesture PLACIDA flings the bouquets into the arms of the nearest virgins…*)

PLACIDA: It is not death…

It isn't…
IT IS NOT DEATH…!
(*She strides to meet LEONORA's hand. She stops.*)
Sing…!
Sing…!
(*The virgins look at one another. The light goes from the scene…*)

ACT THREE

1

A woman singing a psalm. The sword, wrapped, lies on a table.
CYNTHIA, still blindfolded, still bound, sits in a chair. LAMENTINA
does not cease singing as LUCAS enters. He sits in a second chair. He
puts his fingers together. He listens. LAMENTINA ceases at the end of
the psalm. She is taut as a wire...

LUCAS: I've lost face.
   (*Pause...*)
   So what?
   (*Pause...*)
   A prince loses his face.
   (*Pause...*)
   Let him find another my old face what was it after all some
   pride some youth some arrogance I've seen it on street
   corners I've seen it lying in the road oh it's no disaster no a
   better face awaits me chiselled out of stone humiliation is a
   gift from God.
   (*Pause...*)
   In what sense, did you say?
   (*Pause...*)
   I think –
   (*LAMENTINA, following an instruction, breaks into the psalm*
   again. LUCAS hears it to its end...)
   I think the humiliation of a soul must purify it
   I think it is strengthened by shame
   AND I AM ASHAMED
   I am
   I am
   And always will be to recall it horribly ashamed
   (*Pause...*)
   You understand
   How well you understand the damage that's been done me
   I can see it in your eyes
   Possibly you are yourself ashamed to have so shamed me

IT'S HARD ON ALL OF US
(*He jumps out of his chair…*)
All right, go now, go…!
(*LAMENTINA assists CYNTHIA out of her chair…*)
What made her mad, the river?
(*LAMENTINA shrugs…*)
It can
It does
The river
Go
Go
(*The women hurry out…LUCAS grips the back of his chair…he is barely aware of URSULA, entering, but becoming aware of her, he draws back the chair for her to sit in. With perfect decorum URSULA takes the chair. Her long hair falls down her back. He observes it for a long time…*)
I've lost face
(*Pause…*)
So what?
(*Pause…*)
A prince loses his face.
(*He moves away…*)
Let him find another…!
(*He takes the other seat.*)
My old face what was it after all some pride some youth some arrogance I've seen it on street corners
I've seen it lying in the road oh it's no disaster no a better face awaits me chiselled out of stone humiliation is a gift from God…
(*She observes LUCAS…*)
I think the humiliation of a soul must purify it
I think it is strengthened by shame
AND I AM ASHAMED
I am
I am
And always will be to recall it horribly ashamed
(*Pause…*)
You understand

How well you understand the damage that's been done to
me
I see it in your eyes
Possibly you are yourself ashamed to have so shamed me
IT'S HARD ON –
(*LUCAS begins to laugh, shaking his head side to side. He leans his
head on the table, over his arms, as his shoulders shake. URSULA
watches with mixed fear and bemusement…*)
Ursula fuck with me be a bitch I'll be your dog open your
limbs I'll swallow every river of your underneath and howl
and howl be my bitch I smell your odours and I know you
can smell mine pull your skirt over your yellow hair pull it
pull it up what are skirts for
(*She remains quite still…LUCAS waits…*)
Your father sent a letter
What a nice old man
Under the politeness underneath the etiquette he felt an
almighty fool all the same I do appreciate good manners
I am the prince-bishop incidentally and not merely the
prince of this place do tell his secretary should he ever
want to write again a trifling distinction but
(*Pause…*)
I know the gospels…
(*Pause…*)
I know the solitude of Christ…
(*Pause…*)
My own also…
(*Pause…*)
Ursula, you are not naked as you wish to be…
(*Pause…*)
URSULA: We would prefer it if our lodgings were together,
some of the girls have never been away from home before
and –
LUCAS: I know –
URSULA: Some are in the castle and the rest –
LUCAS: I know –
URSULA: Are in the town –
LUCAS: All the guest rooms have got leaking roofs –

URSULA: As for the sailors –

LUCAS: Our poverty embarrasses me –

URSULA: They have been arrested –

LUCAS: (*Affecting ignorance.*) The sailors?

URSULA: Arrested and our boat removed –

LUCAS: Removed?

URSULA: It isn't at its mooring –

LUCAS: I'll investigate it –

URSULA: Thank you and what is that thing on the table?

>*(LUCAS does not remove his eyes from URSULA…)*
>
>I don't mean what is it
>
>I know what it is
>
>I mean why is it there?

LUCAS: To frighten and to reassure you. Simultaneously.

>*(Pause…)*

URSULA: It does neither.

LUCAS: Excellent…! Why is your hair like that if you won't fuck?

>*(Pause…)*
>
>Tumbling. Falling. Loose.
>
>*(Pause…)*
>
>Loose and yellow, what –

URSULA: A virgin does not dress her hair –

LUCAS: Is that so?

URSULA: Christ abhors all vanity –

LUCAS: Christ does and yet you brush it…

>*(Pause…)*

URSULA: The Mother says –

LUCAS: (*Scoffing.*) She brushes hers…!

>*(Pause…)*

URSULA: (*Patiently.*) She's clean…

>*(She looks at LUCAS…)*

LUCAS: Say you like me, Ursula…

>*(Pause…)*

URSULA: I don't dislike you, Lucas.

>*(Pause…)*

LUCAS: (*Bemused…*) I'm not disliked…

URSULA: And it would give me great satisfaction to know we met in temper but parted friends…

LUCAS: (*Contemplatively…*) Friends…

BUT YOU HAVE YELLOW HAIR…!

(*The distant singing of the virgins…URSULA leans forward in her chair…*)

URSULA: Lucas…the act is false…

LUCAS: False…?

URSULA: Ecstasy but false. Never can we be parted from ourselves except in Christ…!

(*Pause…*)

LUCAS: And that is what you yearn for, is it? To be parted from yourself?

URSULA: Yes.

LUCAS: ME TOO I LOATHE ALL THAT I AM AND YOU MUST MAKE ME NEW

NEW LUCAS

FROM THE CELLARS TO THE CEILINGS

URSULA: Through Christ –

LUCAS: THROUGH YOU

YOUR BELLY

(*He stares at her. URSULA rises to her feet…*)

URSULA: The painter, oh, how accurate he was… Sadness streams from you as storm-water gushes from a ferry's figurehead…

(*He glares…*)

LUCAS: You may not leave…

URSULA: (*Leaving.*) Talk with Mother Placida, please –

LUCAS: URSULA, DO NOT LEAVE…!

(*She goes out, passing LEONORA, who stands still, her eyes on the wrapped sword. LUCAS recovers, leans back in his chair…*)

LEONORA: Whose sword is that?

(*Pause…*)

LUCAS: Mine.

LEONORA: It's monstrous.

LUCAS: Monstrous, yes.

(*She does not remove her eyes from the weapon.*)

Monstrous and it isn't mine I borrowed it I borrowed it
for its monstrosity and had it wrapped it is the sword of
execution I can barely lift it he can however do all sorts
of things with it the executioner grotesque shoulders
grotesque wrists he cut an egg in half boiled egg but even
so remarkable I like him he is professional I do admire
that on weekdays he helps in the bakery do you require to
know much more I think some former intimacy between a
woman and a man confers no rights –

LEONORA: Former intimacy –

LUCAS: On either party to be forever privy to their –

LEONORA: FORMER INTIMACY –

LUCAS: Privy to their secrets, surely…?

(*LEONORA bites her lip, turns away…seethes…recovers…turns to
him again.*)

LEONORA: You must release the sailors.

LUCAS: Must I?

LEONORA: The sailors and the ship.

LUCAS: The ship too?

LEONORA: Yes –

LUCAS: BUT THEN THEY'LL SAIL AWAY, WON'T THEY?

(*He glares at her…*)

LEONORA: Talk with the Mother, Lucas –

LUCAS: THE MOTHER WHY WHY TALK WITH THE MOTHER IT'S
ALL I EVER HEAR

(*LEONORA is patient…*)

LEONORA: Because with her all that makes no sense acquires
sense. And all that's turbid becomes clear. As for lying,
it's impossible…! Her voice…! Her eyes…! You can't…! I
confessed to her my blindness was a lie. Always my gaze
was drawn to her and to persist with the pretence I could
not see the kindness that is written there, oh, impossible…!

(*Pause…she is embarrassed. She shrugs…*)

LUCAS: You love her…

(*LEONORA shrugs again…*)

LEONORA: I shrug… Why do I shrug…? Yes…!

(*She bites her lip…*)

I require love, Lucas, and you dragged yours out of me

DRAGGED
DRAGGED
AS IF IT WERE THAT SWORD THAT SOME ENGINE INCH BY
INCH DREW THROUGH MY BOWEL
Leaving me this rag of clots and stains called
FORMER INTIMACY
(*Pause…he lifts a hand to her, which she does not take…*)
Why is it wrapped, the sword…?
(*LUCAS stands, falters, walks slowly out. The sound of psalm sung by the virgins…*)

2

They assemble. The singing falters. They look around, swiftly.

PHYLLIS: What does he say?
   (*Pause…*)
LEONORA: No, he says.
PERDITA: No?
LEONORA: He insists we stay.
   (*They are subdued…*)
JANET: I think this.
   (*Pause…*)
I do not like this thought but it occurred to me therefore
I will however ugly it is speak it and if it wounds you
all apologise for having the impurities of character that
harbour such things anyway it's this
(*Pause…*)
As we came nearer to this place it seemed to all of us that
we might die. And whilst it horrified us still we believed
this death might be an ordeal necessary for our faith. For
we know there is a pain to be extracted for a faith, or the
faith's not proven. We know above the doorway to a faith a
single word is written. That word is suffering.
(*Pause…she shifts…*)
Is it not suffering to be taken into bed against your will?
(*She forces herself on…*)
Is such a hideous violation not Ursula's ordeal? Her private
space made ruin by this man's appetite? Her body nailed

to his desires as cruelly as Christ was hammered to the
tree?
THE BED'S THE TREE
Yes
I won't go on
You follow me
I've spoken
God forgive me
I want to go home –
LEONORA: (*Kindly.*) Shh –
JANET: I want to go home –
LEONORA: Shh –
JANET: But that is not the reason why I spoke –
LEONORA: No –
JANET: Absolutely not, no…

(*Pause…everyone is uncomfortable…*)

URSULA: (*At last…*) Janet wishes to go home –
JANET: I do, but that is not –
URSULA: She says she wishes to go home –
JANET: (*Crossly.*) I HAVE SAID SO BUT THAT IS NOT –
URSULA: IT IS NOT THE REASON THAT YOU SPOKE NO.

(*Pause…*)

I also wish to go home. And this desire for home has
splashed and washed against my faith as tidal rivers pluck
iron bolts from timbers. It rots. It excavates me. Where I
place my hand for solid hope there's no solidarity, just –
OBVIOUSLY I CANNOT MARRY I CANNOT PUT MY OATH
WHERE CHRIST INHABITS ME –
JANET: I said forgive me if –
URSULA: I do, I do forgive –
JANET: Ursula, oh…

(*They embrace each other…the rest stand, crestfallen…PLACIDA
appears, and stops, observing them. Their heads turn, one after
another…PLACIDA laughs, a low, mild laugh…*)

PLACIDA: Oh, you…

(*She shakes her head…*)

Oh, you…

(*She draws her mouth in…*)

141

MELANCHOLY FLOCK...

(*Almost on an inspiration they hurry to her with little cries and wails...*)

(*As they oppress her.*) My hat...!

(*They laugh, encouraged, relieved by her own radiance...*)

LEONORA: (*Who has stood off.*) These arguments...these theological and liturgical arguments...are only about home...

(*She looks at* URSULA, *who also has stood back...*)

The Mother is home...!

(*She laughs...the virgins stand away from* PLACIDA. *As* LEONORA *goes to move towards* PLACIDA, URSULA *is suddenly overcome, seized by a fit of weeping and shuddering, as if convulsed by a sickness...they watch, horrified. She heaves, she appears to choke. She cries out as* PLACIDA, *moving through the virgins, takes* URSULA *in her arms...slowly,* URSULA's *ordeal subsides...as they stand in this shocked silence, the footsteps of* LUCAS *are heard from the depths of the stage. They are frozen with anxiety.* LUCAS *appears holding a great tray of fruits and flowers, a toppling cornucopia...he stops...he is silent a long while...*)

LUCAS: I've an

(*Pause.*)

I've an

(*Pause.*)

Appointment

(*The virgins are still. They look at once to* PLACIDA, *who inclines her head once. They depart, leading* URSULA...)

3

LUCAS: Take the sword, please.

(PLACIDA *looks up...*)

The sword.

(*She looks at the table and the sword...*)

The sword is heavy but so is this tray...

(PLACIDA *goes to the table and draws back the sword, making space for the tray.* LUCAS *places the tray on the cleared space...*)

The table has room for a sword or a tray...but not for a sword and a tray...

(*Pause…*)
Ridiculous table…
(*He stares at the floor…*)
Ridiculous tray…
(*Pause…he seems fixed…*)
PLACIDA: The sword is –
LUCAS: Never ridiculous, no.

(*LUCAS gazes at the floor. PLACIDA holds the sword by its handle. He hesitates. He seems to experience a rage. He flings the tray off the table with a clatter and a cascade of fruit. At the end of it, he leans on the edge of the table, write-knuckled. PLACIDA remains holding the sword by the handle, the tip on the surface, unshaken…*)

I've lost face.
(*Pause…*)
So what? I've lost face.
(*He takes the sword and heaves it squarely onto the table…*)
Help yourself to fruit I understand you have not been supplied with oranges or lemons that is an oversight and not policy on my part please sit don't slip however what a mess the whole lot bruised there is so little fruit here it's too cold on the estuary but a ship came in from I don't know Morocco is it the figs certainly come from there one ship a year I have a contract with the Sultan one a year what a coincidence I never eat such things myself I send him timber by return bog-oak and beech he makes the most preposterous furniture outlandish and uncomfortable he has yet to meet with Christ if he met Christ would he make better furniture I ask myself…

(*A long pause elapses…PLACIDA sits…she places one leg over the other, adjusting her skirts…she does not meet his eyes…*)

PLACIDA: Ursula is –
LUCAS: The humiliation of a soul must purify it, surely?
(*Pause…*)
There is no doubt in my mind the soul is cleansed by shame.
(*Pause…*)
I am ashamed.

(Pause…)

Ashamed for having placed upon another the burden of
my hopes…

(Pause…)

PLACIDA: Ursula is –

LUCAS: *(Not unkindly.)* It doesn't matter what Ursula is.

(He draws back the second chair and sits.)

The error's mine.

(He looks at PLACIDA…still her eyes remain lowered…)

PLACIDA: I have never slept with a man

(Pause…)

Never

(Pause…)

Never

(Pause…)

And I am not without a certain am I

(Pause…)

Older than I was but still I find the years have

(Pause…)

Possibly enhanced those things men find

(Pause…)

I've known no ecstasy but nor have I known shame

(She looks up at last…)

It is so lonely here I said imagine sunset on a winter
afternoon one curlew crying on the mudbanks rotting
hulks etcetera I did not call it beautiful perhaps because
I knew how beautiful it would turn out to be it is it is
beautiful I can't breathe

*(She half-stands, supporting herself on the arms of the chair…and
sits again…)*

I have your picture what am I to do with it one night I took
it from the nail and slipped it underneath my pillow and
do you know of course you don't I slept the whole night
through I never have I never do I take a draught

*(Suddenly she half-stands again…she breathes awkwardly…and
subsides again in the chair…she laughs a short laugh.)*

Look at the darkness round my eyes

Terrible nights

YOU SPEAK NOW
(*LUCAS is silent…*)
It is the only means by which we can ascend to
Christ
The rope
The cable
Is virginity
(*He looks into her…*)
Do with me what must fail
Why don't you speak
And if it fails.
IT WILL FAIL AND IF IT DOES FAIL
IT MUST FAIL OBVIOUSLY
(*She closes her eyes in her desperation.*)
When
When
When it fails
(*She stops…*)
LUCAS: What is this…?
What is this?
(*She is silent…*)
I am betrothed
I greet my bride
My bride is
I don't know what my bride is
Her mother comes
Her mother says
I DON'T KNOW WHAT HER MOTHER IS
PLACIDA: Give me a peach –
LUCAS: A peach –
PLACIDA: I saw a peach –
LUCAS: A peach –
PLACIDA: Or did I imagine it –
LUCAS: What is a peach?
PLACIDA: It's soft –
LUCAS: (*Going down to look for one.*) Soft?
PLACIDA: Not like an apple –
(*He extends a fruit.*)

145

No, that's an apple –
(*He looks again...*)
All right, an apple –
(*He is still...he does not offer an apple...he remains on his knees...*)

LUCAS: Your voice is terrible...

PLACIDA: Terrible, why...?

LUCAS: Because nothing it proposes can be denied...
(*Pause...*)

PLACIDA: And if I lacked this voice...
(*Pause...*)
If this voice were –
(*To her surprise, LUCAS falls to clasping her feet...*)
Some accident befell my voice –
(*He lifts her skirt over her knees...*)
It –
(*Her speech falters...*)
It –
(*She swallows...*)
Failed –
(*Her breath is uneven...*)
Me –
(*She struggles with LUCAS, attempting to remove herself from the chair.*)
Lucas...
(*He overpowers her...*)
Can't breathe...!
Can't breathe...!
(*He draws her to the floor. In the failing light of the afternoon, the single curlew cries...*)

4

They are still. The blindfolded figure of CYNTHIA is discovered, sensing her way over the stage. She stops suddenly.

CYNTHIA: Ugh...!
I've –
Ugh...

SOMETHING STICKING TO MY SHOE
(*She lifts a foot…her shoes drops off.*)
LOST MY SHOE…!
(*Being tightly bound she cannot retrieve the shoe…she feels with her naked foot…*)
Whoever's in here give me back my shoe
(*PLACIDA and LUCAS do not move…*)
Please whoever's in here
TROD IN SOMETHING ELSE NOW…!
(*She half-laughs, half-sobs…*)
My poor shoes…
(*Pause…*)
The Mother says we must wear shoes but what if they are
SHIT SMOTHERED
(*She laughs…she smothers the laugh…*)
The Mother says we must be clean but what if
WHY IS THERE SO MUCH SHIT IN HERE
Shit
Shit
DON'T USE THE WORD
Or fuck
Two awful words
I'll fuck
I'll shit
I'M BEGGING TO BE GAGGED AGAIN
(*She shudders…*)
Clara, find my shoes…
(*PLACIDA rises to her feet. She goes across the floor. She retrieves CYNTHIA's discarded shoes. She lifts each of CYNTHIA's ankles and replaces the shoes…*)
Thank you
Not – Clara thank you
Which room am I in
I am looking for Lucas
I know Clara when I see her
I know Clara when I smell her
LUCAS PLEASE NOT – CLARA
He wants to open me

Never mind the ropes he says
Never mind the blindfold
Or the gag
He wouldn't care about a gag
There are so many parts to kiss not roped or gagged
Lots left
Oh, lots
Not – Clara point me to his room
(*LUCAS has risen. He walks to the women. He stops beside CYNTHIA…*)
This is his room…!
(*He swiftly picks up CYNTHIA. She is silent. He looks at PLACIDA. He carries CYNTHIA away. The curlew cries. PLACIDA is still. She seems suddenly to have to vomit. She holds on to the table. The sensations subside. The virgins, singly or in pairs, cautiously enter the room. They look at the fallen debris…*)

PLACIDA: Do pick this up…
Horrid mess…
Somewhere there's a tray…
(*She leans back against the table, her hands behind her, as the virgins gather the damaged fruit…but they sense her frailty, and almost as one, swiftly enclose her in their arms…*)

LAMENTINA: Oh, are we safe…?

BENEDICTA: Are we…?
(*PLACIDA sobs loudly…*)

PHYLLIS: We're not, then…safe…are we…?
(*Only URSULA has not joined them, but stands with PLACIDA's little hat in her hand…*)

CLARA: Mother…

BENEDICTA: We are so young, so young, aren't we…?
(*Pause…*)

PLACIDA: Yes…
(*She separates their arms…*)
You are…
(*She observes URSULA…*)
Go, all of you, go, now…
(*They disperse. URSULA observes her for a long time…*)

URSULA: And does it…

OH, DOES IT FAIL…?
(*PLACIDA wipes her hands on her skirts…*)

PLACIDA: Does what fail –

URSULA: Oh –

PLACIDA: My little hat, have you –

URSULA: Your legs opened
Funny posture
Open legs
Your heels went up
Higher and higher went the heels

PLACIDA: Ursula –

URSULA: The shoes dropped off
First one
And then the other
Such high heels
Oh
Ugly
Ugly

PLACIDA: Ursula –

URSULA: Ugly because it's loathed by God
(*She goes to PLACIDA.*)
The self
The self comes back again
(*URSULA replaces the hat on PLACIDA's head, clumsily. PLACIDA
endures this.*)
It fails
Obviously it fails
(*She goes to leave, but looks back at the discomforted image of
PLACIDA.*)

PLACIDA: Ursula –

URSULA: Oh, the solitude of the estuary…
(*She goes out…PLACIDA is alone…the curlew is heard…she
places her hands on the wrapped sword…with a spasm of energy
she plucks it up in her arms and holds it, burdensome as a heavy
child…until she balances its weight, it staggers her…then she
is still…in her stillness, she hears the soft shuffling footsteps of
CYNTHIA who, still bound and blindfolded, enters the room,*)

and stops. PLACIDA looks at her…CYNTHIA, as if feeling this
observation, directs her face towards PLACIDA…)

CYNTHIA: Mother…?

(*Pause…*)

Mother…?

(*Pause…*)

Mother…?

(*Pause…*)

Mother…?

(*LUCAS enters, and stops…*)

Mother…?

(*Pause, then with urgency.*)

Mother…!

LUCAS: I'll return that to the armoury…

PLACIDA: Return it, why?

CYNTHIA: Mother…!

LUCAS: Return it for the reason I –

CYNTHIA: Mother…!

LUCAS: No longer require its –

PLACIDA: Don't require it, why…?

(*He strides swiftly to her and kisses her. They turn in an*
embrace…)

CYNTHIA: Mother…!

(*He ends the embrace, leaving her still in possession of the sword,*
but unsteady…)

Mother…!

PLACIDA: (*To LUCAS.*) DO I NOT NEED PROTECTING?

ACT FOUR

1

PLACIDA, alone.

PLACIDA: I'm marrying…!
> (*She gnaws her hand. The sound of chairs dragged over flagstones. The virgins enter, pulling chairs behind them. They assemble about PLACIDA, and sit. They are each blindfolded…a pause elapses…*)
Marrying and…
Afraid
Afraid oh, so afraid
Thank you I could not bear your scrutiny I could not bear your eyes to travel over me to settle on my breasts my lips I have been kissed already kissed in every place and kissed again
ALL RIGHT LOOK AT ME NOW
> (*They are quite still…*)
You do not want to…
You do not want to see my ecstasy…
> (*Pause…she bites her lip…*)
On the contrary, you wish me dead, you wish my body bobbed and plunged in the cold waters of the estuary
> (*Pause…*)
Mother Placida gnawed to bone her belly open to the rinsing seas
MEN LIKED ME AS AN INFANT
YES
AT SEVEN YEARS
AT FIVE
One said to me my eyes were sharp to cut the ropes of all legality his phrase not mine
Another said my mouth was Hell's red flower
Twelve times my age these men
You don't forget
HE KISSED ME HERE, LUCAS

(*They are still…*)
AND HERE
(*She deceives them…*)
I'm naked
Here
And here
My undone thighs
My belly
And my hair
Naked
NOTHING TO DISGUISE
(*Pause…they are immobile…*)
You still don't look
You still
You still

LEONORA: I'M BLIND…!
(*She tears off her blindfold…*)
I'M BLIND…!
(*She stands, horrified…*)
I am
I am
CAN'T SEE
BLIND OH CHRIST IN HEAVEN BLIND
(*She tips over her chair in her loss…*)

URSULA: Christ spares you…

LEONORA: (*Colliding.*) BLIND…!

URSULA: He spares you, Leonora…
(*LEONORA is still…*)
He spares you what each one of us will shrink to see…what
scalds the eyes as if the boiling pans of some mad kitchen
had been flung into the air by howling mastiffs whose yells
grew shriller agony by agony
NOT DEAF ALSO THERE'S THE PITY
(*She stops…*)
No
No
Better we hear the whole
And in this voice which we revered

Better altogether
However in this darkness we smelled yes smelled the
odour of anxiety which clings to you
Your breath
If not your accent
Is not clean
MOTHER...
(*She feels away her blindfold...*)
That absurd hat
That neck exposed beyond the line of hope
Christ stands you there as if
I CANNOT BEAR IT
He props you there like some
I REALLY CANNOT BEAR IT
Some testament to
OH
(*She looks away...*)
The collapse of every love...
(*She stands, she stumbles, she holds her chair.*)
THANK GOD FOR CHRIST
THANK GOD
THANK GOD FOR HIM WHO IS FOREVER
Leonora...!
(*She extends her hand, she finds LEONORA's. She leads the virgins away. As they depart they are heard to sing...PLACIDA stands without moving until they fade. Her hand is seen to rise before her. It clasps a small mirror. The footsteps of LUCAS...he watches her...*)

PLACIDA: This hat is not...
(*She touches it...*)
Is it...?
It is a sweet hat, surely...?

LUCAS: Naked it suits you best –

PLACIDA: (*Flinging it off her head.*) Time for another...!
Time for one which
KISS ME PLEASE
One which expresses
KISS ME

153

My
Yes
Why not
Extravagance
KISS ME WHEN I SAY SO
(*Pause…she laughs at her presumption…*)
No, don't I have bad breath…
(*She turns a little away. He goes to her.*)
Apparently I –
(*He kisses her profoundly…he parts again…*)
Have bad breath…

LUCAS: Bad, and your neck's imperfect –
(*He seizes her, thrusting his hands into her skirts.*)
THAT'S A QUEEN –
(*He drives her backwards in his passion.*)
And your breasts soft, papered and declining –
THAT'S A QUEEN –
(*He flings up her skirts, then stops in his rush.*)
Listen…
(*He lets the skirts fall…*)
Our marriage is a sin…

PLACIDA: A sin, is it…?

LUCAS: A sin, and therefore perfect…

PLACIDA: Yes…

LUCAS: In every scornful eye I'll stare as if it were a mirror…

PLACIDA: (*Half-laughing.*) Yes…!

LUCAS: And all the stiff jaws I will march along as if they were
a pavement…! LUCAS HIS BANNER TRAILED BETWEEN
THEIR TEETH… You have not said if you are pregnant…
(*Pause…she is bewildered.*)

PLACIDA: Pregnant…?

LUCAS: Yes, you know, is my child leaping in your belly?

PLACIDA: I do not think so, not yet, I –

LUCAS: Good, be sterile –

PLACIDA: I am not sterile, so far as I –

LUCAS: BE STERILE YES –

PLACIDA: Be sterile…?

LUCAS: Yes, you're scraping forty, let them howl and giggle in
the taverns, and the silver-tops, the hags, suck their gums
while scratching underneath their aprons
THE PRINCE HOW FINE HE IS BUT SHE...!
They'll make you responsible and your image will be
smeared in the urinals songs sung rhymes rhymed ditties
libels slanders
I'LL HANG FIVE IN A ROW
Placida
Am I not handsome
I love you
Am I not beautiful
It's you
My sterile virgin flood my fingers
FLOOD ME
(*He goes to her to thrust his hand under her clothes but she tightens
her dress, pulling it like a bandage about her hips...*)

PLACIDA: But Ursula...
(*He ceases...a pause...she goes to move away...he goes at once to
intercept her and at once she pulls her skirt tight again...*)
But Ursula...
(*Pause...she walks further...he pursues her and again she tightens
her clothing.*)
Ursula however...!
(*He looks at her. She lets her skirt fall loose...*)
She was my dear...!

2

*The estuary. LEONORA stands in the water. The waves. The birds of
the estuary.*

URSULA: (*Entering...*) Yes, drown...! It's logical...! Every
human love betrayed...! And sightless...!
Quick, you'll meet the ebb-tide, and these skirts, they take
up water and turn into lead, in twenty seconds you'll be
under, disappearing light and the silence of the river bed,
do part from all that hurts you, it's perfect sense...
(*LEONORA is still...*)

Death…
(*Pause…*)
It is
Oh, certainly
It's the solution, death…
(*LEONORA has not moved…URSULA sits on the ground, and
draws up her knees…*)
We did not like each other, did we? We were – in a purely
objective sense – opponents – yes, one might say we were
placed in opposition to each other rather like chess pieces
– do chess pieces harbour hatreds for each other – I can't
think they do – after all, at the end of the game they are
thrust back into the same box and –

LEONORA: Shh…

URSULA: And are obliged to share the dark for days, for
weeks, until on some whim of the players they are stood
again –

LEONORA: Shh…

URSULA: Stood up to quarrel when there is no quarrel –

LEONORA: Please…!

(*URSULA is silent…a pause…suddenly it is she who weeps, her
face buried in her knees. Her tears swell into a wail…LEONORA
does not move…*)
You speak
The rhythm
Even the tone
As she did

URSULA: Yes –

LEONORA: Find another –

URSULA: I will –

LEONORA: Another tone –

URSULA: I will –

LEONORA: A new voice –

URSULA: A new voice altogether –

LEONORA: Yes –

URSULA: I like you –

LEONORA: I like you, but –

URSULA: I must find new accents –

LEONORA: Yes –

URSULA: To speak Christ in –

HOLD ME LEONORA AND I WILL KISS YOUR EYES –

(*She embraces LEONORA.*)

Your eyes which died which shrivelled in your head for
horror of the thing they could not bear to see…

(*She encloses LEONORA in her arms, and as she does so, finds her
attention draws to a movement in the water…she straightens up
as LUCAS, naked, wades in from the estuary…*)

LUCAS: BOTH WAYS…!

(*He shakes, he wraps his arms about himself…*)

BOTH WAYS…!

(*He laughs, knee-deep…he is still…he looks at the women…*)

A man, what is it…?

(*Pause…URSULA stares at LUCAS…*)

Both ways and last time the single crossing tore the lungs
from me…!

(*Pause…*)

A man, what is it…?

(*Pause…*)

Ursula I thought, will put an end to such absurd activities
but Placida –

SHE DOUBLES MY INSANITY…

(*Pause…*)

A woman, what is it…?

(*The women are silent…*)

I'm cold…

(*He shudders…he goes to walk off…*)

URSULA: Return the mother to us, please…

(*He stops…*)

LUCAS: Return her? She's lying in my bed and already
drawing up her knees…

(*Pause…*)

No…!

No…!

I pull that sentence back, I drag it back across my teeth
I never said such coarse things of a woman who knows no
coarseness

AND EVEN THAT'S UNTRUE
I NEVER HEARD WORSE LANGUAGE FROM A WOMAN'S
MOUTH
But it's
It's
HOW HARD IT IS TO SPEAK THE TRUTH
It's
It's

URSULA: Madness –

LUCAS: Not madness no –

URSULA: You said yourself –

LUCAS: Not madness –

URSULA: Insanity you said –

LUCAS: IT'S LOVE IT'S WHAT LOVE DOES

(*Pause…*)

I'm not dressed, I –

I'm –

URSULA: Give her back, Lucas –

LUCAS: Lucas…? Lucas…? You have this way of addressing
me which –

AND I'M NOT DRESSED –

LUCAS…? WHO ARE YOU…? TO LUCAS ME…?

(*Pause…he looks uncomfortable…*)

I'm cold…lend me a…lend me something to…lend me…!

(*URSULA tosses him a shawl. He drapes it over his nakedness…*)

I love her –

I love the woman –

URSULA: So do we –

LUCAS: Then wish her happiness –

URSULA: Happiness, yes, but not this spoiling of a –

LUCAS: SPOILING –

URSULA: Of a once-perfect woman –

LUCAS: I NEVER SPOILED HER

HER VIRGINITY SHE THREW AT ME

(*Pause…*)

I am the prince here and I do not tell my life to you.

(*He turns to go…*)

LEONORA: Lucas…

(*He is still…*)

What's blinded me…?

LUCAS: How should I know…?

(*He turns…he shakes his head with disbelief…*)

You –

You –

Ascribe your misery to me…

You –

(*He seems lost for words…*)

Identify me as the –

LEONORA: My blindness is a sign.

LUCAS: A sign, is it…?

I'VE DONE NO WRONG BUT LOVED SOME ADDER SPAT IN
YOU AS YOU LAY SLEEPING POSSIBLY OR HAWK AS YOU
PEERED SKYWARDS SHAT A TOXIN IN YOUR GAZE I'VE
DONE NO WRONG BUT LOVED

A sign of what…?

LEONORA: The evil of your marriage.

LUCAS: Oh.

LEONORA: Yes.

LUCAS: Oh.

LEONORA: Lucas –

LUCAS: LET IT BE EVIL AND THE STREETS CHOKE ON ITS
SULPHUR

I swam the estuary both ways what's that evil I charm
children off the swings and old mothers pluck their
shopping up and dump it at their doors what's that evil two
felons due for hanging I branded out of pity what's that
what's that I so regret your blindness I so regret it my dear
love if I could buy your sight I'd buy it but

(*He lifts his hands…pause…*)

I'll free the sailors and unquarantine the boat…

URSULA: We must take the mother, Lucas.

(*He is still…the curlews cry…*)

If necessary tied with ropes…

(*He looks at the horizon…*)

We love her and she's ill…

LUCAS: (*Without rancour…*) It's sickness, is it, to cause a prince
to transport an old woman's bag…?

LEONORA: They think you're mad. And jeer at you.

(*He looks at her…he goes slowly out…the women do not move. A
certain tremor passes over them, of joy which at last is released in
a sobbing and a kind of laughter…shyly, the virgins appear and
stand in attendance…*)

URSULA: We laugh…

(*She bites her lip…*)

We laugh as Christ might have…

(*She looks at them with a radiance.*)

If Christ had ever laughed…

3

The portrait of LUCAS on a stand.

PLACIDA: The painter

Let's discuss his attributes

The triumph of

His failure where

It is a work of art and therefore partly true and partly false

You are the same

A work of art

Me also

This voice I made

I was not born with it

AND YOUR INVENTIONS LUCAS, WHAT ARE THEY?

(*He is still…pause…*)

If they won't go then they must stay

The virgins

THEY HAVE THE SAILORS AND THE BOAT

Do they not love their parents?

LUCAS: They love you more –

PLACIDA: How can they I've betrayed them –

LUCAS: All the same –

PLACIDA: Absurd –

LUCAS: Nevertheless –

PLACIDA: Expel them –

LUCAS: They tie themselves together –

PLACIDA: THEN HOIST THEM IN A NET –

(She is shocked at herself...)

Oh, listen, I –

This is so –

LUCAS: You took possession of them. And what is so possessed can't be disowned. They cleave to you.

PLACIDA: I am your bride –

LUCAS: You own their souls –

PLACIDA: Your bride, I said –

LUCAS: Their bowels –

PLACIDA: Lucas –

LUCAS: Their vomit and their blood –

PLACIDA: I WASH MY HANDS OF THEM –

LUCAS: YOU CANNOT WASH YOUR HANDS OF LOVE

(Pause...)

It sticks

It goes all

It coagulates

(Pause...)

PLACIDA: The painter his

I do admire him

His rendering of temperament

With such economy he

In so few strokes

Triumphantly describes

(Pause...)

THE FEAR OF PRINCES

(She goes to the panel...)

Look

The Prince

Even he

Believes in debts

Hear me, Lucas

You are marrying me

What is out that window

I am your bitch

The window what's beneath it?

Water?

Water?

LUCAS: The estuary

PLACIDA: Good

(*She tosses the panel through the aperture. A pause.*)

No more professionals

Such skill is awful and it hurts

(*He stares…she smiles…*)

For our wedding picture we'll employ an amateur

KISS MY HEART NOW THRUST YOUR TONGUE INTO ITS MUD

Stir its sediments

Dredge my darkness, Lucas

(*She offers herself…he holds her, burying his face…*)

No…

Dredge…

Dredge…

(*She moves him away.*)

Later…!

Later, obviously…!

(*He goes to leave, swiftly…*)

Darling…!

(*He stops.*)

It is not white…my wedding dress…

LUCAS: Not white…? How could it be…? You are no virgin.

(*He lingers, looking into her. Then turns and goes out…*)

ACT FIVE

1

The virgins are careered on stage, each strapped to a steel trolley. They collide. They pile against one another. At last they are still, in the peculiar peace that follows upon an accident. The curlew is heard. Suddenly, as if on a signal, they sing a snatch from a psalm. They stop, as suddenly.

URSULA: He's here…
> (*Pause…*)
> Christ is…
> (*Pause…*)
> HE SAYS…
> MY WOMEN
> MY WOMEN
> (*They sing again, and stop as suddenly…*)
> CHRIST HIS WOMEN
> (*PLACIDA enters, in a bridal gown of scarlet. They are unable to see her, but hear its swish on the floor. She moves around them. She stops. The curlew cries…*)

PLACIDA: He cannot lift it.
> (*Pause…*)
> Lucas…
> (*Pause…*)
> Cannot lift the sword…
> (*Pause…*)
> Not with one hand…
> (*Pause…*)
> Not with two…
> (*Pause…*)
> AND HE'S THIS PRINCE THIS WARRIOR AND SWUM THE
> ESTUARY NOT ONE WAY TWO
> (*She swishes as she walks…*)
> Whereas
> (*She listens to the sound of her train…*)

Whereas

(*She stops. The sword descends, unravelling itself from its wrapping, and twisting as it falls. At the end of its descent it hangs, the blade naked. It swings infinitely slowly like a great crane in a wind…the virgins breathe in unison, in horror…*)

Because I have the need I can lift it

(*Pause…*)

Not with one hand…

(*Pause…*)

Two…

(*Pause…the breathing…*)

PERDITA: Mother…

PLACIDA: Not mother yet…

PERDITA: Oh, Mother –

PLACIDA: I SAID NOT MOTHER YET

SHALL BE

SHALL BE HOWEVER

His splash

His torrent

I am watered hourly

His river in my sea

PERDITA: Mother…!

PLACIDA: WE ARE THE ESTUARY

CYNTHIA: Mother…!

LAMENTINA: Mother…!

PLACIDA: And it is inevitable I shall conceive

A perfect child

Exquisite

Pale as him

Pale as me

One only

And then die

Yes

Not the child

JANET: Mother…!

PLACIDA: Me

(*She raises her hands to the sword.*)

You see

It is not heavy
It resigns its weight to me
Oh, do admire this
Its perfect balance and the air is not offended by its cruelty
any more than your hair will be but parts…
(*The virgins breathe in unison, profoundly…*)
Parts for its passage…

URSULA: FIRST ME

PLACIDA: Ursula, always you are first, how else should it be?

URSULA: First, please
I suffer your voice
It's rough as buckets scraped on floors
Glasses trodden into roads
Dogs driven over
Shattered bones
FIRST ME
To hear it grinding tortures me…
(*A snatch of psalm.*)

PLACIDA: My voice? But it's unchanged…

LEONORA: Love…oh love the mother…
(*They sing. PLACIDA draws the blade over the neck of the first virgin.*)
LOVE / LOVE
(*And another.*)
LOVE / LOVE
(*As the staccato psalm and the cries continue, LUCAS advances into the scene step by step, mesmerised, flinching but staring. He holds a bottle and two glasses. The female voices decline as PLACIDA works her way along the trolleys…she ends with the sword raised. Only URSULA remains alive.*)

PLACIDA: Ursula…
(*She sways, the sword now heavy.*)
Say my voice is not changed
Say
Oh, say…
(*URSULA is silent. She lifts one arm into the air. She declines to speak.*)
How cruel you are…

(*PLACIDA laughs sweetly.*)

I do like you…!

(*With an effort of will, PLACIDA draws the blade across URSULA's neck. LUCAS lets fall the bottle and glasses, which shatter on the floor. Then PLACIDA releases the sword which clatters, echoes through the hall. Silence returns. The curlew…*)

LUCAS: (*At last.*) They owned you, Placida…

How could you give yourself when so much was their property? I owned the smallest part…

PLACIDA: And now…?

LUCAS: I have the whole, surely?

(*PLACIDA lifts the hems of her gown, and wrings dark blood from them.*)

PLACIDA: A virgin, Lucas, what is she?

(*LUCAS watches her, transfixed.*)

LUCAS: Christ said

The night that he was taken

Watch with me

They fell asleep however

Three times he pleaded watch with me

There was virginity

PLACIDA: It's hope, then? And their hope is safe now. Their hope is safe because of me. What more can a mother do?

(*LUCAS yearns towards her.*)

LUCAS: Love me, Placida…! Love me…!

(*A figure dimly appears, with a bucket and mop. He drops the bucket noisily, begins to mop the floor. PLACIDA extends a hand to LUCAS. He goes towards her but careers on the blood. He is shaken.*)

I slipped…!

(*He laughs uncomfortably. He goes to her again, but slides a second time, almost losing his balance.*)

I slipped again…!

(*He is aghast. PLACIDA departs. LUCAS follows her. The figure with the mop kicks the bucket along the floor, a curlew calls…*)

HE STUMBLED

Characters

DOJA
an Anatomist

SUEDE
his Assistant

PIN
his Assistant

BERLIN
a Nun

LAYBACH
a Priest

TODD
a Courtier

BALDWIN
a Prince

TURNER
a Queen

NIXON
a Servant

FIRST / SECOND PRIESTS
a Chorus

TORTMANN
a King

Knights

A Crowd

He Stumbled

A high wall. The grieving of masses. A rising sun fingers the top. An aperture appears. A naked arm emerges and tips a pan of fluid onto the ground. It disappears again. The grieving continues. A second aperture opens, and a second arm tips a pan of fluid onto the ground. No sooner has it withdrawn than a low door opens in the wall. A novice, fugitive from the miasma of death, flings herself onto the stage. She gasps the fragrance of uncontaminated air. She is restored. Her hands explore the surface of the stone. A third aperture opens. A bowl of blood is flung down the wall. The novice, stiff with disgust, slowly draws up her clothes until they are gathered over her head. She maintains her posture as, at intervals, further containers splash dark fluids down the wall. A second door opens. A novice emerges, retching, his hand clasped to his mouth. He also inhales the morning air. He also recovers. His gaze falls on the motionless nakedness of the girl, pressed to the wall and flecked with visceral muck. He stares. He is inexorably drawn towards her. His hand reaches, withdraws, extends again. He touches her, at first tentative, then more confidently. She chooses not to welcome or deny him, but remains with her head covered, motionless. At the moment he flings up his cassock to take her, the intoxicated cries of a maddened crowd flood the stage. The novice drops his garment and turns his face to the wall. A mass of figures surges past, streaming banners and bawling. Their impetus blinds them to the two novices, who stand stock still. As their cries fade, a further pan of sickness cascades down the wall. The grieving continues. The youth peers sideways to see the girl in the identical posture she had adopted before the interruption. He tears up his garment, exposing his own nakedness, and goes to embrace the girl from behind. He is stopped in his rush by a single shout. Slowly, with a profound reluctance, he allows the robe to fall. He sits, and with an air of resignation, draws up his knees. Blood runs down the wall. A man enters, grey, powerful. He goes to the naked girl, and lifting her in his arms, carries her away. The youth stares fixedly ahead. At last he climbs to his feet, pulls his cowl over his head and returns through the little door to the death chamber. The sound of grief swells, and falls as the door is closed again. The running mourners pass in a frenzy. The girl, now covered by her cassock, returns and opens the door by which she entered. The sound of grief swells but is suddenly silenced. She freezes in her movement.

BERLIN: You're God…
   (*The grey man inches onto the stage, adjusting his clothing…*)
   From now on…
   (*He looks at her…*)
   God's you…
   (*She slips through the door. Immediately the other door opens. The grieving surges as a woman emerges, closes the door swiftly and leans against the wall, flattening her hands behind her.*)

TODD: Still not over…
   (*A pan of fluid cascades…the grey man looks at her. She walks forward…*)
   By no means over and you're premature or possibly he senses your presence rather as a collapsed heifer smells a wolf and struggles miserably to rise from its puddle of excrement slips slides falls again do you like to be a wolf be a wolf if you want and kiss me I must go back soon kiss me your wolf smell I will transport on my skin perhaps he will die inhaling you perhaps it will abbreviate his agony…
   (*He looks without moving.*)
   Don't kiss then obviously your tender sentiments are bruised by such a proposition why should you kiss a stranger when your nerves are strung perhaps more tightly strung even than my own after all your task is delicate infinitely more delicate than anything I am obliged to do I am ashamed to have described you as a wolf far from it no wolf is not the animal not the animal at all will you wait for the body to be cold or slice warmly through the lungs the bowel the viscera I've heard the flesh comes swiftly from the bone but only if the blood still moves whereas cold flesh adheres
   (*A pan of fluid is tipped out.*)
   As if you'd tell…!
   (*She laughs, falsely.*)
   Never mind the kissing then and next time you see me you will say could that be surely not not possibly the woman

who and I shan't even meet your eyes or if I do with such
a grey indifference you will thrash your memory for lying
not her not her surely you'll

(*The running mourners stream past, yelling. When they have
gone, TODD is revealed against the wall in the same state of
undress as the novice. For a few seconds she is still. A pan of fluid
is thrown down. The grey man goes slowly to her and proceeds
to penetrate her. His hands reach to the wall over hers. They are
still, intimate. The second door opens with a crash and two priests
emerge, gasping for air, light and liberty. The surge of mourning
accompanies them. They do not observe the lovers in the ecstasy of
their relief.*)

FIRST PRIEST: I was

SECOND PRIEST: I was

FIRST PRIEST: Up my throat came

SECOND PRIEST: Torrents

FIRST PRIEST: Flooding

SECOND PRIEST: Saw your mouth go

FIRST PRIEST: Saw yours

SECOND PRIEST: Choking

FIRST PRIEST: Sick

SECOND PRIEST: And laughter

FIRST PRIEST: You too

SECOND PRIEST: Laughter

FIRST PRIEST: You too

SECOND PRIEST: Sick and laughter

FIRST PRIEST: Both at once

SECOND PRIEST: Everyone

FIRST PRIEST: Christ

SECOND PRIEST: Stench and

FIRST PRIEST: Agh

SECOND PRIEST: Stench and

FIRST PRIEST: Agh

SECOND PRIEST: Agh

(*They collapse in a fountain of laughter during which TODD
departs through the door they had left open. The sound of
mourning is muffled. The grey man is immobile. The running
mourners stream by, but on their departure, one remains. She
gazes at the grey man…*)

FIRST PRIEST: And then

SECOND PRIEST: Teeth all

FIRST PRIEST: And then

SECOND PRIEST: The teeth

FIRST PRIEST: Horrible teeth

SECOND PRIEST: Snap

FIRST PRIEST: Snap

SECOND PRIEST: His teeth and we were

FIRST PRIEST: Agh

SECOND PRIEST: C Minor

FIRST PRIEST: In Deo

SECOND PRIEST: Snap

FIRST PRIEST: Fidemus

SECOND PRIEST: Snap

FIRST PRIEST: Agh

SECOND PRIEST: Saw you

FIRST PRIEST: Snap snap

(*They collapse again, in each other's arms, wheezing and hooting. The woman goes to the grey man and draws up her skirt, revealing herself. He looks at her, without visible enthusiasm, then goes to draw her against the wall. The apertures in the wall open simultaneously, with a clatter, the grieving is instantly silenced and the projecting heads of a chorus of nuns announce the end of the king's ordeal. Simultaneously, a surgical table, suspended from chains, is winched downwards. On this table, the naked body of the monarch lies ready for dissection. Two assistants appear from the wings, holding bags of tools, aprons, buckets. They attend politely on the master. The chorus ceases. The two priests hurry away. The grey man draws down the skirt of the woman with an attitude of resignation, and turning from her, goes to the table and leans on it. The assistants wait. The grey man looks from one to the other.*)*

DOJA: Even I

Yes

I who so assiduously removed himself

Who so undressed himself of all things kind and gracious

Shedding the clinging garments of politeness

And stepping out of manners as a woman lifts her feet

lightly from shoes

Even I
Remain susceptible to
Obligation
(*He turns to the woman, who hurries away…*)
Why
(*The assistants hold out an apron.*)
Why
When this obligation both left her wholly dissatisfied and
created in me a sense of profound resentment
(*He extends his arms.*)
It was as if I had submitted to a discipline the rules of
which my entire nature found repellent and under whose
arbitrary regulation my soul writhed
(*They tie the strings.*)
Bitter
And
Recalcitrant
(*The assistants proceed to unfasten cases of instruments.*)
No
Obligation I must learn to recognize
(*They extend the open cases.*)
And recognizing it resolutely
(*He takes a sharp-bladed knife, but fumbles and lets it fall to the
floor.*)
You see I am distracted
(*He leans on his hands…*)
My infamy whilst making me an object of desire must not
create in me some nagging and reciprocal responsibility to
those who suffer that desire surely
(*He recovers, and takes a second blade.*)
I am not after all a monarch
Only
The
Disemboweller
Of
Monarchs
(*The assistants fetch buckets, pails, pans.*)
Did you get a decent lunch?

PIN: Thank you we did…
DOJA: And your room?
PIN: Clean, thank you…
SUEDE: Flowers
PIN: On the window sill
SUEDE: Austere however
PIN: And the view
SUEDE: You could not honestly
PIN: Describe it as a view
SUEDE: The flowers being
PIN: As so often
SUEDE: A substitute for views
PIN: And the corridor
SUEDE: Yet again
PIN: The corridor
SUEDE: Unoccupied
PIN: Remote
SUEDE: And cold
PIN: As if we were
SUEDE: A disease….

> (*DOJA smiles…he goes to the head of the table, and adjusts the head of the corpse…*)

DOJA: My room by contrast

> (*The assistants laugh.*)

Yes

Yes

You anticipate the luxury of my surroundings

My room is

> (*He is about to make an incision in the neck but stops short, the blade in the air…*)

Plump with furnishings and scented like a whore…

> (*He is still…*)

Why is that?

> (*He reflects, then draws the blade exquisitely from the base of the neck to the navel…*)

Because

Surely

Because

I am perceived to be like flesh itself

Corrupt

Malodorous

And

Indiscriminate

(*He throws the knife into a bucket.*)

I don't disagree

(*He walks away wiping his hands on a cloth.*)

Open him

(*The assistants proceed to draw back the walls of the thorax. A youth stumbles into the room. He leans against the wall. DOJA bows from the waist. The eyes of the youth are fixed on the table…*)

BALDWIN: What's that…?

    (*The assistants look at one another.*)

    On the table what is it…

DOJA: It is the degenerate and spoiling prison of a dead man's soul…

BALDWIN: MAN

    WHAT

    MAN

    MAN

    YOU

    CALL

    MY

    FATHER

DOJA: It is in his mortality that a great king –

BALDWIN: BUTCHER

DOJA: Yes

BALDWIN: CLEAVER

DOJA: Yes

BALDWIN: (*Covering his face.*) I have to be here sorry but I must I must ignore me do your work sorry but it's my desire my desire's law I won't distract you sorry but I need a stool…

    (*DOJA indicates to SUEDE that he should fetch a stool. SUEDE goes off.*)

    I loved him…

DOJA: It's a famous love…

BALDWIN: Is it…

DOJA: Legendary…
BALDWIN: Legendary, is it…
DOJA: But I must cut him all the same…
BALDWIN: You must do, obviously…
DOJA: And you must watch without exclaiming…
BALDWIN: I will I said so didn't I…
DOJA: The flesh is not the man…
BALDWIN: Don't lecture me and we will get on very well
    (*SUEDE enters with a stool.*)
    There
    (*He indicates a place.*)
    Thank you
    Sorry
    Thank you
    I am
    All
    A mass of
    Carry on
    Sorry
    I
    (*He climbs on the stool, adjusts his posture, is still.*)
    MONARCH SILENT ON A STOOL…
    (*DOJA returns to the table. He lifts a blade from the case of instruments. He is about to make an incision.*)
    Stop…!
    (*DOJA holds himself rigid. A pause… BALDWIN slips off the stool, walks contemplatively in a circle, stops…*)
    The flesh is not the man…?
    (*He looks at DOJA.*)
    The flesh is not the man…? What is the flesh, then? Is the flesh not this man's and no other's? If the flesh is not the man, why are you here? I am a boy and vastly ignorant but we have spent huge sums on your services, you are not cheap, your fees are thought by some to be exorbitant, why if the flesh is not the man? A cat would do, surely, a goat ripped off a butcher's hook? A goat's heart in the casket would certainly suffice and let a hundred knights stand guard over a skewered bullock if the flesh is not the man I am a boy and vastly ignorant parks of ignorance

distinguish me from you but why if the flesh is not the man…?

DOJA: (*Patiently.*) I am sorry if my price is thought too high –

BALDWIN: By some, I've no opinion on the subject –

DOJA: My skills such as they are have earned a certain reputation –

BALDWIN: Yes –

DOJA: And as a consequence of this reputation I am not infrequently obliged to choose between one mortality and another –

BALDWIN: Obviously –

DOJA: I had made detailed plans to visit Sicily when the news of your father's imminent decease reached me –

BALDWIN: So I gather –

DOJA: The Queen of Sicily did not protest when I proposed a sum appropriate for this expedition, on the contrary, so anxious was she to acquire my services I was embarrassed by the gifts forwarded to me –

BALDWIN: Yes –

DOJA: It was with the most profound reluctance I bowed to the tide of pleas and promises flowing from this place and cancelled my visit –

BALDWIN: Yes –

DOJA: I was able to propose a substitute –

BALDWIN: Good –

DOJA: But this substitute has sufficient modesty to acknowledge the body of the King of Sicily is unlikely to receive the final privilege of a dissection so refined as that about to be bestowed upon your father –

BALDWIN: Yes –

DOJA: Cheap I would not wish to be for fear of causing embarrassment –

BALDWIN: Yes –

DOJA: Not to myself, but to those whose grief compels them to bid for my services –

BALDWIN: Of course and I –

DOJA: Acknowledge this, I'm sure, as for the flesh, my own opinion can be stated very briefly. It is everything and nothing. May I continue? My arm aches and if I cannot

exert the fullest concentration on my task the perfection for
which I am renowned will certainly be compromised, to
everybody's detriment…

(*Pause.*)

BALDWIN: Yes, I

(*Pause.*)

Yes, you

(*Pause.*)

Please do, I

(*He returns to the stool, climbs on it, and rests his chin in his
hands…*)

DOJA: (*To PIN.*) Dextra…

Inflexit…

Contortum…

Occlusit…

In axio…

In axio…

Dixi…

PIN: (*Working deep in the chest.*) In axio…

(*An atmosphere of tranquillity surrounds the work of the
clinicians, cutting and cleaning with a practised routine, hypnotic
to BALDWIN, who sways on his stool…*)

DOJA: Et implacit…

PIN: Sub sternum…

DOJA: Implacit…

PIN: Implacit…

DOJA: Testoria…

PIN: Fluvio…

Fluvio…

(*SUEDE holds up a pan. DOJA lifts out the heart and suspends it
in the manner of a priest raising the host. It leaks blood. BALDWIN
is a miracle of balance as he inclines in fascination…*)

BALDWIN: My father's heart…

My father's heart…

DOJA: Yes…

(*A door closes…*)

BALDWIN: Mother…!

(*A woman appears, advances into the room, stops. BALDWIN clings
to the stool. She looks…*)

Mother…

This man has turned my father inside out…

(*Pause. The Queen looks without flinching…*)

DOJA: I hesitate to continue…

(*Pause…*)

I hesitate because whereas the extrusion of the heart is relatively clean, I must proceed to lift the bowel from its –

(*BALDWIN emits an audible gasp. Pause. The Queen does not move…*)

BALDWIN: Continue…!

Continue, do…!

(*DOJA looks at the Queen…*)

TURNER: I did not love my husband's bowel.

(*BALDWIN giggles with anxiety…*)

Nor his lungs.

Nor his liver, either.

BALDWIN: The lungs are going to Jerusalem…!

TURNER: All that I loved was visible, Mr Doja.

BALDWIN: And the bowel to Constantinople…! Or the other way round, is it…?

TURNER: It must be the same with the character. We love what we see. But that is rather little of it. Really, life is solitude. We collide with others. We attach ourselves to surfaces. But what is intimacy, Mr Doja? A fiction, surely…

BALDWIN: No, the lungs are staying, it's the brain that must be going to Arabia…

DOJA: Intimacy I know rather little of.

TURNER: Is that so?

BALDWIN: No, that's completely wrong. The bowel is meant for Rome.

TURNER: Perhaps it frightens you.

BALDWIN: I forgot Rome.

TURNER: Certainly it frightens me.

BALDWIN: Can we get on, now…?

TURNER: Knowing how little intimacy there is, we are correct to fear it, Mr Doja…

BALDWIN: We cannot keep talking, we have so much to do…!

(*He looks crossly at TURNER…*)

TURNER: You might give the heart to the dogs for all I care.

(*She walks out…pause…*)

BALDWIN: My mother…!

(*He makes a gesture of hopelessness.*)

Never mind my mother…

She…

Her…

Never mind my mother…

(*He arranges himself on the stool.*)

Do the bowel, please…!

Bowel, next…!

(*PIN lifts a container. DOJA places the heart inside. SUEDE puts a lid on the container.*)

And label everything…! Because how silly if how idiotic and infuriating if the organ having been at huge expense in life and labour transported through so many hostile territories should on arrival be discovered to have accidentally been exchanged the lungs in Lapland and the brain in Ireland for example or the liver somewhere altogether inappropriate the rage the indignation just imagine it so write it very clearly or do you do that anyway here am I reminding you of what is probably a routine probably you do that the label writing is that your task I don't know your name Mr –

SUEDE: It's not my function –

BALDWIN: Whose function is it then not Mr Doja's surely he would not stoop to label writing or possibly he –

SUEDE: Each vessel is a particular shape –

BALDWIN: Yes…!

Yes, that would obviate the necessity for labels I do so admire you Mr Doja I want us to be friends I think at this moment you have a terrible attraction for me and my mother also finds you likeable which is odd she likes so few people I put it down to your silence you do not speak more than is necessary which means that those who would dislike you have little evidence for their offence shrewd and calculating Mr Doja and more effective than whole books of poetry I'm leaving I cannot stomach another minute of this butchery I shall know you better in time and hope oh so sincerely hope you do not disappoint my profound intuition that we shall be friends…

(*He slips off the stool and walks smartly from the room. DOJA proceeds as if the interruptions had never occurred…*)

DOJA: Focasit…

PIN: (*Giving him a tool.*) Focasit…

DOJA: Enterritur…

(*SUEDE goes out…*)

Et excisit…

(*He draws a long incision down the wall of the dead man's abdomen…*)

Tentastes…

PIN: Mihi…?

DOJA: Cum clavi…

(*DOJA withdraws to the head as SUEDE returns bearing a substantial pan to contain the bowels. DOJA takes a saw…*)

Of course this surge of intimacy comes as no surprise.

(*He throws down the first saw and selects another…*)

This deference mingled with desire…

(*He rejects that, also…*)

This morbid appetite for nakedness and the profane…

(*And picks another…*)

I think if any of us is to leave this place alive I must fuck with the Queen…ubi serrula…?

(*He tosses down the last saw…SUEDE hastens to sort through the tools. DOJA is patient…*)

I am not attracted to the Queen…

(*The clatter of instruments…*)

There is an odour clinging to her which…

UBI SERRULA MINOR EST…!

SUEDE: It's here, I know I –

DOJA: UBI

UBI

SUEDE: (*Sifting the instruments in a desperate manner.*) I saw it, it's –

DOJA: UBI

UBI

DIXI

SUEDE: Out of sequence, it's –

DOJA: CUR NOT SEQUENTIA EST...?

SUEDE: I don't know, I don't know, I...

(*He is close to sobbing. He extends the saw to DOJA...pause...*)

DOJA: So what if I do not like her odour? My partiality is
scarcely relevant. Of far greater importance is the necessity
to fuck with her in such a way as to satisfy her curiosity
without awakening a passion the extent of which may
be more threatening to our survival than if I had never
aroused her in the first place, but that's too late, she's
aroused already...

SUEDE: Serrula...?

DOJA: Trepannit...

SUEDE: Mihi...?

DOJA: TREPANNIT...

(*SUEDE looks at PIN in horror...he goes to the head of the
corpse...*)

And the boy's inflamed also...

SUEDE: Trepannit...?

(*DOJA walks away from the table...he contemplates his situation.*)

SUEDE: Trepannit, Magister...?

DOJA: Yes, why not you...?

(*The assistants exchange anxious glances...*)

No, it's complicated. The boy does not like his mother.
The mother does not like her son. Each of them has
discovered in me the alleviation of his solitude. It calls on
all my resources to satisfy these competing claims. But do I
possess the resources? I am not young any more. Recently
I have become susceptible to moods of irritation which
make even common politeness an effort for me, let alone
the affectation of desire, amicability and the like, I think
we erred in coming here but how was I to know the depth
of passion my very appearance would cause to stir, like
some turbid pool a hound had splashed in, throwing up
decaying matter, exotic coloured weed and God knows
what fragments of –

(*The assistants are looking at him. He meets their eyes. Pause.*)

Very well

I knew

Yes

Obviously

It was entirely predictable

(*He walks back to the table.*)

Retract the scalp…

SUEDE: (*With relief.*) Magister…

DOJA: (*Taking a blade.*) Cum fasces, placit…

SUEDE: (*And pleasure.*) Magister…!

(*They proceed to expose the dead man's skull, while PIN works on the abdomen. Two of the high windows fly open and the heads of the priests emerge. Their dialogue is punctuated by the musical effects of the surgical instruments…*)

FIRST PRIEST: Everything's

SECOND PRIEST: Ourselves included

FIRST PRIEST: Everything's

SECOND PRIEST: Peculiar

FIRST PRIEST: As if some miasma of

SECOND PRIEST: Some putrescence possibly

FIRST PRIEST: And this interminable mourning

SECOND PRIEST: Makes me

FIRST PRIEST: You too…!

SECOND PRIEST: Want to scream

FIRST PRIEST: Scream what

SECOND PRIEST: Scream

FIRST PRIEST: TORRENTS

    OF

SECOND PRIEST: We seem

FIRST PRIEST: Not only us

SECOND PRIEST: Things seem

FIRST PRIEST: Even the trees

SECOND PRIEST: The tiles on floors

FIRST PRIEST: Have been seen to move

SECOND PRIEST: TORRENTS

    OF

FIRST PRIEST: As if in a profound embarrassment

SECOND PRIEST: Embarrassed tiles…?

FIRST PRIEST: And when we pass each other

SECOND PRIEST: TORRENTS

OF

FIRST PRIEST: People avert their eyes
SECOND PRIEST: They do
FIRST PRIEST: It's universal this suffocating
SECOND PRIEST: Kiss me
FIRST PRIEST: This asphyxiating
SECOND PRIEST: Kiss me
FIRST PRIEST: And airless
SECOND PRIEST: Kiss me I said
FIRST PRIEST: I heard
SECOND PRIEST: Or I will scream
FIRST PRIEST: TORRENTS

OF

(*They laugh. Their laughter falters. Their eyes go dim.
Simultaneously their bodies are launched from the little windows
and plunge towards the floor. They swing by their feet, to and fro
in a breeze…DOJA and the assistants continue with their labours,
unconscious of their fate…the novice priest enters. He stands
politely, waiting to be observed. DOJA wipes his hands on a clean
towel and goes towards him. Pause. They examine one another…*)

LAYBACH: Obviously I hate you but I must speak.

(*Pause…*)

I have been here on three occasions.

(*Pause…*)

I stood there and –

(*He indicates…*)

DOJA: I saw you.

LAYBACH: Yes and what I have to say is very hard to say so on
each occasion I chose instead to leave, thereby avoiding
the actual purpose of my visit…

DOJA: What you have to say offends you…

LAYBACH: Yes, and I feel even now a powerful desire to avoid
your sight but she would not forgive me a fourth time
there is a limit even to her tolerance and if it offends me
so what so much offends me in this life I am bruised by
everything she pleaded with me so I came bitterly I came I
offend even myself you see she is stricken with you utterly
stricken and cannot move her limbs you have to go to her.

(*Pause. LAYBACH stares at the ground…*)

DOJA: Who…?

   (*Pause. LAYBACH still stares at the ground…*)

LAYBACH: Oh, God…

   (*He shakes his head in disbelief…*)

   Oh, God…

DOJA: Do look me in the eyes. I find this place odd. But the oddest thing is the impossibility of meeting any other's eyes…

LAYBACH: I cannot…

DOJA: Why can you not…?

LAYBACH: I am too…

   I think…

   If I contrived to meet your eyes I would kill you.

   (*Pause…he shrugs…*)

   I exaggerate…

   Certainly I would try to kill you…

   And almost certainly I would fail…

   SHE IS PARALYZED WITH HER INFATUATION AND YOU

   (*He turns on his heel, begins to walk resolutely away, but freezes. He sways, like the dead priests in the wind…*)

   Why should you know, why should the identity of an obscure girl whose face I doubt was even registered by you, why should you stoop to –

   YES I COULD KILL YES

   (*Pause.*)

DOJA: This obscure girl whose face I did not register is loved by you…evidently…

LAYBACH: You are so perceptive, Mr Doja –

   (*DOJA slaps him swiftly over the cheek. LAYBACH reels, horrified… he stares…*)

DOJA: I think…

   By and large I think…

   Whilst I did not wish to strike you…

   The blow has saved us…infinite…perambulations of sarcasm and –

LAYBACH: Yes, probably…

   (*Pause. He rubs his cheek.*)

   I am dreadfully unhappy…

DOJA: Yes…

LAYBACH: Perhaps to be unhappy is my fate. She is at the infirmary. May I tell her you will come…?

DOJA: Yes.

(*Pause…*)

LAYBACH: Pity…

I would much have preferred to carry back your cold contempt.

DOJA: Obviously.

(*BALDWIN enters, stands between the dead priests. LAYBACH leaves…DOJA turns to BALDWIN…*)

BALDWIN: They laughed…

(*Pause…*)

Not on this occasion only…

(*Pause…*)

Frequently they laughed…

(*Pause…*)

DOJA: One must be cautious where one laughs. It is a thing to be rationed, laughter.

BALDWIN: You don't laugh, Mr Doja.

DOJA: I laugh but sparingly. And in the strangest places.

BALDWIN: I've not heard you…

DOJA: Still, I do laugh…

I should not wish you to think me incapable of laughter…

BALDWIN: But not like them…!

DOJA: I have not actually heard the manner in which they –

BALDWIN: NOT LIKE THEM I'M CERTAIN…!

(*Pause…*)

DOJA: No, if you're certain, then I think, probably not like them…

BALDWIN: Oh, good…

(*He seems suddenly shy…*)

When one admires someone…how important it is that he should not in any detail of his character…ever disappoint you…

(*He looks at the ground…*)

A tall order, but…

(*Pause. He extends a paper towards DOJA…*)

You are invited to –

(*He stops.*)

Who was here just now…?

DOJA: Just now…?

BALDWIN: As I came in you were in conversation with
someone –

DOJA: A priest, yes –

BALDWIN: A novice, surely…?

DOJA: I didn't notice that he was –

BALDWIN: A novice, certainly –

DOJA: Yes, he was – I'm not sure who he was –

BALDWIN: I see…

(*He offers the paper again…*)

You are invited to –

No –

No –

There was an atmosphere of cordiality between you, a
manner of –

Not cordiality –

Intimacy –

DOJA: I don't think intimacy –

BALDWIN: Something very like it –

DOJA: Far from intimacy, I assure you –

BALDWIN: ALL RIGHT THE OPPOSITE OF INTIMACY THEN BUT
STILL A –

(*Pause. He sways a little on his feet.*)

Profound passage of feeling, Mr Doja, which I should
dearly like to have shared with you myself…

(*Pause…he extends the paper again.*)

This invitation is –

(*Suddenly, he screws up the paper into a ball and tosses it down.*)

Not an invitation any more…

(*He turns on his heel, takes a few steps, stops again…*)

I MUST BE HELPED…

DOJA: Yes…

BALDWIN: YOU SEE THAT, DO YOU, MR DOJA, THAT I MUST BE
HELPED?

(*Pause…the assistants watch…*)

DOJA: Yes, someone must certainly –

(*He is tentative…*)

Certainly…

BALDWIN: What?

(*Pause… DOJA takes the initiative of retrieving the ball of paper, unwrapping it, smoothing it, and reading it.*)

DOJA: Oh, it's an invitation addressed to me…!

(*A fractional, crucial pause. Then BALDWIN laughs.*)

BALDWIN: Yes…!

Yes…!

That's exactly what it is…! Say you will…!

DOJA: Certainly I will…!

BALDWIN: I knew…! I knew however smothered with attention Mr Doja might be still he would –

DOJA: Oh, yes –

BALDWIN: Find time to –

DOJA: Yes, indeed –

BALDWIN: Thank you…

Thank you…

(*He stares at DOJA, smiling, then walks away. DOJA goes slowly to the table, leans on it…*)

DOJA: Take the horses, now, and ride. Not by the way we came. Find another road. Or rather, do not use a road at all.

PIN: What…?

DOJA: I will finish the dissection…

PIN: What…?

DOJA: Go now. Do not even return to your room.

PIN: What…?

DOJA: Do not say what again. Wipe your hands and leave.

SUEDE: Impossible, we –

DOJA: This is my final kindness, believe me. If it is a kindness. Most likely it is no more than the shedding of an onerous responsibility, and therefore, far from kind, rather another manifestation of my inexorable selfishness. All the same it is the best advice you will ever receive. Leave at once.

PIN: (*Tears rising in his eyes.*) Magister…!

DOJA: GET OUT…

PIN/SUEDE: Mag – ister…! Mag – ister…!

DOJA: GET OUT I SAID...

> (*The assistants fall to their knees, and clutch at* DOJA's *clothes...he observes them...pause...*)

Very well, die...

PIN/SUEDE: Magister...

DOJA: Die, die, if you must...

PIN/SUEDE: Yes...

Yes...

Beside you, Magister...

DOJA: Yes...

Beside me, yes...

> (*Pause. He touches their heads lightly. A servant passes bearing a massive covered tray. A table, identical to the anatomical table, descends. A second servant appears, staggering with a second tray, and then a third. This new table is rapidly piled with meat and offal until it resembles a cornucopia, overflowing, preposterous. The passage of servants is accompanied by the staccato chant of the dead priests.*)

FIRST PRIEST: Killed for nothing

SECOND PRIEST: For nothing

FIRST PRIEST: Not that something

SECOND PRIEST: Would make it satisfactory

FIRST PRIEST: Would it

SECOND PRIEST: Would it

FIRST PRIEST: Be altogether better if

FIRST/SECOND PRIESTS: WE'D SINNED

FIRST PRIEST: Or if

Of if

Or if

FIRST/SECOND PRIESTS: WE SAW THE EXECUTIONER

FIRST PRIEST: That would have helped

SECOND PRIEST: Or

FIRST PRIEST: Or if not helped then possibly

SECOND PRIEST: Lent us an object of resentment

FIRST/SECOND PRIESTS: Oh yes

Oh yes

Oh yes

SECOND PRIEST: HOW THE DEAD HATE

FIRST PRIEST: We do
   We do
SECOND PRIEST: Admit it
FIRST PRIEST: Yes we hate
SECOND PRIEST: And sadly must confess to wanting the
   extinction of the human race
FIRST PRIEST: I do
SECOND PRIEST: Me too
FIRST PRIEST: Admit it
SECOND PRIEST: Yes
FIRST PRIEST: Yes
SECOND PRIEST: How lovely to admit it
FIRST PRIEST: Hold my hand
   (*The dead priests reach out…*)
   And laugh…
   (*In the stillness and silence that follows, the footsteps of a man.
   He stops. He bows towards DOJA. He is formal, dark, as if a
   servant…*)
NIXON: I'll take your coat.
DOJA: I didn't bring a coat.
NIXON: Something else, then.
DOJA: Something else…?
NIXON: Gloves, perhaps?
DOJA: I have no gloves…
NIXON: Please.
DOJA: It's warm, I –
NIXON: Please.
   (*Pause. DOJA examines NIXON. He removes a handkerchief from
   his pocket, and extends it to NIXON. NIXON takes it, thrusts it into
   his own pocket and walking away, positions himself at a distance
   from the table. DOJA, lacking a destination, aimlessly crosses the
   room. The stops. He crosses it in the opposite direction. Again he
   stops, then with apparent decision, goes as if to leave.*)
   You are also a monarch.
   (*DOJA stops.*)
   In your own way, also a monarch.
   (*Pause.*)
DOJA: Arguably…
NIXON: Yes, I feel the quality of monarchy in you…

(*Pause.*)

DOJA: And you...what are you...?

(*NIXON is silent...*)

NIXON: Sometimes the king's assassin bears in himself the
very characteristics of dignity, ambition, and so on, that
characterized his victim. I have observed this time and
again.

DOJA: I am not an assassin...

NIXON: You? No...

(*Pause...*)

And yet how rarely the assassin is permitted to occupy the
vacancy he has himself created...!

(*Pause...*)

That seems absurd to me. Surely he is the candidate most
qualified.

(*Pause...*)

DOJA: I am not however, an assassin...

NIXON: You? No...

(*Pause.*)

The assassin is put to death. And horribly. As if this would
deter all others. Frequently I think, oh, how wasteful
this execution is...we have compounded the loss...two
monarchs are extinguished when we might have suffered
only one...

(*Pause...*)

But you are not an assassin...

(*Pause...*)

DOJA: Me? No...

(*They examine one another...a large door opens in the wall,
sufficient to permit the entrance of TURNER, in an extravagant
dress. NIXON bows to her...*)

TURNER: I put this on. I then wished I had not. I had it taken
off again. I raged before the mirror. Poor mirror. It is party
to such. Silent witness of so many. I pity it. I then –
(*She laughs, a long laugh...*)
Concluded my first instinct was correct. It so often is.
But these instincts are always subject to examination,
judgement, inspection, and so on, which contaminate

the purity of spontaneity. How I would love to rid myself entirely of my second thoughts. And how difficult it is…!
(*Pause…*)

DOJA: Certainly, in this instance, your first thought was immaculate…
(*TURNER seems to examine this compliment…pause…*)

TURNER: Failing to keep faith with my instinct, I paid the price of my unnecessary exertions…
(*She looks at DOJA…*)
I'm dishevelled…
(*Pause…*)
And perspiring…

DOJA: This can only have contributed to the striking quality of your overall appearance, I feel sure…
(*Again, she seems to weigh his compliment…his eyes meet hers…*)
On the other hand…

TURNER: Yes…?

DOJA: Inevitably one cannot but think – excellent as this garment is –

TURNER: You know about garments, do you…?
(*He smiles, thinly…*)

DOJA: One cannot but think, how fortunate the mirror was to have –

TURNER: What do you know of garments, Mr Doja…?

DOJA: (*Persisting.*) To have witnessed your impatience, since the very excess of material compels imagination to contemplate what lies beneath…
(*Pause. He shrugs…*)
I…
(*Pause…*)
Do you wish me to continue in this vein or not…?
(*Pause…*)

TURNER: Yes…
A little longer…

DOJA: I think…
In certain cases…
The bereaved are peculiarly enhanced by grief…
(*TURNER looks at him…*)

TURNER: What grief…?

(*She regrets her words. A pause of painful exposure…*)

Listen, I do not like clever men…

(*Pause…*)

DOJA: My cleverness I promise you is nothing but the brittle shelter of my soul…

(*She stares, bemused…*)

TURNER: Is that so…? What quality of soul, Mr Doja…?

(*She whirls away.*)

Perhaps you do not have a soul at all…!

(*She laughs.*)

Some don't…! Some are quite simply, soulless…! And we should envy them, we should envy their extraordinary capacity for happiness, they live like birds, they leave no imprint on the ground and death, when he collects them, finds them insubstantial as fallen leaves, which satisfies his idleness, my husband died a death of such reluctance, Mr Doja, clinging to life by every thread, as if the banner of one of his regiments were gnawn down the middle stitch by stitch, I did not think it possible, but he made death rage, he made of death a ranting exhibitionist…

(*DOJA examines her…she looks down…*)

I put this on for you…

(*BALDWIN enters, hurried, then stopping, ebullient, and suddenly constrained… Pause…*)

BALDWIN: I so wish us to succeed…

(*Pause…he bites his lip…*)

If you knew the scale of that wish…you'd shrink…!

(*He grins. He lifts his arms, in a gesture of helplessness…*)

My mother…! Her body…!

(*He smiles…*)

I'd intended to bring a present. But what? What present could possibly gratify a man of your discrimination…? I dreaded, more than the shame of giving nothing, the slightest hint of disappointment in your face that what I did give was inadequate in any detail…! Obviously, you would conceal this disappointment –

DOJA: I should conceal it, yes –

BALDWIN: You would…! You would conceal it, and brilliant in concealment I am certain that you are, still I should detect it, so attuned am I to every nuance of your character…
(*He stares…smiling.*)
Not really…
(*He smiles on…*)
Not really but I intend to be…
(*He turns.*)
How does she have this body… She's not young…
(*Pause.*)

DOJA: It's me, surely, who as the guest, should have cudgelled his brains to find the perfect gift, alas, I –

BALDWIN: For example, her legs…
(*Pause…*)
To which she devotes inordinate attention…
Her legs are…
(*Pause…*)
You say, Mr Doja…
(*DOJA looks from BALDWIN to TURNER. He is visibly in the process of constructing a suitable response when TURNER cuts him short.*)

TURNER: Mr Doja is a clever man and far from embarrassing him, which is obviously your intention, you merely provide him with further opportunities to demonstrate his cleverness –

BALDWIN: I am obvious, I admit it –

TURNER: What is the point of it, when what we require of Mr Doja is that he lays aside his cleverness, which he assures me –

BALDWIN: Horribly, horribly, obvious –

TURNER: Is nothing more than a means of fending off his fear of intimacy –

DOJA: Did I say that…?

TURNER: Say…? I don't know about say, you expressed it, and you express it now, Mr Doja…I am the same, which is why I am able to recognize in you the preposterous evasions we undertake in order not to –

BALDWIN: Kiss the legs, then…
(*Pause…*)
If you can't describe them, kiss them.

(*Pause…*)

OH, AM I OBVIOUS…?

(*Pause…*)

But it's quicker…!

(*He laughs.*)

And she washes them in milk…

(*DOJA hesitates…*)

DOJA: I…

(*He lifts a hand in a gesture of bewilderment, lets it fall…*)

I…

(*He looks at TURNER.*)

TURNER: He…

(*She also makes a helpless gesture…*)

He…

BALDWIN: Lost for words, the pair of them…

(*He chokes a laugh, bites his lip…*)

Or not…?

(*He watches their stillness. He turns…*)

Nothing

Nothing

Nothing

Is lost on me

I am

Oh, misery

Oh, melancholy

Intuitive to an inordinate degree

My skin

So thin

I feel a thought alight on me

I feel the mothlike footsteps of a curse uttered in distant places

And vision

Vision, oh

My sight is such agony to me I could court blindness for a day's relief from this

PITIFUL TRANSPARENCY OF OTHERS

I dread maturity

The nakedness of things will scald my soul

God shield me with a clever liar soon

God give me a liar
A great liar
Oh, a tower of prodigious mischief, please
(*He clicks his fingers at* NIXON, *who surges forward with a plate
and serving tongs.*)

NIXON: Pike from the high pools of the Isonzo poached in the
pale wine of the Carnic Alps –

BALDWIN: Yes –

NIXON: Served on a field of primrose dashed with honeyed oil
and kernels of –

BALDWIN: Yes –

NIXON: The Tyrolean pine and swept in sauces –

BALDWIN: Whatever you say –
(*He turns back to* DOJA…)
Can't kiss, Mr Doja…?
(*Pause…*DOJA *looks at the floor…*)

DOJA: However much my instinct urges me –

BALDWIN: Instinct…?
(*Pause…*)

DOJA: However much my will commands me to –

BALDWIN: Will…?
(*Pause…*)

DOJA: However much my appetite is stimulated by your
invitation, some modesty restrains me…

BALDWIN: What modesty is this…?
(*Pause…*)
Oh, it's me…!
(*He feigns surprise…*)
You –
My –
The –
(*He laughs, as if in disbelief.*)

NIXON: (*Touring the table and piling a plate.*) Haunch of venison
in a light-baked sleeve of polished pastry garnished with
pressed anchovy, drained, smothered and sun-dried in –

BALDWIN: You put your hands inside my father, Mr Doja…
(*Pause…*)

DOJA: Yes…
(*Pause…*)

And you are now proposing…
(*Pause…NIXON clears a serving spoon by tapping it against a plate…DOJA looks to TURNER…*)

NIXON: Or breast of guinea-fowl marinaded in a flood of Grappa, cherry and Swiss cheese, reclining on a lawn of finely-chopped red peppers of Trieste –

BALDWIN: Yes…
(*Pause…*)
I witnessed one, why not the other…?
(*NIXON makes the same sound with the spoon…*)
And my mother's warm…
(*A fraction of a pause…*)
Oh, Mr Doja, everything conspires to make me intimate with you…!
(*He turns to NIXON.*)
Stool…!

DOJA: Wait…

BALDWIN: No, don't wait, Mr Doja –

DOJA: Compliments aside, I –
(*NIXON goes to fetch a stool.*)
Profound as my respect both for your father and your mother is –

BALDWIN: I know, I know these things –

DOJA: To require of me such an appalling trespass of –

BALDWIN: TRESPASS AND BE DAMNED…
(*Pause…*)

DOJA: (*As NIXON returns.*) You violate my liberty…which is not proper in a king…
(*He looks at TURNER…*)
Though in this instance…
(*He shrugs…he is in a crisis of diplomacy…*)
Violation might be…the doorway to a different liberty…

BALDWIN: (*Climbing on the stool.*) Yes…! Oh, excellent, that is so typical of you…if I may say – at this stage of our friendship, if I may dare to say what's typical of you…that is so…typical of you…!
(*He clasps his head in his hand, crossing his legs as he did in the anatomy clinic…*)

NIXON: (*Returning to his function.*) And a mousse of birds, lark, thrush and capercailie –

BALDWIN: Yes, but little…!

Don't pile the plate…

(*Pause…NIXON serves the mousse of birds. DOJA, with infinite tact, advances towards TURNER, who is still, observing him, he extends a hand, stops…*)

DOJA: I –

BALDWIN: Shh…

(*He yearns…*)

Don't you see how beautiful this is…?

How proper…?

How correct…?

(*DOJA places himself behind TURNER, his hands spread on her torso. He kisses her neck. NIXON taps the serving spoon…*)

Shh…

(*They are all still, NIXON's spoon in the air…*)

DOJA: Manifestum…

et…

Mammarum…

Exposito…

(*He unhitches her dress…her breasts are exposed…she is immobile…*)

I've no desire to…

I've no –

(*TURNER kisses him, placing one hand behind his head and drawing his mouth to hers…BALDWIN is a miracle of balance for the second time, a picture of curiosity and repulsion, in which by degrees, the repulsion triumphs until he throws himself from the stool and, close to suffocation, runs offstage… The light fades on the scene, to the sound of a distracted youth hurling objects about a room. NIXON removes the handkerchief given him by DOJA from his pocket, and holds it to his nose…*)

SUEDE: We carry on

PIN: We carry on as if

SUEDE: Precisely in the manner we are used to

PIN: Calmness

SUEDE: The triumph of routine

(*They are placing the organs of the dead king in containers with a peculiar urgency.*)

PIN: Being the finest antidote to

SUEDE: HORROR

PIN: HORROR

SUEDE: And anyway he would have wished

PIN: It was his rule

SUEDE: No job should last more than –

(*Dropping a lid with a clatter, clasping himself in his arms…*)
Twenty…four…hours…
(*He watches the lid roll idly over the floor…*)

PIN: I've done nothing with my life…

(*Pause…PIN stares at SUEDE…*)

SUEDE: We have seen several cities…

PIN: I had planned to do things, but later…

SUEDE: We saw a thousand geese fly overhead…

PIN: Later, when I was more prepared…

SUEDE: Five thousand, possibly –

PIN: When I was qualified I was waiting to be qualified –

SUEDE: Few can have seen that many geese –

PIN: Then I would have –

SUEDE: The sky was full of them –

PIN: Certainly then I would have –

SUEDE: Wings beating –

PIN: Done extraordinary things I was merely waiting to be –

SUEDE: Racket in the sky –

PIN: Qualified…

(*They stop, forlorn…DOJA enters…they lift their eyes to him…*)
Oh, Master, we were talking of you in the historic tense…
(*He looks at them, silent. PIN goes to collect the dropped lid but before he can retrieve it, DOJA sends it flying with a kick. The assistants stiffen…*)

SUEDE: We waited on you at your door…three times we knocked but…

(*Pause…*)

PIN: You weren't there…

(*Pause…DOJA goes slowly to the table, leans on it with both hands…*)

Talk with us, master…

DOJA: Talk with you…?

PIN: Why not, master…?

DOJA: How should I be the master, if I talked with you…?

(*They shrug their shoulders…LAYBACH enters…*)

LAYBACH: You didn't come…

(*DOJA's head turns slowly to him…*)

You assured me you would come and then did not come which only confirms my instinctive antipathy for you what kind of man –

SUEDE: Shh –

LAYBACH: Knowing the misery to which his careless action has reduced a harmless girl –

SUEDE: Shh –

LAYBACH: Would stoop to further injure her by –

SUEDE: (*Going to usher him away.*) Shh –

LAYBACH: (*Avoiding him.*) HUSH YOURSELF –

(*He goes to DOJA.*)

I came to abuse you and I will abuse you my fear of violence notwithstanding I find it vile that someone so arrogant, malevolent, so – so –

I'VE FORGOTTEN WHAT I WAS GOING TO SAY –

(*He shakes his head furiously.*)

Please see her I don't think I can come here again…

(*Pause…*)

DOJA: There is a smell on me…

(*Pause…*)

A smell which nauseates me and yet…

A smell I –

LAYBACH: Death…

DOJA: Is that what it is…? It's from a woman's body…

(*LAYBACH struggles with an impulse to strike DOJA, but turns and hurries away, passing TODD as he does so…*)

TODD: I have to speak with you.

DOJA: Do you…?

TODD: Now. Yes.

DOJA: This urgency to communicate with me appears to have afflicted the entire population –

TODD: Is that so?

DOJA: People cannot stay away, they are driven by some
terrible compulsion, children climb on the roof, old
women put their eyeballs to the cracks, and the excuses,
the preposterous and exaggerated fictions just to get one
foot inside the door, my assistants are exhausted, they
go to bed wrung out from their exertions, and they are
specialists, they are anatomists, not doormen, the flesh of
monarchy, what is its fascination and I only
WHAT IS IT YOU WANT I HAVE NO TIME
(*Pause...she looks at him...*)

TODD: You are in danger...

DOJA: Is that so, I have always been in danger, one gets
accustomed to such things, now forgive me, I must finish –

TODD: God help you when you do...
(*Pause...DOJA looks at her...he is still...*)

DOJA: The removal of the organs is only the first stage of a –

TODD: Good –

DOJA: Complex and exacting series of procedures which –

TODD: Good –

DOJA: Might take anything up to –
(*Pause...*)
A year...

TODD: A year...?

DOJA: At the very least...a year...
(*Pause...the assistants gawp...*)
In some awkward cases...five or...
(*Pause...*)
HOW MANY YEARS DO YOU THINK WHAT DANGER I
CANNOT SLEEP WITH EVERYBODY WOMAN MAN AND BOY
WHAT DANGER
Very well
I'll come to you
I know your room
I've seen it
Lit all night
Perhaps the danger's you
Oh yes
Quite possibly
Red curtains

Never drawn
I don't miss anything
Eyes peeled
Thin skin
A butterfly of nerves
That's me
Yes
I'll come
And washed
And fragrant
All you require I'll be and

TODD: We don't require your nakedness, Mr Doja...

(*Pause...*)

DOJA: Don't we...?

(*Pause...*)

Who's we...?

(*TODD goes out. A wind shakes the doors. The sound of children laughing and jeering. A cry. Piercing...*)

BERLIN: God...!

Oh, God...!

DOJA: If ever I was God I think I am not now...

(*He walks past LAYBACH, who stands sentinel-like, some yards from the bed on which BERLIN is sitting.*)

God is not coerced, surely?

BERLIN: Pity coerces him. Pity is his weakness. Why did your pity take so long?

DOJA: I thrust it away.

BERLIN: From those who love you...?

DOJA: Those especially. There is a youth there who adores you...

BERLIN: Yes.

DOJA: Relieve him, then. His life is a furnace of frustration.

BERLIN: I used him. As a means to you. His frustration is no concern of mine.

DOJA: Is it not?

BERLIN: None, even if I am the cause. You are the sole object of my life.

DOJA: Pull the blanket over you, it's as cold as death in here –

BERLIN: No –

DOJA: No, why no –

BERLIN: You will warm me. You or nothing. If I die, so be it, I am in God's hands.

DOJA: This is blackmail…

BERLIN: Blackmail…? Why, it's love…

DOJA: PEOPLE MANIPULATE ME AND I WON'T BE

    (*BERLIN laughs…shaking her head…*)

BERLIN: That is the proof…!

DOJA: Of what? The proof of what?

BERLIN: Your divinity…! It is the very cry of Heaven…!

DOJA: Yes

    Well

    God

    Also

    Squirms

BERLIN: He does…! He squirms to know the depths of abjection that his creatures plumb to know one second even of his intimacy…! Kiss my hands, they have waited too long for your blessing…!

DOJA: I –

BERLIN: Do kiss…! Do kiss…!

    (*She extends her hands to him…*)

DOJA: (*Hesitating.*) This is precisely what I –

BERLIN: Oh, kiss…!

    (*Pause. He leans forward and taking her hands, kisses them…*)

DOJA: (*Retaining a grip on them.*) I must tell you…I must warn you…that whilst I may be God…I am not kind…

BERLIN: No…

DOJA: No, and furthermore, to put the least faith in me would be to open yourself to an appalling wound…

BERLIN: Yes…

DOJA: A martyrdom…

BERLIN: Yes…

DOJA: A crucifixion…

BERLIN: Yes, because whereas many have faith in you, you have none in yourself…

    (*He leans over her, kissing her mouth…*)

DOJA: I exist…

BERLIN: You exist, and to ask more of you than mere existence
would be…heresy…
*(He covers her with his body…in the silence, the footsteps of
BALDWIN…he appears, stops, examines LAYBACH from a
distance…the assistants cut, swab, displace lids and pans…)*
BALDWIN: It is so horrible, being me…
(LAYBACH inclines his head a little…)
When I come near people they undergo some change,
some mineral disintegration, colour, structure, odour, a
puddle underneath my gaze I hate it whole individuals
men of character women of integrity pulped to a goulash
of apology I don't require it what possible pleasure could
there be in such a spectacle for me…?
(Pause…)
Why are you standing alone in the night?
(Pause…)
It is so excellent being me…
(LAYBACH inclines his head for a second time…)
The pride, the posture, even the vulgarity they must shed
as thieves ditch treasure when encountering the law,
they shiver like shaved hounds in the chill wind of my
interrogation, I love to see it fall, the crust of practised
personality, the manners and the see-I-have-no-manners,
artifice and calculation, flung to the floor, they are so
naked, oh, so naked and so poor, I'm certain I should
cease to find such pleasure in it, speaking from a moral
point of view, but I am not moral and I do
(He pauses…)
Find pleasure in it…
*(The sound of a woman in coitus, faint, recognizable. BALDWIN
reacts with a slight move of his head…)*
You love someone…
Oh, let me sit…! Oh, let me study you…!
*(He snaps his fingers. A figure emerges from the obscurity, places
a stool behind BALDWIN, and withdraws again. BALDWIN
sits, crossing his legs in a rapture of anticipation. LAYBACH is
mortified…)*
LAYBACH: I –
BALDWIN: Shh…!

(*LAYBACH sways. Out of the silence, the faint sound of BERLIN…*)
Oh, is that terrible…?
(*LAYBACH suffers…*)
Is that the most terrible sound in the world…?
(*Pause…*)

LAYBACH: Yes…

BALDWIN: And that is why you stand alone…I knew…! He
does not stand alone for nothing…! Oh, I knew…!
(*Pause. He concentrates. The sound of BERLIN, notes and
breath, barely audible. The sound of the assistants, faintly
accompanying…BALDWIN stands, goes to the anatomy table,
and returns with a cruel knife. He tosses the knife at LAYBACH's
feet…he then sits to contemplate the effect…LAYBACH stares at
BALDWIN…BERLIN gasps… LAYBACH studiedly turns his back on
BALDWIN…he lifts his hands and covers his ears…*)
Exquisite man…! You love your pain…!
(*He jumps up, lifting the stool by a leg and is about to leave…*)
Who is in there?
(*LAYBACH turns, uncovers his ears…*)
Who…?
(*LAYBACH lifts his shoulders in mock-ignorance. BALDWIN goes
into the obscurity. The assistants clang lids as they heave the metal
buckets of remains into a descending order of size…*)

LAYBACH: Stop now…
Stop now…
Stop now…
(*BERLIN is silent. DOJA still…*)
I'm after all a youth which whilst not an excuse yet still
might be an explanation for – no, curse youth, pulp
youth, rot youth, never again shall I parade the thing
called youth as vindication for my tempers – I would
rather perch on a bough, a hen, a parrot, squawking and
shitting my indignation – no, less whining, less pleading,
less everything – I HEARD EVERY BREATH OF YOUR WHAT
SHALL I CALL IT FORNICATION FORNICATION YES WHAT
ELSE IS IT AND –

DOJA: Fornication, it must be –

LAYBACH: Yes and –

DOJA: The word's good –

LAYBACH: Perfectly –

DOJA: The act good also –

LAYBACH: Possibly –

DOJA: Assuredly –

LAYBACH: I couldn't say –

DOJA: Being a youth –

LAYBACH: HE OFFERED ME A KNIFE AND I DECLINED TO USE
IT WHY.

(*DOJA looks at him, for the first time.*)

Why when

Why if

Why

It was my instinct and I

(*Pause…*)

DOJA: Offered you a knife…?

(*Pause…*)

LAYBACH: Somebody…

(*Pause. DOJA gets up…*)

DOJA: I must not come here again…help me not to come
again…

(*BERLIN sits up…*)

BERLIN: Tomorrow.

DOJA: There is not the least chance I –

BERLIN: Tomorrow.

(*Pause. LAYBACH laughs, a peculiar laugh, which is
unrecognizable to him…he stops…DOJA departs, pulling his coat
round him…the dead priests erupt.*)

FIRST/SECOND PRIESTS: HEY

HEY

DEATH'S AN EDUCATION

DOJA: Is it? Then there's something to look forward to.

FIRST PRIEST: Sarcasm –

SECOND PRIEST: Is the first thing we dispensed with –

DOJA: Pity, I find great comfort in it –

SECOND PRIEST: And humour, that is useless too –

DOJA: It's not the place for me, that's obvious –

FIRST/SECOND PRIESTS: DEATH IS THE END OF FREEDOM,
DOJA…

(*Pause…*)

DOJA: The end of it…?

FIRST/SECOND PRIESTS: AND THE BEGINNING OF

>*(Pause…)*

DOJA: What…?

>*(Pause…)*

>The beginning of what…?

>*(The priests sob, in a subdued, suffocated way…)*

>I don't think you should be –

>These –

>Left –

>Unburied, I –

>*(TURNER appears, also in a dark coat…DOJA shrugs…)*

>It's not my country but…

>*(Pause…)*

>I don't criticize…

TURNER: Have you been looking for me?

DOJA: I –

TURNER: I was looking for you –

DOJA: You were looking for me…!

TURNER: You weren't in your –

DOJA: No –

TURNER: Me neither, so –

DOJA: Absurd –

TURNER: Both of us –

DOJA: Out looking –

>*(They laugh, as if with modesty…)*

TURNER: I've –

>I've –

>I so want to tell the truth –

>For the first time, possibly, in my existence, wanted to tell the truth and –

>*(Pause…)*

>It's like being naked but –

>No, worse, God knows I have been naked and with many so that's such a redundant metaphor, no, not naked –

>*(Pause…)*

>Flayed…

>However, I…

(*Pause…*)

I interpret your silence as permission, I –

(*She laughs shrilly.*)

FLAYED I SAID

NOW THAT'S

FLAYED

You see even the word I choose is yours, an aspect of your own profession

I have thought of you since you parted from me

Never mind exaggeration

THOUGHT OF

Adequate

Adequate

Word

You say something now, will you

Too bad if I'm humiliated…

(*Pause…her eyes rise to meet his for the first time…*)

DOJA: Too bad for whom…?

(*She frowns…*)

TURNER: I have no sense of humour…forgive me, it is not
    something I –

(*She shrugs…*)

Ever required before…

DOJA: It is not compatible with…

TURNER: It is not necessary –

DOJA: Not necessary, no –

TURNER: In queens…not being weak…we scarcely need to
    laugh I DO FEEL WEAK WITH YOU HOWEVER how shall we
    make love a second time how you say I find the second
    time a problem the second anything a problem do you
    want me here now possibly the landscape its cruelty its
    indifference being such a contrast to the last luxurious and
    private place how hard it is to know you everything I say
    may be offensive everything a false step and driving iron
    bars between us but if you refuse to speak I must I must
    articulate the feeling or strike you yes I can do that
    (*She slaps him.*)

WHICH IS PREFERABLE TO A SENSE OF HUMOUR IN MY
JUDGEMENT

(*Pause. DOJA rubs his cheek…they exchange long looks…*)

DOJA: I'm circumspect…

TURNER: Yes…

DOJA: Because I am a slave…

TURNER: Yes…

DOJA: And slaves live only at the whim or possibly the
indifference of their masters –

TURNER: Very well, I'll do the talking –

DOJA: Anything I say –

TURNER: Or fail to say –

DOJA: That also, yes, might cause offence and therefore –

TURNER: YOU HAVE KISSED ME WHERE THE DAYLIGHT HAS
NOT VISITED.

(*Pause…she shrugs…*)

Even so, one might, such intimacies, and still, the most,
profound, and then, next day, despite the, with a new
sunrise, even

EVERYTHING THAT OCCURRED WAS NOVEL TO ME

EVERYTHING

THE DRESS

THE MANNER

THE CONVERSATION

NEVER

NEVER

BEFORE

I WAS A STRANGER TO MYSELF

(*Pause…DOJA looks into her stricken face…he leans into her and
breathes the odour of her body…the assistants, with a clatter,
wash the instruments.*)

PIN: I've no desire to go home…

SUEDE: (*Filling a pan from a tap.*) Home…?

PIN: Home, I called it home…! The room…

SUEDE: The room's not home.

PIN: Not home and I'm peculiarly reluctant to…for some
reason unwilling to…

SUEDE: It's not a nice room…

PIN: It's –

SUEDE: They've tried –

PIN: They've tried but still –

SUEDE: It's bleak –

PIN: Very bleak and in many ways I find this place every bit as
congenial as –

SUEDE: Or the room, to put it the other way round, no more
congenial –

PIN: No more congenial than this –

SUEDE: Which is a damning verdict on their hospitality –

PIN: Yes…!

    (*A pause like the stroke of a knife.*)

    Yes, we'll stay here –

SUEDE: PUT A CHAIR AGAINST THE DOOR –

PIN: (*Infected.*) OH…!

SUEDE: (*Dropping the pan.*) Yes…!

PIN: Quick, a chair, quick…!

    (*They collide in seizing a chair. SUEDE recovers and jams the
chair-back under the door handle.*)

    Christ, oh, Christ…!

SUEDE: The lights…!

PIN: Lights…?

SUEDE: OFF…!

PIN: Off…? Why off…?

SUEDE: LIGHTS OFF…!

PIN: Wait –

SUEDE: SURELY OFF –

PIN: No, on, because –

SUEDE: Oh, quick –

PIN: Because –

SUEDE: THEY KNOW WE'RE HERE –

PIN: Yes, but –

    (*He fathoms swiftly.*)

    All right…!

    (*He turns off the lamps…a profound gloom settles over the room.
A silence also. A pause…*)

    I think they should be on because…

    (*Pause…*)

    Where are you…?

(*SUEDE taps a knife on the ground…*)
It's all right, we can speak –
SUEDE: Shh…!
PIN: Surely we can –
   (*SUEDE taps again, as if to silence him…pause…*)
   What have you got…?
SUEDE: The eight-inch scalpel…
PIN: I'd better get some –
   (*He scrabbles…*)
SUEDE: Shh…please…shh…
   (*The sound of blades shifting on a tray…*)
   please…please…
PIN: THEY WON'T COME HERE…!
SUEDE: (*In despair.*) Oh, please…!
   (*Pause…*)
PIN: They won't come here…
   (*Pause…*)
   Which is why I argued for the lamps…the lamps
   illuminated because…
   (*Pause…*)
   Because of him…
   (*Pause…*)
SUEDE: Who…?
PIN: Him.
SUEDE: Who…?
PIN: HIM HIM WHO DO YOU THINK HIM
SUEDE: Shh –
PIN: ON THE TABLE HIM OF COURSE HIM IN THE BUCKETS –
SUEDE: Shh –
PIN: IN THE PANS OLD OFFAL STINKING HIM WHO ELSE –
SUEDE: (*With a new chill.*) Be quiet or I will stab you.
   (*Pause…*)
   Light the lights.
   (*Pause…*)
PIN: What…?
SUEDE: I will.
   (*He gets up. He kicks a bucket. A muffled oath. The lights glow.*
   SUEDE points an accusing finger…)
   You are the curse.

PIN: Curse…?

SUEDE: Yes, you. You are the origin.

PIN: Of what…?

SUEDE: THE MORTAL DANGER WE ARE IN. YOU.

(*He lifts the scalpel.*)

Don't come near me. Not that I fear you. But I would think
myself contaminated by your blood.

PIN: Would you, and how should that be…?

SUEDE: (*Going to the door, removing the chair.*) And I was looking
outside…! How mistaken, and yet how quintessentially
human to seek the origin of horror in the outside world –

(*He tosses the scalpel onto the tray with a studied nonchalance.*)

When always, always it is –

(*The door opens. DOJA enters.*)

Near

Oh, very

Near

PROXIMITY IS ITS VERY CHARACTER

(*He turns to DOJA…*)

Master, I wish to discuss with you the character and
suitability of my colleague –

DOJA: Why –

SUEDE: His long association with us makes me reluctant to
initiate such a –

DOJA: (*Rolling up his sleeves.*) Apron…

SUEDE: (*Fetching it off a hook.*) Painful and possibly humiliating –

DOJA: I'm working nights –

SUEDE: Inquisition but –

DOJA: My nights have been too free, nights only from now on,
the lamp's low –

(*PIN adjusts the wick.*)

NIGHTS AND ONLY NIGHTS

PIN: We were thinking the same thing…!

SUEDE: (*Persisting.*) He has revealed traits and attitudes –

PIN: We were seriously considering sleeping here –

SUEDE: Quite incompatible with –

PIN: Weren't we…? A mattress on the floor is perfectly –

SUEDE: (*To PIN.*) BE QUIET I AM INDICTING YOU.

(*Pause. DOJA looks at SUEDE…*)

Master, my colleague lacks that character of spirituality
that you have always insisted is the pre-requisite in any
student of anatomy –
(*He turns his gaze on PIN.*)
It gives me no pleasure to announce –
PIN: IT GIVES HIM HUGE PLEASURE –
SUEDE: None at all –
PIN: VAST –
SUEDE: None I said –
PIN: AND VICIOUS PLEASURE –
SUEDE: WE'RE UNDER A CURSE…!
(*He turns to DOJA.*)
And he's the reason. He has no reverence for flesh.
All these years and we did not suspect –
PIN: Suspect what –
SUEDE: (*To PIN, cruelly.*) SUSPECT YOUR INFIDELITY…!
PIN: To what –
SUEDE: Oh…!
PIN: Infidelity to what –
SUEDE: (*Shutting his ears with his hands.*) I can't listen –
PIN: TO WHAT TO WHAT AM I UNFAITHFUL –
SUEDE: OUR COMPACT WITH THE DEAD.
(*PIN screws up his face…in the silence, DOJA lifts a tool from the
tray…pause…*)
DOJA: Things are bad here, certainly…
(*He throws it down, picks up another… this also he tosses down…
he leans on the table…*)
I'm not myself…
PIN: None of us is –
SUEDE: YOU SAY THAT TO PROTECT YOURSELF…!
(*PIN stares at SUEDE, horrified by his vehemence…*)
DOJA: I think for example, whilst I am able to lie with my
usual dexterity…
(*Pause…*)
I am not certain if these lies are lies at all…
(*Pause…*)
I cannot conceal from myself the possibility…that these
lies…are…

(*Pause…*)

Aspects of the truth…

(*Pause…*)

The odour of the Queen, which I described as uncongenial to me…

(*Pause…PIN completes DOJA's sentence.*)

PIN: (*Cheerfully.*) You're gasping for…!

(*Pause…he regrets his impetuosity…*)

Forgive me, master, I –

(*He drags his hands through his hair.*)

Oh, I –

NONE OF US IS HIMSELF…IT'S TRUE…

(*He turns, makes a short, absurd walk, stops…dogs bark in the distance. In despair, PIN extends a hand to SUEDE. SUEDE ignores it…at last, the hand falters.*)

DOJA: It's not too late, you can still –

SUEDE: (*Panicked.*) I'M NOT LEAVING THIS ROOM…!

(*Pause…DOJA looks up at him…*)

If what you're saying is – if you are – whatever you are saying with the Queen I think – no wonder we – of course you are the master and will always be the master in my eyes – nevertheless – the curse I think could be quite adequately explained by – you must sleep where you wish but –

(*He waves towards the body on the table…*)

THE DECEASED ARE CAPABLE OF PAIN…

(*He looks at the dissected body…*)

And therefore, surely…of resentment…

(*He bites his lip…*)

He fought death…you can tell that from the condition of the tissue…

(*Pause…*)

I daresay because…

(*Pause…*)

He knew…of your…

(*He falters…*)

I'll make a bed over there…if no one else wants that… particular…

(*He drifts away, throwing a coat onto the floor…the sound of sobbing comes from his obscure corner…slowly, daylight penetrates the scene…*BALDWIN *is discovered with a basket of laundry.* DOJA, *summoned, goes to attend to him. He inclines his head…*)

BALDWIN: Good day for a dry…

(*Pause…*)

A dry they call it…the laundry women, how I like to speak their tongue…did you bring the pegs…?

DOJA: Yes…

BALDWIN: They never mind me…! Nor the cooks…! I drift about their premises, and I am not the king in there…! No, they are the queens of the copper tubs, but so supreme in their authority they do not think to shut their mouths… the oaths…the bawdy…swimming in the steam…! This morning, for example –

(*He points to an item in the basket.*)

You take one end –

(DOJA *lifts a sheet…shakes it about in search of the hems.*)

This morning it was –

(*He pauses…*)

The stubbornness of stains…

(DOJA *is half-upright…pause…he rises. He holds out a sheet hem towards* BALDWIN…)

Not anybody's stains…!

And me there…!

Me, a leaf of tenderness that tumbled on the wave of their extraordinary speculations…

(*At last he takes the sheet. They proceed to hang it on the line, pegging it…*)

Don't I have feelings…? Oh, the density of them, the strata of my feelings…but they go on…! I blush, I squirm, and they…!

(*He shakes his head…he shrugs…*)

STEAM ON…

(*He returns to the basket.*)

You have to admire such an extravagance of coarseness, they are made of leather, and that's the subtle ones, no, they're brick, souls of brick and gobs of clay…!

(*He stoops to the basket.*)

217

I like them…

(*He pulls out an item of underclothing…female…he opens the garment with his fingers…*DOJA, *with an attempt at casualness, extends his hand to take it to the line…*BALDWIN *counters by remaining in possession…*)

She went with many, many men…

(*His eyes rise to* DOJA's…)

And these men had to die…they knew it…! Oh, they were fully apprized, they went into it with their eyes open…! They understood my father had no option, they were stricken, obviously but none complained…

(*Pause…*)

They knew if she was not to die, then it must be they…

(*Pause…*)

Given that my father…

(*He throws the pants to* DOJA…)

Doted…

(*Pause…*DOJA *proceeds to peg the pants to the line.* BALDWIN *stoops for another item…*)

DOJA: Her skin…

(BALDWIN *stays low…*)

Has that peculiar…

(DOJA *pauses to contemplate the effect of his speech.*)

That simultaneously…

(BALDWIN *remains stooping…*)

I can only describe it as possessing the identical extremes of fecundity and decay associated with…

(*He observes* BALDWIN's *unyielding posture…*)

Compost…

Manure…

Ordure…

Spoiled fruit…

Drenched hay…

Intoxicating…

Nauseating…

I can only spend a little time with you today my assistants are not experienced in the techniques of organic preservation…

And opening her legs she…

(*He watches* BALDWIN…)

Exhales this…

(BALDWIN *is fixed…*DOJA *enjoys his pain…*)

They are not incompetent but whilst the removal of the viscera is merely the organization of formlessness, the forestalling of corruption calls for altogether…

(*Pause…he himself squirms…*)

This…

This…

Breath of rivers, blood and human floors to which my lips are drawn as if steel cables hauled me in, a barge inexorably brought into its berth…

(*Pause…*)

I stink of her even now…

(*Pause…*)

I stink…

(*Pause…*BALDWIN *lifts another garment on the end of an extended arm, his body still fixed…pause…then* DOJA *takes it, and pegs it to the line. Simultaneously, they both erupt into laughter,* BALDWIN *rising at last and shaking with the exertion of it. The laughter fades…* BALDWIN *shakes his head…*)

BALDWIN: It's me you love…!

(*He is still. He looks at* DOJA *under his eyes…*)

All this –

Oh, I understand it…! I am the same…! This forestalling and false signalling, I am the same…! HOW HARD IT IS TO SAY…

(*Pause…his eyes remain on* DOJA…)

And I don't ask you to say…on the contrary, I would perhaps forbid your saying, because I know for you saying is so – practised, such an art, whereas your silence…! There's a tribute to a choking love…

(*Pause…his eyes fall…*)

On the other hand, an action, possibly indiscreet…

(*He shrugs…*)

I don't know…

(*He bites his lip…*)

I don't know how to advance…

(*He looks up…*)

Do you…?

(*DOJA shakes his head…*)

Not even you…

Know how…

(*He affects an exasperation…*)

AND WE'RE KINGS…THE PAIR OF US…!

(*He laughs, stops, looks hard into DOJA…*)

If kings can't do…what they most want to do…I'm
shedding monarchy…and like some crusted quarryman
blaspheming from the canteen I'll abuse you…words of
one syllable…the thought unqualified by manners or by
poetry, I'M HOWLING, MR DOJA, KISS MY ARSE AND I'LL
KISS YOURS…

(*DOJA is suspended between politics and revulsion, but BALDWIN
allows him no time to reflect, flinging himself on DOJA and
dragging the sheet with him. DOJA is the more powerful, however,
and in the ruins of the laundry, topples BALDWIN…the dead
priests squeal with mingled horror and delight…*)

FIRST/SECOND PRIESTS: OH, MAJESTY…OH, REVERED
    MAJESTY…!

FIRST PRIEST: The blue sky never was more blue

SECOND PRIEST: The sheets like sails

FIRST PRIEST: On plunging schooners

FIRST/SECOND PRIESTS: Crack… Crack…!

FIRST PRIEST: And you

SECOND PRIEST: Are so much closer to your execution

FIRST/SECOND PRIESTS: A FINE DAY FOR A DRY THE WIND
    FILLS SKIRTS AS IF THE OCCUPANTS WERE PRANCING

SECOND PRIEST: On an avenue…

(*A silence descends, the wind alone stirring the few hanging
garments… DOJA climbs to his feet, extricating himself…*)

BALDWIN: Kiss, I said…

(*He moans…*)

Kiss, I said…

(*DOJA is aware that another has entered and is observing him…*)

TODD: How you have loved to be beyond…keeping your
    intimacy for the dead…and visiting, as it were…just
    visiting…the living…

(*Pause.*)
But now…
(*Pause.*)
How you have stood as crows stand…on the rim…and watched through unpitying eyes the antics of we who deserved no pity…untouched by weathers and with each flight casting memory away as some thing undigested…
(*Pause.*)
But now…

BALDWIN: (*Wailing.*) Kiss, I said…!

TODD: We wait for you…but not infinitely…

DOJA: Yes…

TODD: NOT…INFINITELY…
(*She turns to BALDWIN…with a pretence.*)
Oh, what has happened here…!
(*She hurries to him.*)
Oh, Lord, the line has come down and the prop…oh, some wind dislodged the prop and…oh…grass and goose muck…!
(*She shouts off, to the launderers.*)
Boil up, the whites are ruined…!
(*DOJA surges through the disorder to find TURNER, who is bathing. NIXON holds a towel…DOJA recovers, dictating a silence…at last he speaks.*)

DOJA: I came by forty graves…
(*TURNER squeezes a sponge, thoughtfully…*)
Shaded and the whispering descent of pine needles… polished but unnamed…
(*She draws a comb through her hair…*)
You'd know the names…but not the order of the names…I daresay…
(*Pause…*)
Always I have preserved the most clinical and frozen distances between myself and the material remains of the –
(*He shakes his head…*)
Please, this affectation of –
(*She stops…*)
This studied and contrived languidity, I –

(*Pause. She holds the comb still in the air.*)
Murderers, torturers, cannibals who put whole cities to
the sword and stewed the infants in the ponds, nothing to
me…! Revered archbishops, fratricidal usurpers, guts in the
pan and –
(*He stops…his eyes close…pause…*)
In this case however…a profound loathing for this
degenerating flesh makes me recoil from the most
mundane professional activity, I –
(*He sees, and is transfixed by, the spectacle of SUEDE murdering
PIN in the anatomy room…as PIN fights for his life, the pans
and buckets are swept over, instruments are strewn over the floor
in an appalling ballet which concludes with PIN's death from
innumerable wounds. SUEDE, exhausted by his exertions, collapses
onto a stool, head in hands…TURNER is not aware of this, but in
the returned silence, her weeping is heard…DOJA turns to her…his
eyes travel to NIXON, who shrugs his shoulders…TURNER weeps
out loud…*)
Stop that…
(*She excels herself in grief.*)
Stop that…!
(*He turns to hurry away.*)

NIXON: Don't go, Mr Doja…

DOJA: (*Stopping…*) Don't go…? Why not go…? The Queen's a
liar…

NIXON: And can you not be lied to, Mr Doja…?

(*Pause…NIXON encloses TURNER in a towel, as she emerges from
the bath…*)
This tenderness with regard to a deception might be seen
as certain evidence of love…
(*He dries her body…*)
But equally, so might the deception that created it…
(*He ceases…leaving TURNER enclosed in the towel.*)
Love and the world…
(*He shrugs…*)
The one abhors the other…
(*He smiles…*)
I lecture you…! I, the ignorant and –

DOJA: Don't go on –

NIXON: Servile agent of my master's whims, I –

DOJA: Don't go on, I said –

NIXON: Lecture you…!

> (*He goes, drawing away the towel in which TURNER is enclosed, she is perfectly still, her back exposed to him, her head inclined…*)

DOJA: All things here…even the confessions…are manifestly false…

> (*Pause…*)

TURNER: Yes…

DOJA: And nakedness…far from being…a testament to truth is…further –

TURNER: Yes…!

> (*Pause…*)

DOJA: Manipulation –

TURNER: I manipulate you, yes –

DOJA: Not only you –

TURNER: Not only me?

DOJA: IT'S UNIVERSAL I AM PLUCKED AND PULLED AS A DOLL IS TORTURED BY A POISONOUS CHILD –

TURNER: DOLL YOU DOLL WHAT DOLL IS THIS…?

> (*She is silent…*)

I cannot argue naked if you wish to argue dress me find a towel my skirt I cannot let my nakedness be spoiled like this –

DOJA: SPOILED IT'S A FOOTBALL FIELD OF FORNICATION –

TURNER: My skirt – my towel –

> (*She extends a hand in desperation.*)

DOJA: A SODDEN QUARRY OF COPULATION –

TURNER: My skirt, I said –

DOJA: TRODDEN, SLIPPERY AND FORLORN AS GRAVEL PITS IN WINTER –

TURNER: My skirt

Oh skirt

Skirt

Please

My

(Her hand hangs in he air. DOJA watches, then seizing the hand, kisses it desperately…SUEDE, climbing with an air of resignation off the stool, begins to collect the scattered lids and implements. He ignores the body of PIN, even when LAYBACH enters…LAYBACH stares at the body…)

SUEDE: I don't know where the master is…

(Pause…he tidies…)

He left notes at one time…little notes in this exquisite hand…black ink…and dated…the day fully described…no numbers…Tues – day…the whole word…!

(He wipes a blade on a cloth, places it on the tray.)

Fri – day…

Excellent, I wish I'd kept them because he not only informed us as to the nature of his absence but announced as well the precise time of his arrival…! Yes, and he would not fail to appear…!

(He collects, organizes…)

An extraordinary man I am honoured to have served him at what we must now recognize was his – apotheosis – and it was not brief – no, in this state of perfection he continued many years, I learned so many things from him –

(He stops in mid-movement…)

MANY THINGS…?

(He shakes his head.)

I learned it all…

(Pause…LAYBACH stares…DOJA, parting from TURNER, enters the anatomy room…SUEDE pays him no particular attention…)

LAYBACH: I –

DOJA: Yes, I was expecting you –

LAYBACH: It's been considerably longer than she anticipated, and her –

DOJA: Health, yes, is deteriorating –

LAYBACH: Health and not only health –

DOJA: *(To SUEDE.)* Where's my apron…?

LAYBACH: Her character –

DOJA: Apron…?

(SUEDE ignores DOJA.)

LAYBACH: YOU KNOW HOW I RECOIL FROM THESE HUMILIATING ERRANDS BUT –

DOJA: APRON...!

(*Pause. SUEDE stops...*)

SUEDE: Are you addressing me...?

(*Pause...*)

DOJA: I can't address...the other...

SUEDE: No...

(*He shrugs...*)

The other...as you call him...the other's dead...

(*Pause. He busies on, ignoring DOJA...*)

The other...! Funny...! And we were amicable once...And now he is merely – the other...

LAYBACH: (*Patiently.*) Never, never will I allow myself to be so racked and ridiculed by an unreciprocated love of this description, never, never –

DOJA: (*Turning on him as if to swat a fly.*) IT'S THE LOVE YOU LIKE...!

(*He returns to SUEDE.*)

This corpse is for the river...

(*SUEDE stops...an iciness afflicts his mouth...*)

SUEDE: This –

What...?

(*A pause settles...*)

This –

DOJA: Carcass...

(*SUEDE adjusts his glasses...*)

Sacks...

Stones...

(*SUEDE chews his tongue...*)

Or no stones...?

(*Pause...*)

No stones...

(*Pause...*)

No stones and no sacks, either...

(*Pause...*)

There's a bend three miles downstream where every suicide and unlucky boatman fetches up in the reeds...

(*Pause...*)

The sun beats down...

(*Pause…*)

The storks go –

SUEDE: I'm so sorry –

DOJA: The storks' beaks go –

SUEDE: So sorry –

DOJA: Sharper than butcher's knives –

SUEDE: TO SEE YOU ROT LIKE THIS –

DOJA: He rots, not me –

SUEDE: AND I REVERED YOU ONCE…!

(*DOJA stares into SUEDE…*)

DOJA: This vile character…

(*He indicates the body, his eyes still fixed on SUEDE…*)

is not for preservation…

(*Pause…*)

TIP HIS BITS INTO THE RIVER…

(*SUEDE holds out for some seconds, then his face collapses and he stamps his feet…*)

SUEDE: IT'S MY PROFESSION…!

(*He grabs a wicked blade from the table and levels it at DOJA…*)

How sad how terrible how sad and terrible to have to kill not one but two oh what a place oh what an atmosphere we never should have come here but we did too bad too late too everything the poison came from him it seemed but no not only him you too you are the source to call a king a corpse a what a corpse and a cadaver no you're ill so very ill I'm sorry I alone appear to keep faith with an honourable profession if you insult the dead they shout they also have their tempers –

(*He nods towards LAYBACH, who is staring wildly…*)

RUN TO THE CASTLE RUN AND TELL…!

(*He makes a lunge at DOJA, who steps back, and follows it with another.*)

RUN AND TELL I SAID…!

(*DOJA trips in retreating from SUEDE's jabs…*)

LAYBACH: (*His ecstasy unstopped by DOJA's frailty.*) STAB HIM, STAB HIM, STAB…!

(*He goes to seize DOJA in his arms…*)

God fingers me…! God fingers me…!

(*DOJA evades LAYBACH's impetuous rush, grabbing up the wooden stool to protect himself…LAYBACH takes a knife from the tray. The young men menace DOJA…*)

I am saving a life…

(*He advances a step…*)

In taking your life…I am saving a life…

(*He advances another step…suddenly he seems to fold at the middle…the knife drops to the floor…he shudders and wails…*)

I'll run to the castle…

SUEDE: Go on, then, run…

LAYBACH: (*Incapable of movement.*) I'll run to the castle…

(*SUEDE is about to rage at LAYBACH when BALDWIN enters, casually. SUEDE replaces his knife on the tray with exquisite composure. DOJA places the stool on the floor and perches on it in a single movement.*)

BALDWIN: (*Observing LAYBACH's wretchedness.*) Always you repudiate the knife, when the knife is precisely your requirement. Always you fail to act, when action is the very –

(*He stoops, retrieves LAYBACH's knife, and places it on the tray…*)

Or not…?

(*LAYBACH sobs…*)

With you, the knife is perhaps, the mirage that shimmers on the horizon of your life…the alibi for ecstasy never quite attempted

I TALK OF ECSTASY

ME

ME MR DOJA

ECSTASY…!

(*Pause…he wanders to the table, and lifts the corner of the sheet…*)

I have my fifty knights. Ten with the liver to Kiev. Ten with the heart to Riga and so on. IT IS A SHAMBLES IN HERE IS IT NOT and one of the experts dead dead on the floor what kind of and you are not cheap you said yourself hardly the lowest tender Mr Doja

I AM A CHANGED MAN

No

Not changed

Oh, preposterous and incredible claim is anybody is
anything changed no not changed merely reassorted I am
reassorted

(*He flings back the sheet.*)

I was a boy and now I'm reassorted what does that make
me Mr Doja last time I looked upon my father I shuddered
not today however some reassortment surely…?

(*DOJA climbs off the stool…*)

DOJA: I have abandoned my vocation.

BALDWIN: Can you abandon a vocation, Mr Doja? Perhaps it
has abandoned you?

DOJA: It's fled, certainly…

BALDWIN: Fled and my father in a dozen parts…!

DOJA: The necessary reverence for the dead I found in this
particular instance rapidly diminishing –

SUEDE: HE TOLD ME TOSS IT IN THE RIVER…!

DOJA: I experienced disgust –

BALDWIN: Disgust?

DOJA: Disgust, which is the –

BALDWIN: Disgust, Mr Doja?

SUEDE: IN THE RIVER, TIP IT IN, HE SAID…!

(*Pause…DOJA completes his sentence…*)

DOJA: The nightmare of anatomy…

(*BALDWIN lets the sheet fall back on the body…*)

BALDWIN: My knights, however, have their own exigencies. I
cannot think your squeamishness will find much sympathy
with them, they ache to gallop with my father's bowel,
a pennant, a banner flying in the wind, WHAT SUDDEN
HORROR OF A MAN'S INTERIOR IS THIS MR DOJA…!

(*He stares at DOJA…*)

SUEDE: If I may –

(*BALDWIN and DOJA are fixed…*)

If I could –

(*Pause. LAYBACH runs off…*)

I think I can say without false modesty that I alone possess
the necessary – spiritual authority – for this task, having –

(*BALDWIN goes towards DOJA, and takes his head between his hands...*)

discovered in myself the courage to –

(*He kisses DOJA on the mouth...*)

to murder even where sacrilege had poisoned the atmosphere, and...

(*He moves to the table and begins work with the knives...*)

so on...no...nobody I think...is better qualified to...

(*He works on, with a detailed attention to his craft, as BALDWIN's kiss lingers...*)

Serrula...

(*He extends a hand...*)

Ubi serrula...?

(*BALDWIN's kiss ends...DOJA goes to the table and hands SUEDE the tool... BALDWIN silently withdraws...*)

Et inflexit...

(*DOJA assists...*)

Dextra...

Dextra...

LAYBACH: (*To BALDWIN, who passes at a distance.*) I cannot hurt, it is my problem...

(*BALDWIN stops, wipes his mouth...*)

I long to hurt...which some would say...is just the same as hurting, but...

(*He shrugs...*)

Perhaps the world is made of those who can and those who only wish to...

(*Pause...*)

Hurt...

(*BALDWIN moves to go...*)

HE HAS YOUR MOTHER AND OTHERS TOO NUMEROUS TO MENTION

I merely

I just

I

I

No that is

Forget I said

That is so
(*He makes a dismissive gesture with his hands…*)
An utter
Pure calumny
I am sick with jealousy it makes me lie
Preposterously lie
I perjure myself
SICK MY LIFE IS EBBING OUT OF ME…
(*BALDWIN cogitates…LAYBACH gathers his resources from the bottom of his soul…*)
Perhaps…
(*He shrugs…*)
Perhaps in submitting to an ordeal a man…finds powers which…had he resorted to an instinct…he never could have assembled…
(*He shrugs again…*)
Perhaps…
(*He turns to leave.*)

BALDWIN: The death of Mr Doja is certainly the solution…I am painfully aware of it…
(*LAYBACH turns…*)
At my first glance I knew…much sleep would be lost as a consequence of Mr Doja…and sleep's precious, I am an advocate of sleep…

LAYBACH: It is a rare commodity round here…

BALDWIN: It is…! One shuts one's eyes, but on the lids, oh, racing rivers, cascades brighter than the sun, how I wish I could relieve you, it is after all among a monarch's many obligations that he grants his subjects the facility of sleep HAD MY MOTHER WHERE EXACTLY lamps are burning at all hours and kettles boiling in the dead of night it is a plague that Mr Doja brought in with him a plague of insomnia IN WHAT POSTURE WHERE SHOW ME –

LAYBACH: What –

BALDWIN: Now –

LAYBACH: Show you –

BALDWIN: The place –

LAYBACH: The place? I –

BALDWIN: HE TOOK MY MOTHER IN –

LAYBACH: I have not personally –

BALDWIN: THE PLACE, SHOW ME –

LAYBACH: I can't, I haven't –

BALDWIN: INVENT IT, THEN…

> (*Pause…LAYBACH is strung between horror and resourcefulness…*)
> The rumour…make it…live…
> (*BALDWIN is patient…*)

LAYBACH: I…

> (*He strains…*)
> One afternoon…between the abbey and the hospital…was –
> (*He is aware of a third party standing in the penumbra of the light…*)
> On an errand and…
> (*He swallows…*)
> I think this will be the death of me…
> (*His eyes search BALDWIN's imperturbable features…*)
> Came upon this –
> (*The figure enters. It is TURNER. She sits on the ground, taking BALDWIN's fingers in hers…LAYBACH observes this with a terrible unease…*)
> Spectacle…
> (*He covers his face with his hands…*)
> This violates my soul –
> (*The dead priests shriek with laughter.*)

FIRST PRIEST: His soul goes ow…!

SECOND PRIEST: Ow…! Ow…! His soul…!

FIRST PRIEST: Wrapped round a drum and –

SECOND PRIEST: Ow…!

FIRST PRIEST: His soul is more elastic than –

SECOND PRIEST: ST ELMO'S BOWEL…!

FIRST PRIEST: Ow…! Ow…!

> (*Pause…*)

FIRST/SECOND PRIESTS: Let out…let out…your soul…as a fat woman…loosens her bodice…or you…will never be a bishop…but die…a novice…

(*BERLIN crosses the stage in a wheelchair, propelling herself.*
She stops in the vicinity of the anatomy room...DOJA senses her
patience...he goes to leave the room.)

SUEDE: Non exeat...

(*DOJA stops...pause...*)

Non exeat...

(*SUEDE works on...*)

If every passing bitch can draw you from your labour
where's the

(*Pause. He cuts...*)

The sign of our profession is its immunity to every passing
instinct, every transient circumstance...

(*He proceeds without looking...*)

This might be a battlefield.

(*DOJA is still.*)

A battlefield

A kitchen

Or

A

Brothel

BERLIN: I MOVED...!

SUEDE: Still our whole attention would be on the task in –

BERLIN: MY LEGS REFUSED SO I COERCED THEM...!

My legs declined therefore my arms were forced to serve
me and if my arms dare mutiny my teeth will be enlisted
THAT IS THE POWER OF MY WILL

DOJA: The master –

BERLIN: Master...?

DOJA: Will beat me certainly if I –

BERLIN: Master...?

DOJA: Unfortunately yes –

BERLIN: You are the master...

DOJA: He's far from kind, and lashes out sometimes with a
bare fist, which I put down to his limitless dedication,
demanding as he does the same devotion in his assistants
that he –

BERLIN: YOU ARE THE MASTER –

DOJA: Shows himself...

(*Pause. A low laugh comes from* BERLIN*...she shakes her head... her laugh rumbles on...*)

BERLIN: Oh, Doja, you think...

(*She laughs still...*)

You think to smother your...

(*And laughs again...*)

I ADMIRE IT...

To escape the notice of the world you –

ACT DEAD

(*With a swift exertion she rises out of the wheelchair and walks into the room.* SUEDE, *disconcerted, looks up with irritation.* BERLIN *jabs a surgical instrument into him. The priests erupt into a staccato laugh.* SUEDE, *incredulous, staggers in a grotesque dance...*DOJA *stares...*BERLIN *crushes him in an embrace...* LAYBACH, *intuitively perceiving the murder, rushes into the anatomy room...he stares in disbelief...*)

BERLIN: He's mine...!

I saved him from obscurity...!

HE MUST BE MINE, THEREFORE...!

(SUEDE *crashes into* LAYBACH'*s arms and dies...*LAYBACH *holds the body for some seconds, then lets it slide to the ground. Silence returns...*)

And pale...! How pale he was becoming, like a leaf in the first chill of autumn, no, he would have shrunk, become transparent, disappeared, and –

DOJA: It is not you I love...

BERLIN: Passing carriages could have splashed through his brains unknowingly, as some frail bird's egg fallen from the nest is smothered in their wheels...

DOJA: I said it is not you –

BERLIN: Shh...! I know...!

LAYBACH: (*To* BERLIN.) YOU ARE MAGNIFICENT AND I DETEST YOU.

(*Pause.* BERLIN *looks at* LAYBACH...)

BERLIN: Detest me...? Why...?

LAYBACH: (*Grimly.*) Did you think...

(*He wipes his hands on his cassock...*)

Oh, did you really, really think my little fountain of pure
devotion could just flow and tinkle day and night like some
spring bubbling in a market square, century on century
of loyal provision, WHOEVER THANKS THE FOUNTAIN
RATHER THEY PISS IN IT
(*She puts out a hand. He dashes it away.*)
No…!
I HAVE TURNED TOXIC DO NOT DRINK FROM ME…
(*He glares at her. She by contrast, is kind-faced to him…*)
BERLIN: But of course…! How else could you be…?
(*She bites her lip…he weeps…his hand goes up and down…*)
LAYBACH: Oh, sick…oh, sick of this weeping…
(*He waves in his despair…*)
Cut me open, Mr Doja…take out my liver and plant the
place with some black bear's bile instead…
(*He walks slowly out…*)
DOJA: How the little priest consoles himself for his weak
character…he applauds his sensibility…and asks us to
applaud it, also…
(*He looks to BERLIN…*)
I've nothing to offer you…neither gratitude…nor love…
even the instinct that our nakedness might DON'T UNDO
YOUR GARMENTS possibly inflame OR LET YOUR LIP
PROTRUDE would be lower than a guttering candle dying
in its wax I'VE NOTHING NOTHING –
(*He stops, as NIXON enters with a hand-cart, which he drops in a
business-like manner alongside the body of PIN…*)
BERLIN: Nothing is precisely what I ask…
(*She goes out, ignoring the wheelchair…NIXON puts his arms
under the dead man's shoulders…*)
NIXON: The dead, oh, listen to them…!
DOJA: Yes, they give us no peace…
NIXON: (*Jerking the body onto the cart.*) Like wolves behind a
wire…
DOJA: Yes, very like wolves –
NIXON: Baying –
DOJA: (*Of the dead monarch.*) Him especially…

NIXON: (*Pausing.*) The assassin is free in one sense only. He is free to become an assassin…

(*He looks at DOJA…*)

It is a destiny…

(*Pause. He lifts the legs on the cart…*)

Characteristically, he squirms, for assassination offends him also…

(*He looks at DOJA…*)

He shrinks…he shuns the light…

(*He picks up the cart handles…*)

Only at the moment when, donning – so to speak – the garments of his destiny – he admits his character, does the assassin experience the calm assurance that attends on all those who have abandoned the struggle to resist what they are chosen to –

DOJA: ASSASSINATE WHO…?

(*He points to the body on the table…*)

He's dead…!

(*NIXON lifts the handles and pushes the cart away…pause…*)

Or not…?

(*A chill wind rattles tin roofing. DOJA laughs…*)

He's dead because I disembowelled him…!

(*He shakes his head…*)

What kind of evidence is that?

(*He goes to the remains…*)

And washed his heart's blood off my fingers…

EVIDENCE, YOU CALL IT…?

And splashed the yellow fluids of his brain over my cuffs, my shirt front splattered it with tissue…

JUST THE STUFF OF JUST THE SUBSTANCE WHICH

And put him into seven jars

DIFFUSION WHAT'S DIFFUSION

(*He takes a flying kick at a can, which spills as it clatters against a wall…pause…*)

It's up the wall…long fingers of his succulence…

(*He turns…*)

CALL THAT DEATH I DON'T…

(*TURNER is looking at him…*)

How clean you look today each time I see you I say that
woman is so clean her eyes even as if they had been taken
from their sockets bathed in dew and restored with scented
fingers to their places my assistants knew they'd die they
dreaded it and so they have perhaps in their anxiety
brought down on their heads the very thing they most
(*Pause…*)
Do you still love this
(*Pause…*)
MAN OR MEMORY DO YOU STILL
(*Pause…*)
MESS OR MONARCH
(*Pause…*)
And the lying here is –

TURNER: I cannot help the lying…
(*Her eyes meet his…*)
The lying is –
(*Pause…*)
Me…
(*Pause…*)
So answering your question…for all that my love compels
me to…might yield you nothing but a further terror to go
marching through your sleep –

DOJA: I GET NO SLEEP –

TURNER: Me neither –

DOJA: (*Seizing her by the wrist.*) I WAS THE MONSTER, ME…!
(*Pause…*)
And this place…dwarfs my frigidity…what is that smell on
you…?

TURNER: My flesh –

DOJA: (*Pulling her close to him.*) No, your flesh, no, you're
smeared with something –

TURNER: Nothing, I assure you –

DOJA: Lying –

TURNER: No –

DOJA: No? Not lying? What, then?

TURNER: In this matter, not –

DOJA: Not lying in this matter?

TURNER: Not in this – you're hurting me –

DOJA: Hurting a liar?

TURNER: Yes –

DOJA: Oh, liar, now it's stronger, oozing from every pore –

TURNER: Fear –

DOJA: Fear?

TURNER: Fear of you, perhaps –

DOJA: Why me, I'm innocent –

TURNER: Innocent, you –

DOJA: OH, APPALLING INNOCENCE –

    (*He forces her head steeply back…*)

    Drink your husband…

    (*Pause…the tin roof rattles in the wind…TURNER is rigid with horror…*)

TURNER: Drink –

DOJA: I'm your physician, do take my advice…

    (*He holds her still…*)

TURNER: Drink –

DOJA: I say advice, in cases of this gravity I think advice is not –

TURNER: Drink –

DOJA: The word, advice, no, it's imperative –

TURNER: Drink –

DOJA: Your health depends on it –

TURNER: DRINK MY –

DOJA: AND MINE THE SURGEON'S SICKNESS ALSO MUST BE CURED…

    (*He continues to grip TURNER with one hand, and with the other lifts a beaker of fluid from the anatomy table to TURNER's lips…a long pause…*)

TURNER: Of course I loved him…

DOJA: Loved him, yes…

TURNER: Obsessive –

DOJA: Yes –

TURNER: And implacable –

DOJA: Yes –

TURNER: Madness of –

DOJA: I have no rivals, drink –

TURNER: Insoluble –

DOJA: I tolerate no rivals, drink –

TURNER: Horror –

DOJA: DRINK

DRINK

(*She gulps the fluid…*)

DRINK

(*The sound of her swallowing. She drains the beaker. It falls to the floor. DOJA sinks to the floor with TURNER in his embrace. He takes her from behind in a faltering light as the dead priests whisper…*)

SECOND PRIEST: About Death, now…

FIRST PRIEST: The very best perspective…

SECOND PRIEST: Believe me…

FIRST PRIEST: From which to see…

FIRST/SECOND PRIESTS: THE SHEER EXAGGERATION OF THE WORLD…

FIRST PRIEST: Especially with regard to…

SECOND PRIEST: Sad to say…

FIRST PRIEST: Emotions, Mr Doja…

(*Pause…TODD enters…she leans on the back of the abandoned wheelchair, watches as DOJA and TURNER, their act completed, disengage. DOJA sits on the floor his knees drawn up…TURNER, unsteady, moves to go…avoiding DOJA's eyes…she stops…*)

DOJA: Lies, obviously…

(*TURNER shakes her head violently…goes out…*)

TODD: The new…

(*She walks in…*)

Always made of the old, unfortunately…

(*She folds her arms, gazing at him…*)

We could have been such…!

(*Pause…*)

A permanent source of regret to me –

A DYNASTY I THINK…

(*DOJA shrugs, lifts his hands…*)

Instead of this less brilliant thing, a COMMON INTEREST…

(*She half-laughs, shaking her head… NIXON returns with the hand-cart…*)

NIXON: I put them side by side…

DOJA: Side by side...why not...?

NIXON: (*Hauling SUEDE onto the cart.*) The fact they quarrelled violently should not deprive them of the possibility that in death they might be reconciled...

DOJA: Yes, let them educate each other...

NIXON: I think if death is good at all, it must be from the point of view that its infinity eradicates all friction...

(*Pause...*)

DOJA: How sentimental servants are...I've observed it over and over again...

NIXON: Yes...and a proper servant has no ambition for himself...in the deepest places of his heart he feels a loyalty to things beyond self-interest, even beyond the interest of his master...to order itself, perhaps...

(*He starts to move out the cart, but stops...*)

The knights will take three months to escort the royal remains...

(*Pause...*)

The sooner they go the sooner...

(*Pause...*)

DOJA: I've discovered an antipathy for my old profession which –

NIXON: Yes, of course...! Some greater purpose is asserting its dominance over your soul...it was obvious to me from the moment I laid eyes on you, here is a man who cannot be content with surgery for long...!

DOJA: I AM HOWEVER DISSOLUTE.

(*Pause...*)

Skilled

And

Dissolute...

NIXON: Yes...

DOJA: Hardly the figure who could bring order to a world whose – disorder – appalls your servant's sensibilities...

NIXON: (*Smiling...*) Mr Doja, you do not like your life...

(*Pause...*)

DOJA: Do I not...?

NIXON: Under your repudiations and disavowals, a stern critic
　　sits…
　　(*Pause…*)
DOJA: Does he…?
NIXON: Oh, yes…! It's obvious…!
DOJA: Everything is obvious to everyone, and nothing is
　　obvious to me…
NIXON: How could it be…you have for such a long time
　　cultivated a supreme indifference to the panics and
　　pretentions of the governing life…I admire it, and yet, the
　　nature of perfection is precisely – its own redundancy…
　　(*He picks up the handles of the cart…*)
　　Do you want any – for these gentlemen – any –
　　solemnities…or…
　　(*DOJA hesitates…laughs…*)
　　You choose…
　　(*NIXON bows…goes out with the cart…*)
　　I love the Queen…the Queen I will not have assassinated –
　　ASSASSINATED…I HAVE SAID THE WORD…you see, I am
　　drawn in to your…I think your thoughts when I was
　　perfectly contented with my own –
　　(*He shakes his head…*)
　　GET YOUR THOUGHTS OUT OF MY HEAD…!
　　I am fifty years old and have a farm with three hundred
　　acres, gardens, fountains and the like, a tessellated
　　pavement, most beautiful and a wall of blue mosaics I
　　had transported from an antique site to rest my gaze upon
　　in my retirement, a summerhouse to make love with my
　　neighbours' daughters in, I am in all ways –
TODD: You cannot go –
DOJA: Satisfied with my –
TODD: You cannot go, Mr Doja –
DOJA: I RINSE YOUR THOUGHTS OUT OF MY HEAD…!
TODD: (*Relentlessly.*) The question is not whether you will go,
　　but how you will stay…my own desired one…
　　(*DOJA slowly extends a hand towards TODD…*)
　　No…
　　For us…

That is not possible…
(*His hand falters…*)
Our union is of another sort…
(*He looks at his extended hand…*)
DOJA: I…
(*He turns it…*)
Must find a different use for it…
(*A cry from TURNER…DOJA turns his hand again…she cries out again…he looks at it from another angle…TODD walks out…*)
BALDWIN: My mother…!
(*DOJA immediately begins thrusting the remains of the deceased man into assorted pans and buckets, banging down the lids with a clumsy indifference.*)
My mother's hanged herself…!
DOJA: Knights…! The knights for Cracow, where are they…?
(*He hammers down the lid of an urn…*)
And Dijon…!
BALDWIN: Mr Doja…!
DOJA: THE KNIGHTS FOR DIJON…!
BALDWIN: (*Entering.*) Hanged herself but failed…!
(*DOJA stares at BALDWIN…the hammer in his hand…*)
DOJA: Failed…?
BALDWIN: FAILED…!
(*Pause…*)
DOJA: THE KNIGHTS FOR LUBECK, WHERE ARE THEY…!
BALDWIN: Don't visit her.
DOJA: (*Hammering down a lid.*) Why not…?
BALDWIN: She's been restrained –
DOJA: THE KNIGHTS FOR ESTRAGOM…! How restrained…?
BALDWIN: Horribly, horribly restrained, I can't look at her –
DOJA: Can't look at her –
(*He hammers wildly at a lid.*)
But looking's love –
THE KNIGHTS FOR OLMUTZ AND FOR ROME…!
(*He scrambles to his feet.*)
These knights, they are, if I may say so, hardly clamouring with impatience for their sacred task, the organs are sealed in their caskets –

BALDWIN: (*Scrutinizing.*) Sealed –

DOJA: Sealed in their caskets and rapidly acquiring those aspects of religiosity with which all relics are endowed –

BALDWIN: Not sealed, Mr Doja…

DOJA: And where is this blessed band, this fraternity of excellence whose entire existence has prepared them for this lofty honour –

BALDWIN: (*Kicking a can with his toe.*) Not sealed at all…

DOJA: Tumbling…! Tumbling on the grass…!
(*Pause…*)
Not sealed, no…the one who sealed…can't seal today…
(*He turns to BALDWIN…*)
They insist I kill you…me…whose journeys in the living flesh have been…for the most part…fruitful and benign…
(*He turns the hammer in his fingers…*)

BALDWIN: (*Nervous, smiling…*) Your – presumably your
– surgical skills –

DOJA: Second to none –

BALDWIN: And anatomical –

DOJA: Oh, I know where the veins are –

BALDWIN: (*Laughing but weakly.*) Expertise has…impressed itself upon their –

DOJA: AND I'M IN TWO MINDS ABOUT IT…
(*Pause…*)

BALDWIN: Are you…? In two minds…?
(*Pause…*)
You must love me, then…
(*Pause…with a swift move, BALDWIN grabs a chair and drawing it to him, sits in it. DOJA's response is too slow and BALDWIN is seated, facing DOJA, and with folded arms and crossed legs almost before DOJA perceives this action…*)
You must know, of all the hands that would now and will with passing time acquire the itch to send me reeling into darkness yours alone would I admit to be elected to the deed KILL WHAT'S YOURS, MR DOJA since you arrived I've not slept a whole night through WHO'S PRINCE HERE ME OR YOU and I have hardly governed yet a signature endorsed a regulation here and there the opening hours of

the tennis courts scarcely draconian but what's the pleasure
of coercion if I can't coerce your thoughts in my direction
I think to have my brain sent splashing would be to know
I'd moved you have you a first name I've always been
afraid to ask…

(*Pause…*)

Observe me seated in the puddle of my father I do not
exaggerate though exaggeration pleases me the certain sign
my life is poor I do not exaggerate however when I say his
stains his fragments might cling to my shoe and I would
not stoop to scrape them with a stick or wipe the sole on
grass THAT IS THE MEASURE OF YOUR OBLITERATION MR
DOJA MEMORY'S DEAD and I revered him did you not say
yourself my love was legendary it was it was a legend and
so are you you fill my brain a tumour a sprouting plant that
squeezes my character against the inside of my skull and
empties it what character I am only fifteen fifteen and –

DOJA: Stop now –

(*BALDWIN ceases…*)

Stop…

(*Pause…*)

Do stop…

(*The wind rattles the shutters…*)

How brilliantly you lie…how dazzling…you skate on
fictions…you gasp at the craftsmanship of your invention
like old women gawping in museums…I've seen it…oh,
I've seen it…in dancers…and in athletes…sheer adoration
of the self and as you say FIFTEEN…! I genuflect…I…yield
to it…

BALDWIN: I'm hurt that you should feel…that in my agony I
have attempted to –

DOJA: Shh –

BALDWIN: Mislead or consciously deflect you from –

DOJA: Shh –

BALDWIN: Whatever act you –

DOJA: SHH.

(*Pause…*)

The perfection of it requires no further elaboration…

(*He looks at the hammer…*)
And I have not done…
(*He bites his lip…*)
What certainly should have been done…
(*He winces…*)
AND STILL
YES
STILL
MIGHT
YET
BE
DONE…
(*Pause…they look at one another…with a crash, a door flies back on its hinges. Two armoured men stand in the entrance…*)
Too late now, however…!
(*He flings the hammer against the iron wall of the anatomy room. The priests erupt…*)

FIRST/SECOND PRIESTS: THE PLEASURES OF THE DEAD
FIRST PRIEST: Consist in witnessing
SECOND PRIEST: Your passage to oblivion
DOJA: Is that so…? I feel sure you will be thoroughly entertained…
FIRST PRIEST: The heart attack
SECOND PRIEST: The passing peacefully away in sleep
FIRST/SECOND PRIESTS: Would not have let you off
    NO DEATH ON THE CHEAP
DOJA: Nothing less than an ordeal would be appropriate…
FIRST/SECOND PRIESTS: YOU CRAVED IT…
DOJA: Did I…?
FIRST/SECOND PRIESTS: CRAVED IT…
DOJA: Possibly…I craved it…yes…
    (*He looks to the immobile knights…*)
    The knights for where…exactly…?
    (*They do not reply. BALDWIN gets up from the chair and going to a brimming bucket, flings water over the anatomy table, deluging it, washing away the blood and offal. In the following pause, NIXON enters. DOJA lifts a hand in disbelief…*)
    But you…

BALDWIN: Apron…!

(*Dumping the bucket, he runs to the hook…*)

DOJA: (*To NIXON.*) You are the one who…

BALDWIN: Apron…!

(*He extends the apron to NIXON…*)

DOJA: WHAT DOES HE KNOW ABOUT ANATOMY

HE'S A COOK

A BUTLER

A BATH ATTENDANT

(*He appeals to BALDWIN…*)

Honour me with expertise…

(*NIXON wears the apron. BALDWIN ties the strings. TODD enters, stands with folded arms…*)

TODD: The assassin, having been nominated, yet declining to assassinate…so naturally endowed with the necessary qualities, yet defying nature…can only be compared to a great physician who, possessing the power to heal, withholds his gifts and with a cruel detachment, studies the sick and lets them perish…

(*She looks at DOJA…*)

Such things can never be forgiven…

BALDWIN: Oh, let me have his heart…!

(*They wait, with repressed impatience, for DOJA to submit. He indicates his torso with a finger…*)

DOJA: You cut from here to –

(*A woman's cry comes. DOJA recognizes it to be the cry of TURNER…his head does not turn…*)

From here to –

(*It comes again…*)

Oh, perfect liar…

(*He goes to walk swiftly to his fate, but trips on an abandoned canister of royal organ…he nearly falls, but in regaining balance, turns to see TURNER's cries are the consequence of an act of love. The lid of the can rolls away…DOJA, drawn by the spectacle of TURNER's nakedness, moves a few, agonized paces towards her… as he does so, the man who has participated in her ecstasy, lets out a terrible cry of solitude and melancholy, shame and despair…*)

FIRST/SECOND PRIESTS: Doja…

(*He ignores them…*)

Doja…

(*DOJA strains his eyes and mind…*)

Much easier to die than see…

(*He goes nearer, afraid…*)

Who gives the Queen…her ecstasy…

(*His mind races. He fathoms. He plunges to the depths of an idea. He repudiates, and then submits to the idea…he looks to the attendant group…*)

DOJA: Who could so gratify a queen…? Only a king, surely…?

(*A wind. With the excruciating sound of an unoiled winch, the priests are hauled slowly into the air, back to the apertures from which they plunged…DOJA turns to the table…*)

And this was…

(*He shrugs…*)

Some dog…of…adequate obscurity…on whom my skills could play…uncontradicted…

I CUT ONLY KINGS…!

(*He smiles…*)

My own decay had long set in, obviously…or I should have known, through the scalpel's infinitesimal vibration, this was…vulgar flesh…

(*The king, leaving TURNER, comes down into the anatomy room. DOJA bows…*)

Oh, how painful your life must be…

(*The king looks at DOJA…*)

I have flayed kings…but in your case, there is no skin that I can see…the nerves are naked…and wind even, gives you agony…

(*He remains in the bow…*)

WHY DON'T THEY BOW…?

(*He resolutely refuses to rise. The assembled court does not bow…*)

ETIQUETTE

ETIQUETTE

ETIQUETTE

Why don't they…?

(*Pause…then he rises swiftly…*)

Obviously, you don't exist…outside the bedroom…

I'M RECRUITED TO A GAME
I WHO
I THE MASTER OF
AND ERUDITE
CYNIC
SCEPTIC
AND TRIUMPHANT EVASIONIST
I WITH NEITHER PARTY NOR A WIFE AM
(*Pause…a strange laugh comes from him…*)
Part of a game…
And not my own game, either…
(*One of the knights takes a single step…*)
Do I object…?
(*And another.*)
No, wait…
(*And a further step…*)
WAIT
WAIT
LET A MAN DECIDE IF
WAIT
(*The knight is still.*)
If he concedes…or if he finds it…humiliating…and
preposterous…
I DON'T KNOW
For if some weapon loosed at random can splatter my
brain or tripping on an unlit path I topple in a cold canal
my screams ignored by courting couples slippery fingered
and
WHOSE GAME IS THAT
SOMEBODY'S
(*To the knight.*)
No don't rush me I'm half-way to understanding –
(*He drags his shirt over his head, stopping half-in, half-out…sobs
come from within…he staggers…he wails, fighting his horror in
the dark…the court observes, unmoving…at last the writhing
ceases. DOJA completes his disrobing. He is naked to the waist.
Suddenly, the appearance of LAYBACH, breathless…*)
LAYBACH: I stabbed…

(He looks around, from face to face…)
I STABBED AND…
Having stabbed…experienced…
(He shrugs, enormously…)
RELIEF…!
(No one reacts to his passion…)
And she was guiltless, guiltless obviously, but this
guiltlessness was…
(He bites his lip…)
POSSIBLY THE CAUSE OF MY RELIEF…!
(He looks from one to another…)
Whilst my hatred did not shift from its original and
habitual target…while Mr Doja remained the object of my
envy and contempt…in stabbing her I sensed, oh, such a
draining of my misery, as if some tide had raced away and
left me solitary on a wide and undisputed beach, the squeal
of gannets and
(He stops…)
I expect to be punished with the utmost severity…
(He dares them…)
This is not to say however, that I admit to even the
slightest sentiments of shame or guilt…
(They are still deaf to him.)
ON THE CONTRARY I –
DOJA: Shh…
LAYBACH: I AFFIRM MY –
DOJA: Shh…
*(He looks at LAYBACH, a smile of unfeigned kindness on his face…
LAYBACH is stopped…DOJA goes to the anatomy table. He picks up
an instrument, looks at the blade, tosses it in a bucket. He repeats
this with the next, and so on…the sound is rhythmic, relentless, as
the light fades from the scene and rises on two windows which fly
open in the wall…)*
FIRST PRIEST: A king's night…!
SECOND PRIEST: The window open and a light breeze
FIRST PRIEST: Stirs the beeches
SECOND PRIEST: Moon
FIRST PRIEST: Moon and

SECOND PRIEST: The laughing leaves

FIRST PRIEST: Under a single sheet he lies

SECOND PRIEST: White

FIRST PRIEST: Laundered and white

SECOND PRIEST: He lies

FIRST PRIEST: A bell

SECOND PRIEST: Stiller than death

FIRST PRIEST: A bell

SECOND PRIEST: Naked

FIRST PRIEST: The fountain falters in the breeze

SECOND PRIEST: The crawling hours of his agony

> (*The light returns to the anatomy table, where DOJA lies. Seated beside him, head in hands, TORTMANN. They are alone…*)

TORTMANN: (*At last.*) An obsession…what's an obsession, Mr Doja…but a privilege…? And because I was a king…my privilege was itself privileged…because I was a king my ecstasy has been…extraordinary…an ecstasy akin to God's…

> (*TURNER slowly enters, and sits at a distance. TORTMANN senses her, but does not turn…*)

For she is impossible to own…which for a king…is infinite – is unrelieved – torture…we are so unbalanced by possession…

> (*Pause…*)

DOJA: Execute her, then…

TORTMANN: That was my first inclination…but you will have deduced I am no common husband, Mr Doja…I hoarded pain as some hoard money…and through hoarding it…I found in pain whole realms of pity and excess that butchering cuckolds know nothing of…

DOJA: And we – while we –

TORTMANN: I kept my distance…oh, distance, Mr Doja, distance is everything…to know…to see…what's that but sordid witnessing…? I walk by the wide river, whose fullness races like my blood…

> (*He rises to his feet…*)

I'll keep your heart…a thing no doubt you've long since ceased to revere, but I…

(*He shrugs…*)
believe me, study…
(*He goes out, leaving* TURNER *alone with* DOJA…*she sits in perfect stillness…*)
DOJA: Heart…?
(*Pause…*)
What heart…?
(*Pause…*)
WHAT HEART I'VE NONE NONE NOTHING THE CAVITY THE
HOLLOW CHAMBER UNDERNEATH THE RIB THE VAULT THE
CRYPT THAT ECHOED TO A WOMAN'S HEELS WALK WALK
THE TILED FLOOR OF ITS ABSENCE DO WALK
(*TURNER does not move…*)
I'm impatient
Oddly impatient
To be another remnant of your passion yes another rag of
your extraordinary love
I've seen the graves a pleasant spot do you walk there
not unlike the cemeteries of war whose occupants must
surely grumble more than I shall at the futility of their
extinction to suffer for a flag or book oh nothing nothing
to my martyrdom I'm not humiliated no to perish for the
pleasure of
(*He stops…*)
It is not pleasure, is it…you two share…
(*Pause…*)
But terror…?
(*She remains motionless…*)
What's common love alongside that…?
(*Pause…*)
Answer me…
(*Pause…*)
OH, ANSWER…!
No
No
They all say that
They all
They all

They all say that
Don't answer
No
I'LL CUT
I'LL DO THE CUTTING
I
I'LL CUT
THE MASTER ME

(*His hand sweeps for an instrument, spilling a tray which clatters. He gropes. The apertures in the wall fly back. Desperately chattering heads appear, horrified, fascinated. The hysteria of the audience rises. DOJA's hand is seen to make the movements of swift dissection, the other assisting it, nimbly, as if inspired, rapid as a concert pianist, an apotheosis of a skill. BALDWIN, entering in a routine manner, sees, stops, is fixed to the spot, his left knee rising, his arms clutching himself in a slow paroxysm of disbelief. At the moment he is in a position of absolute balance, twisted yet erect, the audience drained of utterance, falls silent. In this silence, the sound of instruments exchanged, the frantic activity of DOJA's hands...a spectacle of will, dexterity, endurance...of magic, therefore, which endures until the sudden entrance of BERLIN, uninjured. DOJA's activity ceases, is suspended...*)*

BERLIN: (*Looking at BALDWIN...*) The priest is mad and locked me in a hut...

(*BALDWIN ignores her.*)

With food...

(*Pause...*)

And great jars of water...

(*BALDWIN does not remove his gaze from DOJA...*)

I said –

(*Irritably, DOJA taps his instrument against a metal bowl... BERLIN's gaze slowly turns in DOJA's direction...*)

I climbed out through the roof...

BALDWIN: Shh...

BERLIN: This roof –

BALDWIN: Shh...

BERLIN: Was thatch –

(*Again* DOJA *taps to silence her…but* BERLIN *is so shocked she can only persist…*)

It seems to me therefore…despite the food and water…he had no desire I should remain in there…on the contrary… he locked me in…precisely in order that I should escape –

DOJA: HE'S HANGED SHUT UP…

(*This information stifles* BERLIN'*s voice. In the resulting silence,* DOJA *reaches for another instrument and proceeds to incise himself…*)

BERLIN: HANGED BUT HE –

(DOJA *raps the blade against a bowl…*)

TURNER: There is a man there who is making his own death…

(BERLIN *sways…*)

And I have not moved one centimetre…

(*Her eyes close…*)

I

Who

Love

Him

NOT ONE CENTIMETRE FROM THIS SEAT…

(*A collective gasp from the public accompanies a stroke by* DOJA… *a profound groan issues from* BALDWIN…BERLIN *takes a violent step towards* DOJA, *as if to remonstrate or restrain him, but* BALDWIN *is swift and seizes her by the wrist…*)

BALDWIN: The flesh is not the man…

(*Pause…*)

BERLIN: The flesh is not the man…WHAT IS THE FLESH, THEN?

(*A further gasp from the public…*)

BALDWIN: Oh, Mr Doja is cutting the strings of my own heart…!

(*A gasp again, an instrument discarded, another taken from the tray…*)

BERLIN: I ALSO LOVE…!

TURNER: Then find a seat…

(BERLIN *turns from* DOJA *to* TURNER *in disbelief…in the suspended silence, an instrument chimes against another…the dead priests appear from the obscurity.*)

FIRST/SECOND PRIESTS: Are we a little premature?

FIRST PRIEST: Anticipating

SECOND PRIEST: Our impatience is so typical

FIRST PRIEST: Of death

SECOND PRIEST: Which longs for more

FIRST PRIEST: A spoiled child

SECOND PRIEST: More

FIRST PRIEST: Death

SECOND PRIEST: Still…

    (*They peer, on tiptoe…DOJA lifts another tool…*)

FIRST PRIEST: Skill…

SECOND PRIEST: Infinite skill…

FIRST PRIEST: In leaving every vein uncut until

    (*A public gasp…*)

    His

SECOND PRIEST: We wait…

FIRST PRIEST: His

SECOND PRIEST: We wait…

FIRST PRIEST: His

BERLIN: (*A cry of revulsion.*) SIT STILL…?

    (*Her cry unleashes a river, a sluice of black fluid which roars
like an unlocked lake, streaming in a profusion from beneath
the table to a downstage drain. The roar continues, a niagara of
sound as the apertures slowly close, the witnesses withdrawing one
after another, leaving BALDWIN, BERLIN and TURNER in fixed
postures…as the last window slowly closes, a sound of running
footsteps, descending iron stairs, fills the silence. LAYBACH,
breathless, comes into the room…*)

LAYBACH: A man…

    A man has flung himself into the river…!

    (*They ignore him…*)

    And I –

    I WANTED TO FOLLOW HIM…

    But…

    But…

    (*He shrugs pitifully…*)

    IN THE RIVER A MAN…!

    (*The mass of grieving figures hurries past, frenzied, as in the first
moments of the play. The light of the sun descends to the rim of*

the wall. As the last of the figures departs, TURNER is discovered on her knees in front of the chair she has been seated in. She is quite still. The mass of figures returns. They pass. The light is reduced to a single blade of light reaching over the wall. An old woman appears with a bucket and a mop. Ignoring the still figures she begins the laborious task of washing the floor. As she finishes a section, she shifts the bucket with one foot. The light, sinking, suddenly drops behind the wall.)

THE LOVE OF A GOOD MAN

.

Characters

PRINCE OF WALES
Heir to the English Throne

GENTLEMAN
his Equerry

FLOWERS
an Army Sergeant

HACKER
an Undertaker

CLOUT
his Assistant

RIDDLE
a Soldier

BASS
a Soldier

TROD
a Soldier

MRS TOYNBEE
a Bereaved Parent

LALAGE
her Daughter

BRIDE
a Commissioner for Graves

COLONEL HARD
a Recruiter

BISHOP

ACT ONE

SCENE 1

A part of Passchendaele in 1920. Looking over a scene of desolation, the PRINCE OF WALES. He wears a bowler hat and clasps a pair of gloves behind his back. Pause.

PRINCE: Feel sick. (*Pause.*) Somebody. (*Pause.*) FEEL SICK!
(*A GENTLEMAN OF THE HOUSEHOLD hurries in and assists the PRINCE into a stooping posture. Pause.
The PRINCE straightens.*)
Want to say something. Want to be apt and truthful. Do you understand? Feel the need for it.

GENTLEMAN: Sir.

PRINCE: For lovely words.

GENTLEMAN: Sir.

PRINCE: Can make it better, if you find the proper words.
(*Pause.*) Sorry, for example.

GENTLEMAN: Sorry?

PRINCE: Yes. Good word. Cheapened by over-use, that's all.
But in this context, perfect. In this context, pure poetry. (*He points to the horizon.*) Get it up there, d'ye see? In hundred-foot-high letters. Spanning Flanders. SORRY. Coloured lights on it at night!

GENTLEMAN: Yes. (*Pause.*)

PRINCE: Wish I spoke better. Wish I had an education. Didn't like Sandhurst at all. There is a man down there. Digging.

GENTLEMAN: Oh, yes. So there is.

PRINCE: Fetch him, will you?

GENTLEMAN: Fetch him?

PRINCE: Up here, please.
(*Reluctantly, the GENTLEMAN beckons.*)

GENTLEMAN: Can't see me.

PRINCE: Shout, then. Please.
(*Pause while the GENTLEMAN clears his throat.*)

GENTLEMAN: Hey.

PRINCE: No. Shout.

>(*GENTLEMAN looks at him.*)

>You know. Shout.

GENTLEMAN: HEY!

PRINCE: Seen us.

>(*GENTLEMAN beckons wildly.*)

>I shall be King of England soon. When Daddy's cancer gets the better of him.

GENTLEMAN: Yes, indeed.

PRINCE: Very funny thing to be.

GENTLEMAN: I don't see why.

PRINCE: Unusual.

GENTLEMAN: Possibly.

PRINCE: Like to be good at it. Like to make a decent go of it. Win the people's hearts and so on.

GENTLEMAN: You already have.

PRINCE: And do things, too. (*Pause.*)

GENTLEMAN: What things?

PRINCE: They do have such a lot of power, don't they? Kings? Daddy chose the generals.

GENTLEMAN: Yes.

PRINCE: Rather badly, I believe...

>(*A MAN in a leather garment enters, holding a spade.*)

FLOWERS: Guv?

>(*Pause. They examine him.*)

PRINCE: T-t-tell me, w-w-were you a soldier of the war?

FLOWERS: I was.

PRINCE: Please may I k-k-kiss your hand?

GENTLEMAN: KISS HIS HAND?

PRINCE: Please?

>(*FLOWERS extends a muddy hand.*
>*The PRINCE kneels and takes his hand to his lips.*)

GENTLEMAN: HE IS A COMMONER!

PRINCE: Do you know who I am?

FLOWERS: I 'ave a rough idea, guv.

PRINCE: I am Edward, Prince of Wales.

FLOWERS: Tha's what I reckoned. (*Pause.*)

PRINCE: I wish you to know that I am sorry.

FLOWERS: What for?

GENTLEMAN: You see, there isn't really any point in this.

PRINCE: Now ask me to rise, will you?

GENTLEMAN: Ask you to WHAT!

PRINCE: Will you, please? The ground is rather wet.

FLOWERS: Rise, please.

(*The PRINCE gets up, brushes his coat.*)

PRINCE: Stained the new coat Mummy gave me.

GENTLEMAN: Dear, oh, dear! Look at it! (*He begins rubbing it with a handkerchief.*)

PRINCE: She can always get another one.

GENTLEMAN: That's all very well, but coats cost money!

PRINCE: His hand had mud on it…

GENTLEMAN: Better let it dry, I think.

PRINCE: Did it get onto my lips?

GENTLEMAN: (*Stands up, looks at the PRINCE's mouth.*) No.

PRINCE: The ground here is alive with tetanus. Suppose I had a small cut on my lip?

GENTLEMAN: (*Looking closely.*) Can't see one…

PRINCE: I might have died from it…

(*He muses on the idea.*

FLOWERS goes out unobserved.)

This will get around, won't it? That I knelt to a common soldier?

GENTLEMAN: Their Majesties will splutter. I shall feel the royal saliva.

PRINCE: It will get in the papers, though?

GENTLEMAN: I imagine he is heading for the nearest journalist.

PRINCE: What was he doing here? All the troops went home, surely?

GENTLEMAN: Some were kept back. To re-inter the corpses. Shall we go?

(*He starts to move off.*

The PRINCE is frozen. Pause.)

PRINCE: Feel sick. (*Pause.*) Somebody! (*Pause.*) FEEL SICK!

SCENE 2

THREE MEN, dressed in Wellington boots and heavy coats, come in, carrying dividers, plans, maps, etc.

HACKER: I took on more labour. I don't like taking labour but there was this contract going begging and I would 'ave been an idiot to pass it up. Silly, I know, but I am timid about labour. I would say there is a ratio between workers and bother. The more workers the more bother. I tried to take the sons of my existing masons but most of 'em were dead, so I 'ave been obliged to take on strangers. I expect wage demands. I expect all kinds of nonsense, but I will deliver. No question of that. Won't I, Clout? I will deliver.

CLOUT: Your strong point, Mr 'acker, is delivery.

HACKER: Loyal, ain't he? Fuckin' parrot. Always says the right thing. No, I love him, I do. Now, what's the situation?

BRIDE: Before I go into that, I wonder if I might ask you something?

HACKER: Fire away.

BRIDE: That you are careful not to swear. (*Pause.*)

HACKER: Swear? Did I swear?

BRIDE: Yes.

HACKER: Oh. Beg pardon.

BRIDE: I wasn't thinking of myself. I was referring to our situation. You see, I don't expect you swear in church. (*Pause.*)

HACKER: Not often.

BRIDE: And this is a church. I think we have to regard this whole enterprise as the building of a church.

HACKER: A church.

BRIDE: Yes.

HACKER: Right. (*Pause.*) That cuts out the swearing, then.

BRIDE: There are a million dead men here.

HACKER: Yup.

BRIDE: A million Englishmen.

HACKER: And as many monuments, of which five thousand will be mine, 'and chiselled in my Peckham factory. It will

be time and 'alf on Sundays for a year, but they will be a
credit to the Empire, Mr Bride, I promise yer.

BRIDE: This is not so much a contract with the government. It
is a contract with our dead people.

HACKER: Mr Bride, I am a rough character, perhaps, but if
you scratch me I do bleed. Clout 'ere will tell you I am
not impervious to grief. I am 'ere to make money, I make
no bones about it. I am in business. But I 'ave a soul. The
idea got around during the war that businessmen do not
'ave souls. But did we not lose our boys as well? Not me
personally, but the business people did. Money was made
on the one 'and, but sons were slain on the other. Now
either we are animals or the system's buggered. Take yer
pick, I 'ave no answers, do I, Clout? I am not a provider of
answers any more than you.

CLOUT: What's the stake-out, Mr Bride?

BRIDE: This ridge we are standing on is about a thousand
yards in length. It changed hands many times during the
war. They do not know how often, but it got very bloody,
being so exposed, you see. And as a consequence, it is very
deep in bodies. I do not want to dramatise, but where we
are standing is not ground so much as flesh.

(*Pause.*

HACKER clears his throat.)

HACKER: Nasty business.

CLOUT: When we got out the taxi, I said to Mr Hacker, isn't
there a smell?

HACKER: All right, Clout.

CLOUT: I know we're in a church, but definitely there is a
smell.

HACKER: ALL RIGHT.

BRIDE: This ridge is designated Number 14 Cemetery. It will
be according to the Commission's specifications. At least
there is no drainage problem here. If you want me, I shall
be here. I am recording everything.

HACKER: A lifetime's work, Mr Bride.

BRIDE: It must be written and recorded. Every death and
every maiming. There is no truth in war except this truth.

HACKER: I wonder if it isn't best forgotten? All that. A decent veil drawn over it.

BRIDE: I am presenting the bill, Mr Hacker. It is my mission. Ignore the dead and you will cheat the living.

HACKER: Cheat, Mr Bride?

BRIDE: This place has been the scene of awful lies. Such lies as nearly swamped humanity. We must not cheat the people of their consciences. We must name names. All million of them! Till we are dizzy with the lists!

HACKER: Yes. Right.

BRIDE: Dazzle them with suffering!

HACKER: Right.

BRIDE: Christ, man, would you draw a veil across all this?

HACKER: No. (*Pause.*) No, of course, I wouldn't. Just a suggestion. A silly one, I see that now.

BRIDE: I am against all veils. Give the dead their voice!

HACKER: Absolutely.

BRIDE: Which is your task, Hacker. You will orchestrate their suffering. (*He looks into HACKER's eyes.*)

HACKER: Yup.

(*Pause, then BRIDE turns and goes out.*
They watch him disappear.)

Bananas. Fuckin' bananas.

CLOUT: Swearing.

HACKER: Fuck swearing!

CLOUT: (*Shrugs.*) All right.

HACKER: I don't want lecturing. I didn't come to Belgium for a lecturing. I 'ave respect. My own respect. Let me do it my way. Not bananas fashion, thank you very much.

CLOUT: Funny. Funny though.

HACKER: What?

CLOUT: Standing on – a million dead Englishmen – did he say?

HACKER: Something like that.

CLOUT: Not so much ground, he said, more 'uman flesh…

HACKER: Give over, Clout.

CLOUT: Creepy, Mr 'acker.

HACKER: Yeah, well, it will be if you give into it.

CLOUT: It's getting dark, Mr 'acker. Shall we get back to the
lodging 'ouse?

HACKER: Yeah, why not? Fleas are getting 'ungry, I expect.

(*They go a few yards.*

HACKER stops.)

Yer know, Clout, this is easy money. Let's be honest
for a minute, this is cream and fucking jam. I can't see
myself going back to ordinary funerals after this. All the
whispering and decorum. Stuff it. It's wars for me in future.
Someone's got to benefit.

CLOUT: Mr 'acker, I'm sorry, I'm getting the creeps.

HACKER: Got to get used to it, ol' son. Going to be 'ere bloody
months.

CLOUT: I know, Mr 'acker, but – WHASS THAT!

(*He grabs HACKER's arm impulsively.*)

HACKER: SHUDDUP!

(*Pause. They are holding each other's arms.*)

Git. Look at me. Made me jump, yer git.

(*He shakes off CLOUT's hand, prepares to move on.*)

CLOUT: THERE IT IS! (*He grabs HACKER again.*)

HACKER: What! Fuck it! What?

CLOUT: 'eard it.

HACKER: 'eard what?

(*There is a faint sound of singing.*)

Oh, bloody 'ell, what do they have to fight wars 'ere for? In
the middle of a bleedin' swamp…?

CLOUT: (*Pointing.*) IT'S DEAD MEN!

HACKER: Clout. Come 'ere, will yer?

CLOUT: (*Starting to run.*) Sorry, Mr 'acker, I can't –

HACKER: CLOUT!

(*CLOUT disappears.*

HACKER hesitates.

The singing gets louder.)

It's only – CLOUT!

(*He tears after him in a panic.*

*The singing grows louder. FOUR MEN enter, dressed in leather
garments which virtually conceal soiled army uniforms
beneath. They carry shovels and each holds the corner of a*

large canvas bag. They sing to the tune of 'She Was Only a Bird in a Gilded Cage'.)

FLOWERS / BASS / TROD:

It was only a corpse in a canvas bag,
A wonderful sight to see,
With no bollocks or legs,
With no arse and no 'ead,
Why is it so fucking 'eavy?

(*They dump the bag unceremoniously.*)

FLOWERS: Our picturesque language. Our funny songs that kept us faithful in the midst of death. Us cockney sparrers. Us criminals and layabouts made decent for a royal kiss. (*He rolls a cigarette.*)

BASS: Still in Flanders. Two years after the armistice. While Vickers, Krupp and Schneider get their scrap metal back, slightly imperfect owing to its passage through the human body, and Belgian whores we fucked in cellars buy up the farms as soon as we have cleared the corpses of their clients out of it.

FLOWERS: If someone 'as to do this job, why not the chinks and wogs? What is the Empire for if this degrading labour ain't given over to the chinks and wogs? (*He lights his cigarette.*)

RIDDLE: Are we ready? I would like to be pissed in time for bed, and twilight's dirty fingers are creeping into our moist crevices.

FLOWERS: Mr Riddle has spoken. We may shove on.

BASS: Before the war I never met a type like Riddle. Then suddenly, there were hundreds of 'em. It opens whole perspectives up, a war. The longer they go on, the more you see. A couple more years and England's innards would have been hanging out, all red and twitching. It would have been a bloody great dissecting room.

FLOWERS: Compared with clearing battlefields, fighting was 'ealthy. It is clearing battlefields that's made young lads like Trod 'ere go mysterious. That is why I urged the use of chinks and wogs. I wrote this to *The Times,* and Riddle 'ere, with 'is command of English, phrased it for me. But widows and vicars were outraged. It made ex-majors' noses bleed. The general opinion was the English soldiers' flesh would shrink from the touch of blacks. I said we could 'ave issued 'em with gloves. In any case, whoever 'eard a corpse protest?

TROD: You have no ears to hear them. I hear them.

FLOWERS: You see what I say about Trod?

TROD: You are frightened of death. Because I understand death you mock me.

FLOWERS: I don't mock you, son, I pity you.

RIDDLE: It is rather damp here and I am thin. I have reason to believe I have rudimentary TB. Shall we push on?

BASS: Silly to die at this stage, Riddle. After what you've been through. You would look a silly bugger to your friends.

RIDDLE: I have no friends.

FLOWERS: Did you not 'ave a mate killed, Mr Riddle? A painter or a poet or something?

RIDDLE: They talk about the friendships of the war, but they were not friendships. They were the whimperings of shared discomforts. None has survived the peace. The mania for bonhomie is the most disgusting fetishism of war. I could fight for twenty years if it were not for the singing.

TROD: I had a friend –

FLOWERS: So you did, son, but we don't wanna go into that now, do we?

BASS: We don't. Shove on.

(*They bend to the canvas bag, each taking a corner.*)

FLOWERS / BASS / TROD:

It looked like a body, but it was all shit,
It was no grave that was marked with a cross,
We shovelled away,
At this fucking French clay,
While the turds giggled in piss, blood and toss!

SCENE 3

Morning. Two English women are staring over the battlefield. Pause.

MRS TOYNBEE: Do you feel anything yet?

LALAGE: No.

MRS TOYNBEE: I do.

LALAGE: I expected you to.

MRS TOYNBEE: In my womb.

LALAGE: But of course.

MRS TOYNBEE: It goes hot. (*Pause.*) Yes! There! (*She takes LALAGE's hand.*) Feel it! (*She places LALAGE's hand on her belly.*) Convulses!

LALAGE: Can't find it…

MRS TOYNBEE: Yes, there! Oh!

LALAGE: (*Turning away, walking from her.*) I suppose this is Hill 60? We have got it right? (*She looks at a map.*) Not that there are many hills. If you can so dignify these miserable humps. (*She turns back.*) Have you finished, Mother, please? (*Pause. MRS TOYNBEE opens her eyes.*)

MRS TOYNBEE: I have never known that before. I will put it in my diary.

LALAGE: What about Mahler's Fifth?

MRS TOYNBEE: What about it?

LALAGE: Look in your diary. It got to your womb.

MRS TOYNBEE:: Don't remember.

LALAGE: Everything seems to get to your womb. I suppose you are that kind of woman.

MRS TOYNBEE: Well, I am a woman, most certainly.

LALAGE: Me too.

MRS TOYNBEE: I'm glad. I'm glad we are women. Bereaved men are a pitiful sight.

LALAGE: Can't cope, you mean? Poor, silly dears?

MRS TOYNBEE: Compared to us, yes. They are poor, silly dears.

LALAGE: I don't have that view of men. Not at all.

MRS TOYNBEE: You don't know them.

LALAGE: Well, of course not. Not like you.

MRS TOYNBEE: They are not used to expressing real feelings.

LALAGE: They have no wombs.

MRS TOYNBEE: (*Patiently.*) It is not sex that draws them towards us. It is the sheer luxury of being sincere.

LALAGE: Well, you seem to know all about them.

MRS TOYNBEE: I've had the opportunity to form an opinion. You have not.

LALAGE: No. And I don't want to. I hate the idea there are things called men. Things which experience will teach you to handle. Like ponies or dogs.

MRS TOYNBEE: We are standing among them. They are lying under our feet. They are lying as far as the eye can see. Ranks deep... (*Pause.*) No two women have ever been surrounded by so much male flesh... When they find Billy they want to put him in the official, standard grave. There is even a uniform headstone. I am not having that for him.

LALAGE: They may not find him.

MRS TOYNBEE: Oh yes, he will come back. And when he does, I am claiming him.

LALAGE: They won't like that.

MRS TOYNBEE: Of course not. But two women can do a great deal. We will take him back to England and bury him under the tree.

LALAGE: Is that what he wanted? I never knew.

MRS TOYNBEE: He worshipped the tree.

LALAGE: He was fond of it, I know.

MRS TOYNBEE: Hills and trees. You knew Billy. Look at his poems. All hills and trees.

LALAGE: Yes, but did he actually say –

MRS TOYNBEE: Lalage, I am bringing my son home! (*Pause.*)

LALAGE: A million corpses coming home. That would be grotesque...

MRS TOYNBEE: I am not bringing a million. Everything is repulsive that everybody does. Every moving gesture, every beautiful thought, is hideous in proportion to its popularity. This is between Billy and us.

(*BRIDE comes in, accompanied by FLOWERS and TROD, carrying plans and ledger.*)

BRIDE: Are you ladies off the Cook's Battlefields tour?

MRS TOYNBEE: Certainly not.

BRIDE: There are unexploded things round here.

MRS TOYNBEE: We aren't afraid.

BRIDE: We have quite enough dead.

MRS TOYNBEE: My son among them.

(*BRIDE stops.*)

BRIDE: Hill 60?

MRS TOYNBEE: Toynbee. Second Lieutenant.

BRIDE: (*Aroused.*) P Toynbee? Scots Guards?

MRS TOYNBEE: No. W Hussars.

(*BRIDE cogitates.*)

FLOWERS: 'e 'as a million names jammed in 'is 'ead. Ask 'im who's prime minister, who won the Derby, when 'e last 'ad a piss, 'e couldn't tell yer, but who died by bayonet and who by bomb –

BRIDE: August the eighth.

MRS TOYNBEE: Correct.

BRIDE: Missing, presumed dead. Aged twenty-eight.

MRS TOYNBEE: Twenty.

BRIDE: (*Shocked.*) Twenty? Are you sure?

MRS TOYNBEE: Of course I'm sure.

(*BRIDE concentrates his memory, starts to go out.*)

Where do we look?

BRIDE: (*Stops.*) Look? He is missing, isn't he? There is everywhere to look. Or nowhere. (*He goes out.*)

MRS TOYNBEE: (*To FLOWERS.*) But he will show up? His body must eventually show up?

FLOWERS: They don't just kill yer. They destroy yer. Where a geezer might have been standing, there is just a black hole in the mud, and a trickling as the water drains back into it. You could argue that somewhere 'e still exists. Matter, I 'ave 'eard, is indestructible. But not impossible to separate, alas.

(*He follows BRIDE out.*

TROD hangs back. Pause.)

TROD: The dead do not die.

(*Pause. The WOMEN look at him.*)

LALAGE: What do they do, then?

TROD: Transhabilitate.

(*They look at him.*)

LALAGE: And what is that?

(Pause. TROD looks to see that FLOWERS is out of sight and sound.)

TROD: I had a friend. Have you got time?

MRS TOYNBEE: All the time in the world.

TROD: He was beautiful. He was holy. I never looked at him without thinking I stood in a fountain of pure light. He had been a shepherd and it had brought him near to God. Not God. Not the God. But another God. Also called God.

MRS TOYNBEE: Yes…

TROD: *(Looking over his shoulder for FLOWERS.)* During his shepherding, the secret of Transhabilitation had been revealed to him by a saintly sheep. The sheep was known as Trotters. Have you got time?

MRS TOYNBEE: *(Cooling.)* I think we have, yes…

TROD: During a trance this holy ewe revealed that England was a segment of the moon, broken off and crashed near Europe aeons ago. The inhabitants of the moon had been herbivorous quadrupeds.

FLOWERS: *(Appearing left.)* Come on, Trod!

TROD: Damn. Bloody damn.

MRS TOYNBEE: They seem to want you.

TROD: To keep it brief, the lunar quadrupeds, breathing the terrestrial ether –

FLOWERS: FUCK IT! COME ON!

LALAGE: Perhaps we could hear a bit more later.

TROD: He meant there is no death, only reordering of spirit –

FLOWERS: TROD.

(TROD turns to go, then stops, looks at MRS TOYNBEE.)

TROD: You are very beautiful. I don't know what you looked like before, but it has touched you with beauty. *(He hurries away. Pause.)*

MRS TOYNBEE: Has it?

LALAGE: Billy's death?

MRS TOYNBEE: Put a little shadow in my face?

LALAGE: Max Factor's Stricken Mum…

(MRS TOYNBEE turns on her, just as CLOUT appears carrying a wooden peg and a mallet. He hammers the peg into the

ground, and begins measuring from it with a linen tape. At
the requisite distance, he hammers in a second peg.
HACKER comes in, reading from the official plan.)

HACKER: (*Quoting.*) Footpaths will traverse the cemetery at
angles corresponding to the pattern of the Union Jack…
fuck…did we bring a Union Jack? I think we can assume
we didn't. (*He reads on.*) With the cross of sacrifice placed
at the confluence…the confluence… THE CONFLUENCE?
Bugger this. (*He reads on.*) Each section thus delineated will
contain sufficient area for one hundred graves, the surface
of each grave to be eight foot by four. Got that, Clout?

CLOUT: Eight foot by four.

HACKER: Correct. And not an inch more, 'ave 'em spilling
over, otherwise. Did yer bring the flask with yer?

CLOUT: (*Measuring.*) In the bag, Mr 'acker.

HACKER: Got to keep the sodding damp out, 'aven't we? (*He
sees the women.*) Morning, ladies. Cheerful business, ain't it?
(*He removes the flask from CLOUT's bag.*) Note the Frogs 'ave
scarcely bothered. Just chuck the spare bits in a bonery.
Mind you, it's their crops stand to benefit. Fertilising on
this scale 'as no precedent, 'ave you an interest in this?

MRS TOYNBEE: A dead boy.

HACKER: Well, no doubt you are thoroughly nauseated with
official sympathy, so we won't add our little voices to the
chorus, will we, Clout?

CLOUT: Sir.

HACKER: There is so much 'ypocrisy about yer could launch a
ship on it. (*He indicates the string line.*) This 'ere will be the
central road of the cemetery, north-south.

CLOUT: West-east, Mr 'acker.

HACKER: West-east, is it? Got ears all over 'im. Good job
I wasn't making an improper suggestion to the lady,
Clout would 'ave been a party to it. No, 'e's a good lad.
I love 'im, don't I, Clout? (*Silence.*) Now pretends 'e can't
'ear. Bloody 'ell, this coffee's disgusting, Clout. It is the
drippings of the stable gutters, son. (*He casts it away, screws
the lid on the flask.*)

LALAGE: Shall we move on?

MRS TOYNBEE: (*To HACKER.*) Are you –

HACKER: 'acker.

MRS TOYNBEE: Hacker. And you are – burying the dead?

HACKER: Building a Garden of the Fallen, actually.

MRS TOYNBEE: I see.

HACKER: I am the contractor for No 81. I put in my estimate and got it. Rock bottom, practically a loss, but a beginning. A man with a government contract shall not starve. I 'ave also tendered for Gallipoli. They say the sunsets over Lesbos are remarkable.

MRS TOYNBEE: All the dead, then, come to you?

HACKER: Funny way of putting it. Sounds like the Day of Judgement.

MRS TOYNBEE: All right. Pass through your hands?

HACKER: I suppose so, yeah. (*He looks at her, closely.*)

MRS TOYNBEE: I see. Mr Hacker.

(*Pause. He cannot take his eyes away.*)

HACKER: Ronald, if you like.

MRS TOYNBEE: We are staying in the village.

HACKER: So are we. Getting fed on Christ knows what at Monte Carlo prices. Bitten by the Belgian flea.

MRS TOYNBEE: I expect we'll see a lot of one another.

HACKER: Every morning, should you wish. Squelching about. Though the Passchendaele mud doesn't seem to stick to you. You are very neat and spotless. (*Pause.*)

MRS TOYNBEE: Well, good morning.

HACKER: Good morning, Madam.

(*The WOMEN start to go.*
MRS TOYNBEE turns.)

MRS TOYNBEE: I am Sylvia Toynbee.

(*HACKER nods, smiles, the WOMEN go out. He watches them disappear.*)

HACKER: Oh, God our 'elp in ages past… (*Pause.*) I could use 'er shit as toothpaste… (*Pause.*) I could crawl across three fields of broken glass just for a piss in 'er bathwater…

CLOUT: Got the plan, please, Mr 'acker?

HACKER: Ronald, you are buggered for concentration now…

CLOUT: Plan, Mr 'acker?

273

HACKER: Fuck it, Clout! The plan, the plan! Did you see that?

CLOUT: Sir.

HACKER: Well, what does that do to yer measurements?

CLOUT: Very pleasant lady, sir.

HACKER: (*Looking down at* CLOUT.) Oh, the little urges of the little man. Never mind, Clout, 'ere's yer plan. (*He drops the plan on the ground.*) Out of all this – filth and squalor – comes forth sweetness. I shall never feel disgusted by a corpse again.

SCENE 4

The same place, late at night. Someone is smoking a cigarette. Pause.

LALAGE: (*Coming in.*) Is that you? (*The cigarette does not reply.*) Is it? (*Pause.*) PLEASE, IS THAT YOU?

RIDDLE: Yes.

LALAGE: Why don't you answer?

RIDDLE: I like the shake in your voice.

LALAGE: I've cut myself. My leg is bleeding.

RIDDLE: There is a lot of old iron up here.

LALAGE: Will you take my hand please? I've come such a long way. My knees are shaking. Take my hand, PLEASE.
(*He stands, gives her his hand.*
They sit. Pause.)
Did you fight here?

RIDDLE: No.

LALAGE: Did you shoot anyone?

RIDDLE: I don't talk about the war.

LALAGE: What do you talk about?

RIDDLE: You want to talk, not me.

LALAGE: Yes, I do. I have to talk. I'm nervous and I have to talk. I haven't been with many men. (*Brief pause.*) What do you think will happen to England now?

RIDDLE: I don't care.

LALAGE: It's bound to change, isn't it, though? There are women doing men's jobs, for example. And more questions being asked. I think it's very good that people ask more questions now. You may kiss me if you want.

(*Pause.*) My mother organises seances. She invites other mothers to our house. They try to reach their sons. They cry and have hysterics. I don't think we should give in to it, do you? The war was superstition, we should –

RIDDLE: Place my hand there. (*Pause.*)

LALAGE: Where?

RIDDLE: You place it there. (*Pause.*)

LALAGE: Do you not really care about England? When you have given such –

RIDDLE: Shh.

LALAGE: I must talk, really I have to –

RIDDLE: SHH. (*Pause.*) There's someone here.

(*BRIDE is standing looking over the battlefield. He has no trousers on.*)

BRIDE: Abbey. Abbey. Abbott. Abbott. Abbott. Abel. Abercrombie. Abernathy. Abraham. Abraham. Ackerley. Ackerley. Ackerley. Ackerley. Ackock. Ackroyd. Ackroyd. Ackroyd. Ackroyd. Ackroyd. Ackroyd. Ackroyd. Acland. Acland. Acton. Acton. Adcock. Adcock. Adcock. Addison. Addison. Adey. Adkin.

(*RIDDLE stands up as BRIDE, gathering momentum, removes a revolver from his jacket pocket and puts the barrel to his head.*)

RIDDLE: Put it down, Bride. (*Silence, for some seconds.*)

BRIDE: Fuck. (*Pause.*) Oh, fuck.

RIDDLE: They go off, you know. When you don't mean them to.

BRIDE: (*His back still towards him.*) Who is it?

RIDDLE: Riddle.

BRIDE: I thought I knew the voice.

RIDDLE: Please put it away, old boy.

(*The revolver is lowered.*)

BRIDE: Resent this. Interference. Very much. (*He turns on him.*) I have a rank! My acting rank! (*Pause.*) God… I forgot to put my trousers on…

RIDDLE: Never mind.

BRIDE: Oh, Christ…

RIDDLE: Nothing really matters. Ranks or trousers. Go home, now.

(*BRIDE starts to go out, stops.*)

BRIDE: It was you last time, wasn't it?

RIDDLE: Yes, I spend a lot of time up here.

(*BRIDE goes out. Pause.*)

There are no bullets in his gun. But it's best to humour him. Everyone to his own agony. (*He looks at her.*)

LALAGE: What do you mean by saying nothing matters?

RIDDLE: Bride thinks the dead matter. I don't. But I don't think the living matter, either. England is having her recurring nightmare, isn't she? Crackerjacks and bangers. Mounted policemen in Trafalgar Square. A lot of angry soldiers asking what happened to their acre and their cow, clinging to some punctured lie. No one will lie to me. Rot England. I will make love to as many women as will have me. That way there is no lie. Will you have me? I have talked too much. (*Pause.*)

LALAGE: You have not said a loving word to me. Or even called me by my name.

RIDDLE: No.

LALAGE: I don't know you.

RIDDLE: No. (*Pause.*)

LALAGE: Good.

SCENE 5

Early next morning. LALAGE is straightening her clothes after a night in the open. MRS TOYNBEE appears, looks at her.

MRS TOYNBEE: You haven't slept in your bed.

LALAGE: No.

MRS TOYNBEE: You weren't at breakfast.

LALAGE: No. (*Pause.*)

MRS TOYNBEE: Well, you must please yourself. What's the matter with your leg?

LALAGE: Barbed wire.

MRS TOYNBEE: You know there is tetanus round here?

(*HACKER and CLOUT come in, followed by FLOWERS, TROD and BASS.*)

FLOWERS: We're one short this morning. Mr Riddle is in bed with a cold, or 'is TB is nagging 'im, or 'is ulcers, or 'is varicose veins.

HACKER: Good morning, Mrs Sylvia Toynbee.

MRS TOYNBEE: Good morning, Mr Hacker.

HACKER: A nice one. A nice pink tinge in the sky. Do you like skies, Mrs Sylvia? I do. I have a set of lantern slides on skies. My favourite is 'Stratocumulus over the Pentland Firth'. (*He gazes up.*) I don't think there is a great deal to be said about these Belgian skies. When you think of Belgium you don't think of skies.

LALAGE: What do you think of?

HACKER: Getting skinned by the inhabitants, Miss.

FLOWERS: Poppies.

(*They turn to him.*)

Supposed to say poppies, aren't yer? Springing out of dead men's eyes? (*He turns to his men.*) Shall we move along, gents?

HACKER: (*As they pass.*) I 'ope you won't be getting under my feet, Flowers.

FLOWERS: We're raising bodies, guv'nor. The longer you leave it, the 'arder it gets.

HACKER: That may well be.

FLOWERS: Earth to earth is a very true saying.

HACKER: Is it? Go on.

FLOWERS: The human substance 'as a tendency to imitate the soil in which it's placed. In Palestine, our dead blokes are made of sand, while 'ere, unluckily, they absorb their weight in water and turn into mud. (*Categorically.*) We are moving west to east. You'll 'ave to lump it.

HACKER: Discuss it with Bride. Bride is Graves Commissioner.

BASS: (*Stopping.*) Mr 'acker. Bride will bend down for a finger. He would put an eyeball in 'is 'andkerchief.

(*MRS TOYNBEE lets out a pathetic sob.*
HACKER turns in alarm.)

HACKER: Clumsy idiot! (*He hurries to her side.*) Sylvia, love, I – (*He see the SOLDIERS watching.*) Don't bloody gawp! Christ,

everything is witnessed! (*He shakes out a handkerchief.*) 'ere,
use this. (*He looks at LALAGE.*) Is she gonna faint?

MRS TOYNBEE: I may just... (*Pause.*) No, I shan't faint.

(*The SOLDIERS drift away.*)

HACKER: She isn't.

MRS TOYNBEE: I'm all right...

HACKER: She's all right.

LALAGE: When my mother was a girl to faint was sexual
provocation. Now it's taken as a sign of malnutrition, but
the habit's very difficult to break.

MRS TOYNBEE: (*In full possession of herself again.*) It gave men the
opportunity to fulfil a need. A need to be powerful. Isn't
that right, Mr Hacker?

(*He clears his throat nervously.*)

It was when I fainted that my husband fell in love with me.
He wasn't a strong man, but I made him feel it. Naturally
he was full of gratitude. When you look at me, Mr Hacker,
don't you feel strong?

(*He shifts uncomfortably.*)

HACKER: Clout, do you need to work under my feet?

CLOUT: Mr 'acker?

HACKER: (*Waving him away.*) More that way, eh?

(*CLOUT removes himself.*

HACKER turns back to MRS TOYNBEE.)

Where were we?

MRS TOYNBEE: I said when you look at me, don't you feel
strong?

HACKER: Yes – I – I suppose I – (*Then, desperately.*) What
happened to your 'usband, Mrs Toynbee?

(*Pause. She turns away a little.*)

MRS TOYNBEE: When the Eastern Front collapsed he switched
all our money into Russian tea. Buying in depressed
markets was his speciality. We acquired the entire crop
until 1960. Then, six months later, while we were at
breakfast, I heard this funny little thud from behind the
newspaper. It was his forehead on the tablecloth. The
Bolsheviks had seized our tea. Coming on top of Billy's
death, he became possessed by the idea we were a cursed

family. He died insane, two days before the Armistice. I have tried to reach him through mediums, but they say he is trapped in the ether...somewhere above Siberia.

HACKER: What a tragedy...

MRS TOYNBEE: Ronald, I want my Billy's body. I want to take him home.

(*Pause. HACKER is confused.*)

HACKER: Your boy Billy – you want –

MRS TOYNBEE: Help me.

HACKER: Well, I –

MRS TOYNBEE: Look into my eyes. (*He looks. Pause.*) Will you?

HACKER: Er...

MRS TOYNBEE: Answer my eyes.

HACKER: Er...

MRS TOYNBEE: Say yes. Say yes to my eyes.

HACKER: Sylvia...

MRS TOYNBEE: Say yes, I beg you.

HACKER: Yes. (*Pause.*)

MRS TOYNBEE: Thank you.

HACKER: Yes what? What have I said yes to?

MRS TOYNBEE: Me.

(*Pause. CLOUT is tapping in a peg.*)

HACKER: I think it's illegal, in fact, I know it is.

(*She looks at him, he shrugs.*)

So what? It's illegal.

MRS TOYNBEE: Will you take my hand?

HACKER: If it's all right with you.

(*She extends a hand, he takes it, is about to kiss it, when she withdraws it. She gives him a slip of paper.*)

MRS TOYNBEE: This is his name and number.

HACKER: (*Deeply aroused.*) Christ, Sylvia, you do –

(*There is a sudden shout of despair from CLOUT.*)

CLOUT: OH, GOD 'ELP US! (*He flings down his shovel and runs to HACKER.*)

HACKER: Control yerself, Clout!

CLOUT: I can't do this! I can't do this!

HACKER: Can't do what?

CLOUT: Dig 'ere! I can't dig 'ere, I won't!

HACKER: If yer want payin', yer will.

CLOUT: JUST PUT ME SPADE THROUGH SOMEONE'S 'EAD!

(*Pause.*)

HACKER: Clout. That is the sort of language that makes a lady faint.

MRS TOYNBEE: I am perfectly all right.

HACKER: You're in luck. She is perfectly all right. Now go and fetch Mr Bride and tell 'im you 'ave uncovered somebody, 'e'll know who it is, I expect. (*Pause.*) Get along, son!

(*CLOUT goes out.*)

MRS TOYNBEE: It could be Billy.

HACKER: Oh, I don't think so.

MRS TOYNBEE: Why ever not? He must be here somewhere, mustn't he?

HACKER: If you say so.

MRS TOYNBEE: I don't say so. It is the War Office who says so.

LALAGE: (*Who has wandered to the place.*) It's a German.

MRS TOYNBEE: (*Turning.*) Darling, do you have to look?

(*LALAGE shrugs, walks back.*)

HACKER: Fine people, the Germans. In many ways. Got to admire 'em, 'aven't you?

MRS TOYNBEE: No, actually you haven't.

(*Pause. He shrugs.*)

HACKER: Maybe not.

LALAGE: What do you mean, 'maybe not'?

HACKER: I've forgotten where I was now.

LALAGE: Why not admire them if you want?

(*He shrugs.*)

I admire them. As much as I admire anyone.

MRS TOYNBEE: They are not like other people.

LALAGE: It was only his uniform that marked him out.

MRS TOYNBEE: That is shallow. It is so easy to say everyone is just the same as everybody else. It is all the craze now. But because it is easy it does not make it true.

HACKER: Hear, hear.

MRS TOYNBEE: I hate the Germans because they don't know when to stop.

(*CLOUT comes in, with BRIDE.*

CLOUT points at the place, BRIDE looks. Pause.)

BRIDE: Unfortunately, I haven't been able to compile a comprehensive German list. They have a different attitude to us. Mass graves and tiny granite tablets. As if there was something to be ashamed of in being dead… (*He comes to the others.*) Of course, they haven't been allowed to raise great monuments.

LALAGE: They can't afford it, can they? They've gone bust.

BRIDE: Is that so? I rarely see a newspaper.

LALAGE: I wonder if we wouldn't have done better by sending them something to eat. Instead of all these endless English cemeteries.

MRS TOYNBEE: No. Let's have the cemeteries.

LALAGE: The dead before the living?

BRIDE: Yes, oh, yes. (*Pause. He is about to go, stops.*) The most repulsive aspect of humanity is the ease with which it reproduces. If conception were more difficult, we would be less contemptuous of our lives. Were we pandas, should we have fought the Battle of the Somme? (*He looks at HACKER.*) Mr Hacker's stones will tell no lies. Count them. Each one had lips to kiss. I loathe oblivion. I loathe the word forget.

LALAGE: They will forget. They will eat sandwiches here, and bring their dogs to shit.

(*FLOWERS, BASS and TROD come in, carrying a canvas shelter.*)

BRIDE: It's a German. I will tell their people.

(*He goes out, as the SOLDIERS erect the shelter round the place. CLOUT is just watching.*)

HACKER: Perhaps you could start that end, Clout? Rather than 'ang about?

CLOUT: Sorry, Mr 'acker. It was a shock.

HACKER: The first one always is, isn't that right, lads? Your first corpse shakes yer, then it's like 'aving a fag?

(*RIDDLE arrives for work. He joins the soldiers.*)

BASS: 'ello, look who's 'ere.

RIDDLE: I overslept.

FLOWERS: 'ave to report it, Riddle.

RIDDLE: War's over two years, Mr Flowers. Report what you like.

(*MRS TOYNBEE and LALAGE start to go out.*

LALAGE hangs back, speaks boldly to RIDDLE.)

LALAGE: It was a beautiful night.

(*They stop working, all look at her, pause.*)

RIDDLE: Was it?

(*She goes out, behind her mother.*

TROD watches them.)

TROD: I could not desire a woman who had not known death.

HACKER: (*Seeing to whom he refers.*) Desire? What's desire got to do with you?

BASS: Trod ain't in a fit condition to desire anyone.

FLOWERS: Six months in the 'ighlands 's what 'e wants. It's shell shock with you, ain't it, Trod?

TROD: (*Still looking after the women.*) A woman like that moves you, turns your bowels…

FLOWERS: (*Looking at BASS.*) Want to see the MO. Get some medicine for that.

HACKER: They are arresting blokes in London for that sort of trench filth, Trod.

BASS: They would not arrest me, the bastards.

HACKER: No, well, you don't talk filth, do you?

BASS: They will not arrest me, I say.

HACKER: In fact, you 'ardly talk at all.

FLOWERS: (*As he digs.*) Is that the daughter? The trembling one?

HACKER: It is Miss Toynbee, yes.

FLOWERS: She's over-ripe. Someone should pluck 'er or she's gonna drip.

HACKER: YOU CAN'T TALK ABOUT PEOPLE THE WAY YOU DO!

BASS: (*Having thrust his spade.*) Gone through the leg.

FLOWERS: Fuck the leg.

BASS: No. Get it up. Don't leave the leg.

FLOWERS: 's a German.

BASS: Do it proper.

FLOWERS: Please yerself. (*He leans on his spade while BASS digs.*) So what about the daughter? On the subject of legs?

HACKER: 'er bum crack you couldn't slip a five pound note in.

FLOWERS: While the mother 'as an arse to swallow a donkey's cock.

HACKER: (*Seething.*) Stick to the daughter, shall we? Stick to one.

BASS: Right. Ready. Are we ready?

(*They place their spades under the remains.*)

– and HUP!

(*Staggering, they transport their burden to a canvas stretcher, withdraw their spades.*)

FLOWERS: Mr Riddle, do your stuff.

(*RIDDLE puts on a pair of rubber gloves and kneels beside the remains.*)

HACKER: That's it, then, is it?

FLOWERS: As soon as Mr Riddle's 'ad 'is delve, 'is nimble fingers 'ave explored vast numbers of 'uman cavities. Some 'ot and female, which 'ave no doubt benefited from 'is tenderness, but more often the rigor-mortised guts of soldiers, accidentally penetrated in the search for valuables.

RIDDLE: Nothing. (*He stands up.*)

BASS: No disc?

FLOWERS: Fuck the disc. Let 'im join the missing.

RIDDLE: (*Feeling again.*) No disc.

TROD: Herr Nichtmann.

FLOWERS: (*Pulling a cover over.*) Mr Nobody it is, then.

HACKER: Is this delving really necessary? I can't see it is myself.

RIDDLE: Eight wristwatches yesterday. Two in good order. A cigarette case. A hall-marked whisky flask.

FLOWERS: In future wars all combatants will be requested to bring valuables into battle. As tips for the poor bastards who will have to dig 'em up.

RIDDLE: We aren't getting the officers, that's the pity.

HACKER: Must be an easier way of earning a few bob.

FLOWERS: No doubt you'll tell us if there is. There is no work at 'ome. The factory I worked for has closed. They switched from bicycles to howitzers, but the market for howitzers has dropped off.

BASS: We will go home, and if there is no work we will
demand it.

FLOWERS: Just like that.

BASS: Exactly.

FLOWERS: You will be put inside.

BASS: I will not.

FLOWERS: 'ow will you not?

BASS: I will refuse.

FLOWERS: 'e will refuse.

BASS: It is that simple, we are the soldiers.

RIDDLE: Bass, they have already got your rifle back. They
have swapped your weapon for a spade.

FLOWERS: Come on, let's move.

(*They bend to the stretcher.*)

HACKER: Gents, one moment, gents. Can I whisper a little
something in your ears? Something related to the ladies we
discussed?

(*They stand upright again.*)

You see, they're looking for a body. Mrs Toynbee is
looking for 'er son. (*He looks over his shoulder.*) This
particular youth is listed missing. Round 'ere.

TROD: She is brought here by his astral body. He calls her and
she has to come...

HACKER: Something like that. So if you could make a
special effort I, for one, would be prepared to make my
appreciation very clear.

TROD: She bears his wound in her. She weeps his blood.

FLOWERS: STUFF IT, TROD!

HACKER: Thank you. What I'm saying is, this particular corpse
would earn you more than a nickel fag-case. (*Pause.*) To put
it another way, can you get 'im this week?

RIDDLE: (*Indicating two points on the horizon.*) There are tens of
thousands between here and there...

HACKER: I never said it was easy. (*He reaches for his wallet,
removes a note.*) I wonder if you could find 'im in a week?
(*He holds the money out.*)

FLOWERS: We can do it.

HACKER: William, he is, William Toynbee. That's 'is number and 'is regiment. (*He hands FLOWERS a scrap of paper, turns to go out.*) Means a lot of work, of course. But there's more money where that came from. I'm not made of money but I admit I'm bloody keen.

FLOWERS: To knob the lady, would 'e mean?

HACKER: (*Stopping.*) I heard that, Flowers. Vile insinuation, vile. Four years of squalor 'as made you cynical, I suppose. (*He walks away, past CLOUT, who is working.*)

SCENE 6

CLOUT is still working here next day. BRIDE comes in, with a copy of The Times. *He reads it out to CLOUT.*

BRIDE: Ferocious argument in the House. Copies of *Hansard* employed as missiles following the Government's decision to enforce the standard model headstone for officers and all other ranks. Described as creeping socialism. As lowering downwards. An further evidence of the persistent erosion of individual choice. Desperate parents have become the body-snatchers of our time. One body only is to be returned, for interment in the place of kings. The Prince of Wales will choose the Unknown Warrior, being blindfold and using a pin. (*He folds the paper and tucks it under his arm.*) There is something gone in my head. If I jerk it quickly, something moves. Have you ever had that?

CLOUT: No, sir.

BRIDE: I'm not married, are you?

CLOUT: No, sir.

BRIDE: Which is difficult, because what happens if I'm ill? Someone has to wipe your bum. I should have thought of this, but I've been racked with work here – (*He moves his head.*) There it goes! WHO WILL WIPE MY SHIT AWAY! (*He goes out as LALAGE appears.*
CLOUT gets up, is about to go out.)

LALAGE: They don't abuse my mother, do they? (*He stops.*) Please tell me she is not the subject of their filthy talk. (*Pause.*) I see.

(*He goes out.*
LALAGE stares over the country.
RIDDLE comes in, looks at her.)

Why didn't you come for me? I was here all night.

RIDDLE: I didn't want you.

LALAGE: All night here. I was so cold.

RIDDLE: What would have been the point in coming? As I didn't want you?

LALAGE: To tell me. That would have been the reasonable thing to do.

RIDDLE: I don't do the reasonable. That's why you like me.

LALAGE: I thought you might be ill. I thought anything.

RIDDLE: Desperate.

LALAGE: Yes.

RIDDLE: In the freezing night. Hot and clamouring in the womb.

LALAGE: No. Sneezing and bloody uncomfortable.

RIDDLE: Quivering from knee to belly.

LALAGE: Look, we must have a talk some time. (*Pause.*) Mustn't we? Get to know each other?

RIDDLE: Ah. So it begins.

LALAGE: I feel like having a conversation. I love your darkness but I am finding it too quiet.

RIDDLE: Nothing you can say will be worth saying.

LALAGE: Try it, shall we?

RIDDLE: Not with me.

LALAGE: I love you, but I cannot go on if we don't learn to speak!

RIDDLE: Go on? GO ON?

(*CLOUT appears pushing a wheelbarrow full of gravel. He takes a rake off the top.*)

LALAGE: If you want to fuck me.

(*CLOUT does not react.*)

If you want to go on doing it.

(*Pause, then she goes out. CLOUT tips out the gravel into a heap.*)

286

RIDDLE: I know her. Through and through I know her. I read what is engraved on every vertebra along her spine. It says I am clean, and I do good.

CLOUT: (*Spreading the gravel.*) Someone 'as to.

RIDDLE: Her good is all to do with ventilation. Ventilated villas in suburbia. Ventilated underwear. She is throbbing with conviviality.

(*HACKER comes in with a Union Jack.*)

HACKER: 'ere we are, son. 'ere at last. Two years after a world war and a million rotting Englishmen, yer can't lay yer 'ands on a Union Jack. Grateful bleeding Belgians turn 'em into shopping bags. It's this way up, is it? (*Spreading the flag on the ground.*) Or is it? (*He points to the pathway.*) This 'ere's the 'orizontal, am I right?

CLOUT: Er…

HACKER: (*Waving his hand.*) This 'ere.

CLOUT: Er…

HACKER: What you're laying, come on, son!

CLOUT: This is the diagonal.

HACKER: What? 'ere?

CLOUT: Sir.

HACKER: Diagonals is four foot wide.

CLOUT: Er…

HACKER: Whatcha mean er? Whatcha mean, er, er? Give us the measure. (*He gets up, takes CLOUT's rule.*) Bollock this up at your peril, Clout. (*He tests the width of the path.*) Well, so it is. Why didn't yer say? This is the diagonal. (*He gives him the rule back.*) Well, I can see I am a burden on your ingenuity. (*He turns to RIDDLE.*) How's things going, Riddle?

RIDDLE: We have him.

HACKER: You what?

RIDDLE: Young Toynbee.

HACKER: You 'ave 'im? You – 'ANG ON.

RIDDLE: Oddly enough.

HACKER: Oddly enough. COME ON.

RIDDLE: War is like that, Mr Hacker.

HACKER: War is like that. COME ON.

RIDDLE: Do you have to repeat everything I say? We have
   him. I can't compel you to believe it, obviously.

HACKER: You can't. You damn well can't.

RIDDLE: Shall we bring him? Or will you collect?

HACKER: Yesterday I ask you, keep an eye open for certain
   remains. Today, remains arrive, on the doorstep like a loaf.
   Come on, it stinks.

RIDDLE: You have to give some credit to coincidence. The war
   has made us all so sceptical. If we were working one on
   you, Mr Hacker, wouldn't we have left a few days' grace?
   That would be cleverer, you must admit. Our spades
   upturned him within an hour of you leaving us.
   (*Pause, while HACKER looks at him searchingly.*)

HACKER: You're a cool one, Riddle. All right, bring him 'ere.
   (*RIDDLE starts to go, stops.*)

RIDDLE: (*Turning.*) There isn't all that much to see.

HACKER: No, of course, there wouldn't be.
   (*RIDDLE goes out.*)
   Smart bastard. Smart bastard, don't yer think?
   (*CLOUT pretends not to hear.*)
   Still, it has its advantages. Bona fide or non bona fide, I
   can't complain. I wonder where you take a woman 'ere?
   Pity they 'ad to knock the coast about. Yer can't take a lady
   like that to an allotment shed. (*Pause.*) Or maybe you can.
   Christ knows what the gentility conceals. Christ knows
   what itch…
   (*The SOLDIERS come in bearing a stretcher draped in tar-
   paulin. They dump it down, stand back.*)
   I would be right in thinking, wouldn't I, there can't be
   much left of 'is 'ead?
   (*FLOWERS shakes his head.*)
   Is there an 'ead?
   (*FLOWERS shakes his head.*)
   Unlucky. Nor nothing in 'is pockets neither?
   (*FLOWERS shakes it.*)
   No pocket?
   (*FLOWERS shakes it.*)

Well, what is there, then? (*Pause.*) I can't sell 'er a bag of
peat!
(*They just gawp.*
He goes over to the stretcher, lifts the tarpaulin.)
Very funny. Fifteen quid for that. I love your sense of
'umour. Come on, lads, you're dealing with a businessman.

FLOWERS: Yer wouldn't be accusing us of cheating?

HACKER: You said the word, not me.

BASS: British Soldiers of the Great War for Civilization?
HEROES OF ARMAGEDDON?

HACKER: Very good, Bass, but can we be serious for just a
minute? (*Pause.*) It is not so much a matter of convincing
me. I am 'appy with a pound of sausage meat. It is Mrs
Toynbee, isn't it? It's 'er feelings I 'ave to consider.

RIDDLE: Look at his disc. Round what was once a neck there
hangs a disc. Otherwise we should not have bothered you.
(*HACKER goes to the remains, looks at an army disc.*)

HACKER: 1127161 Toynbee. Royal Hussars. (*He looks up.*) Well,
I'll be buggered. (*Pause. He gets up.*) Well, I regard that as
conclusive.

RIDDLE: She will be satisfied. We have watched widows weep
on horsemeat supplied by less scrupulous squads.
(*HACKER gazes at the remains.*)

HACKER: To think that – muck – down there came out
between 'er lovely limbs…
(*He bites his lip.*
The SOLDIERS look puzzled.)
That is the measure of war, I think… (*He turns, stops.*)
Christ, that shakes me… (*He walks a little, staggers, stops.*)
Bloody 'ell… Clout… CLOUT!
(*CLOUT drops his rake, hurries over.*)
Bloody 'ell, man, I've come over sick…

CLOUT: Bend over, Mr 'acker.

HACKER: Ridiculous… (*He retches.*) Cor…silly, ain't it, but I…
(*He retches again, dabs his mouth with a handkerchief.*) What
are they gawping at?

BASS: The money, guv.

(*HACKER takes out his wallet, gives CLOUT two notes, which he hands over.*
The men withdraw.)

HACKER: Clout, I 'ave 'ad a vision of death. I saw beyond the grave. I saw Alpha and Omega. Are you listening?

CLOUT: Mr 'acker.

HACKER: I saw a thin 'ole to the bottom of the world…

CLOUT: Sir.

HACKER: (*With sense of horror and discovery.*) I SHAN'T BE 'ERE LONG! (*He holds CLOUT by the shoulders.*) Fuck it, I am scared of death! All these years gone and I never noticed 'em! I got to 'ave a child, Clout! Somebody must give me a kid!

CLOUT: Mrs 'acker, sir?

HACKER: Mrs Hacker? Mrs Hacker? Are you barmy? Mrs Hacker is forty-three and sterile as a collar stud. It's been like shooting into concrete these last twenty years! What's gonna 'appen suddenly? Use yer 'ead!

CLOUT: Sorry.

HACKER: This 'as touched me. This 'as touched me very deep. Who's gonna remember me? What'll 'appen when I'm gone? (*He strides about in despair.*) Shakespeare was a lucky sod. Day and night they're stuffing 'im down schoolkids' gobs. Won't forget 'im, will they? What about me?

CLOUT: The name 'acker, Mr 'acker. Over the shop.

HACKER: Next geezer who takes over the business will 'ave my sign down in the dust.

CLOUT: It's on all the memorials, ain't it? Hacker fecit, it says. In little letters on the back.

HACKER: You said it. Little letters on the back. First bit of moss obliterates it. No, I shall 'ave to 'ave a kid. The common man's immortality, such as it is. You 'ave been busy working, so you won't 'ave noticed an interest I've developed in a certain lady –

CLOUT: Shit as toothpaste.

HACKER: Wha'?

CLOUT: Shit as toothpaste.

(*Pause. HACKER glares at him.*)

HACKER: Clout, I urge you to eradicate that particular phrase from your mind. I most earnestly encourage you to be a tabula rasa as far as Mrs Toynbee is concerned. I do urge you. (*Pause.*)

CLOUT: Get on with the pathway, Mr 'acker.

(*He goes off, starts working, stops, looks at HACKER.*)

SCENE 7

The remains on the stretcher are mid-stage. MRS TOYNBEE and LALAGE stand together, MRS TOYNBEE in a pure white dress. Pause.

MRS TOYNBEE: I shall kiss him. Will you want to?

LALAGE: No, I shan't.

MRS TOYNBEE: Sometimes I wonder if you loved him. (*Pause.*) I mean really loved him.

LALAGE: Really loved him. Loved him. What's the point of qualifying it?

MRS TOYNBEE: Then kiss him.

LALAGE: No. I said.

MRS TOYNBEE: Why?

LALAGE: Because it won't be him, will it?

MRS TOYNBEE: Who will it be, then?

LALAGE: It's two years since he died. Imagine that.

MRS TOYNBEE: Love does not die at the grave. I shall kiss him. In my white dress.

LALAGE: You must do exactly what you want.

MRS TOYNBEE: You think I'm making too much of this? Making a banquet of my grief?

LALAGE: That's about it, yes.

MRS TOYNBEE: I am. You're right. I am drinking it to the dregs. (*She walks towards the body, stands looking down.*)

LALAGE: I think you are making a fool of yourself.

MRS TOYNBEE: Or you, is it? You think I am making a fool of you? There is nothing quite so embarrassing as a parent who can't keep her feelings checked. Especially when your own are so trapped and strangled. Isn't that it?

LALAGE: No.

MRS TOYNBEE: You oppress your spirit too much. Everyone
    does. And the world is an uglier place for it. I loathe
    dourness and grinding teeth. So did Billy. He wrote to me
    that if people hadn't been so stiff-lipped with their grief the
    war would have finished two years earlier.

LALAGE: I didn't mean that. I meant –

    (*At this moment* HACKER *appears, discreet in a dark suit. He
    watches from a proper distance.*)

    I meant how do we know that is him?

    (*MRS TOYNBEE ignores this. She kneels beside the stretcher.
    At this moment, the* SOLDIERS *come in bearing a number of
    empty coffins.*
    HACKER, *trying to preserve decorum, waves them away.
    They do not notice him.*)

FLOWERS: These are getting lighter, or I'm getting stronger.

RIDDLE: They are using thinner wood. Out of consideration
    for our backs.

BASS: Or the maker's profits, could it be?

    (*Seeing* HACKER, *they stop, look at* MRS TOYNBEE, *who, in
    an ecstasy of emotion, leans forward and places her lips on the
    remains.*
    TROD, *with a groan, collapses in a faint, and the coffins
    clatter to the ground as the* SOLDIERS *struggle to hold them.*)

FLOWERS: Hold it!

BASS: Jesus Christ!

FLOWERS: Hold it!

HACKER: You clumsy buggers! Oh, you clumsy sods!

BASS: Trod's fainted!

HACKER: Sod Trod.

FLOWERS: Who are you abusing, guvnor?

HACKER: There is a woman 'ere, paying 'er respects… Christ,
    what is England coming to? What did we fight the war for?
    Women, wasn't it? Women and their feelings?

BASS: I love the 'we'.

HACKER: Christ, appealing to Englishmen to 'ave an 'eart.
    I never thought I'd see the day.

FLOWERS: Come on. Shove off. (*He leads off.*)

BASS: What about Trod?

RIDDLE: He'll recover there as well as anywhere.
(*They go out, leaving* TROD *on the ground.*
After a pause MRS TOYNBEE *gets up.*)

MRS TOYNBEE: Oh…! There is mud on my dress…!

LALAGE: Oh, really, you are so – (*She turns on her.*) WHAT IS IT
FOR?

HACKER: (*Hurrying forward with a handkerchief.*) I wonder if I
might brush it off? This is a brand new handkerchief – (*He
kneels at her feet.*)

MRS TOYNBEE: No.

HACKER: No?

MRS TOYNBEE: It is there forever.

LALAGE: (*Mockingly.*) Surely you realised that?

HACKER: I'm afraid I didn't. But I understand it. I don't think
I 'ave ever been so moved. I think if someone made a
painting of it, it would sell. You might call it 'The Patriot's
Farewell'. I think it would hang in bedrooms all over
England.
(*LALAGE walks out smartly. Pause.*)
I 'ope everything is satisfactory, then? (*Pause.*) Took a bit of
doing, obviously. Finding one person in all this – I think
you're so beautiful – so one way and another we were
lucky, I suppose they – I would give my life to kiss your
arse… (*Pause.*) Did you 'ear me, Sylvia?

MRS TOYNBEE: (*Her back still to him.*) Yes.

HACKER: No doubt others 'ave said similar things.

MRS TOYNBEE: Yes.

HACKER: Naturally. Well. (*Pause.*) Can I? (*Pause.*) What more
can I say? I'm not a poet. (*Pause.*) Can I? (*Pause. Then,
nervously, he extends a hand, at last touching her, running his
hand over her. Then with a groan, falling to his knees and burying
his face in her clothes.*) I am so 'appy! Isn't it easy to make a
man 'appy?

MRS TOYNBEE: Yes. It is. (*Pause.*) Now I think you should get
up.
(*Obediently, he rises, brushing his knees.*)

HACKER: May I book a room, Sylvia? Sorry – a suite? There's this place called Blankenberghe. I 'ave the brochure – (*He goes to take it from his pocket.*)

MRS TOYNBEE: Yes. Why don't you? (*Pause.*)

HACKER: Why don't I? Yes…

(*He looks at her, then hurries out.*

MRS TOYNBEE remains motionless for some time.

There is a groan behind her, then TROD sits up.)

TROD: Blood…

(*She turns.*

He indicates her dress.)

Blood on your dress…

MRS TOYNBEE: Blood?

TROD: I am going to be killed.

MRS TOYNBEE: Oh, no. Not now the war is over, surely?

TROD: Yes. It's the meaning of that blood.

MRS TOYNBEE: It isn't, though. As a matter of fact. It's mud.

TROD: I'm not afraid. You carry death in you but I'm not afraid. Bride and I, we are going to cross over soon…

(*Pause.*)

MRS TOYNBEE: Really. It's mud.

(*She goes out.*

The SOLDIERS reappear.)

BASS: (*To TROD.*) Come on, son. Up on yer feet.

FLOWERS: Herr Nichtmann is done with, then, is 'e?

BASS: What number do we paint on this?

FLOWERS: (*Looks in a book.*) Missing Number 1127161. Then put it with the others in the shed.

BASS: (*With a paint can.*) 1127161.

TROD: We should not have done it…

FLOWERS: Done what, son, exactly?

TROD: She kissed it. With her lips…

BASS: Yeah, well, she is a performer, ain't she?

TROD: We have mocked her pity! We have sinned against the ordinance of death!

RIDDLE: It doesn't matter, Trod. All your conscience. All your guilt. From the right distance all the thundering of bishops is drowned by a rat's squeak.

BASS: Only the rich come 'ere, yer notice.

RIDDLE: They are not rich. It is all appearance with them.

BASS: The poor rich, then. My mother could not come 'ere.
My missus could not.

RIDDLE: Why should they want to? As you're not dead?

BASS: The rich can filch some bastard's body. The poor make
do with telegrams.

RIDDLE: She got nothing for her privilege. For all we know the
corpse she kissed had killed her son. (*He gets up.*) Are we
ready, then?
(*They lift the remains into the coffin and start hammering
down the lid.*)

FLOWERS: Mr Riddle, what plans 'ave you got when it's our
turn to enjoy the peace? I can swallow ten pints at a sitting,
but I 'ave a feeling no one's employing men for that.

RIDDLE: Why don't you emigrate? You like the Empire, don't
you?

FLOWERS: I should like it. I 'ave two brothers killed for it. One
in Palestine shot by the Turks, the other lost 'is footing
racing an Australian down a pyramid. The Australians
lose 'alf their men through dares, did you know that? (*He
hammers in the final nail.*) Yes, I like the Empire. Where do
you suggest?
(*They look up, suddenly aware of a stranger in their presence.
The man wears khaki riding breeches and boots and a police
jacket. He taps a small riding whip against his leg.*)

HARD: Good men. (*Pause. He stares at them.*) Oh, good men. (*He
wanders around them, feasting his eyes.*) Oh, very good.

ACT TWO

SCENE 1

The cemetery is partly built. The gravel path is laid, there are head-stones lining the back of the stage, but a sense of disorder prevails. CLOUT is unloading turfs from a wheelbarrow. HACKER is blowing into his cupped palms and sniffing earnestly.

HACKER: Is it my breath? (*Pause. He blows and sniffs.*) You can say. I won't 'old it against yer.
(*CLOUT works on.*)
Two bookings, both cancelled. I'm the laughing stock of Blankenberghe. (*He sniffs again.*) I've got this idea it's my breath, yer see. Last night I cleaned my teeth so hard I was bleeding. Sink 'ad gone pink. (*Pause.*) She lets me fondle 'er clothes, but I 'aven't actually kissed her. Not 'er lips…
(*Pause.*) Clout.

CLOUT: CAN I JUST GET ON WITH THIS!
(*Pause. HACKER is astonished.*)

HACKER: What? What did you say? Come again?

CLOUT: I'm sorry, Mr 'acker. Can I just get on with this?
(*BRIDE comes in.*)

BRIDE: Mr Hacker.

HACKER: Mr Bride.

BRIDE: If you can finish by the end of this week there is every chance the Prince of Wales will perform the dedication. He is in Paris on a social visit and would like to fit it in. The other cemeteries have drainage problems. What do you think? Can you finish?

HACKER: (*Wide-eyed.*) Yes.

BRIDE: You're certain?

HACKER: I'll swear to it.

BRIDE: How many graves have still to be placed?

HACKER: Forget it. No problem.

BRIDE: I ask because –

HACKER: Easy.

BRIDE: Yes, but –

HACKER: Say a hundred –

BRIDE: A HUNDRED?

HACKER: Less. Definitely less. Say fifty.

BRIDE: You just said a hundred.

HACKER: Dunno why I said that. Wasn't thinking. Fifty at the outside.

BRIDE: That is still a lot of work.

HACKER: I can do it.

BRIDE: Yes, but properly?

HACKER: Obviously properly.

BRIDE: You have the staff?

HACKER: No problem.

BRIDE: And proper turfing?

HACKER: I said yes, didn't I! (*Pause.*) Sorry. Yes.

BRIDE: If he selects this one it must be right.

HACKER: Work through the night if it comes to it. (*Pause.*)

BRIDE: Good. All right. (*He starts to go out.*) I want to be laid here myself.

HACKER: Well, why not?

BRIDE: I am not war dead, am I?

HACKER: No, I suppose you're not.

(*BRIDE goes out. HACKER turns to CLOUT.*)

Did you 'ear that? Did you cop that, Clout? Hacker, by appointment to the Prince of Wales! Oh, the way of the world! You can be shit one mouthful and sugar the next!

CLOUT: (*Dourly.*) Two 'undred, Mr 'acker. (*Pause.*)

HACKER: Two 'undred, is it? Is it? Two 'undred?

CLOUT: Sir.

HACKER: As much as that…

CLOUT: Never do it.

HACKER: Shut up.

CLOUT: Not in a month. Not in three.

HACKER: If you keep on about bloody months, Clout, I will do something I might regret. The word month is not permitted 'ere!

(*Pause.*)

CLOUT: Twelve weeks.

HACKER: All right, clever. Now listen. It is a fact that nothing
is impossible. They said the war was impossible but it
still 'appened. I say we can do it. All we need to know is
'ow. So let's forget the when and stick with the 'ow. 'ow
do we get two 'undred cadavers in their 'oles and two
'undred slabs of Portland laid on top of 'em. In seven days?
'ow? 'ow? (*Pause. He walks up and down.*) Christ, this is a
bugger… (*Pause.*) All this battlefield clearance yer can't get
staff…

CLOUT: I could tell yer.

HACKER: Fire away, then.

> (*Pause. CLOUT just looks at him .*)
>
> Well, let's 'ave it. (*Pause.*) Clout?
>
> (*CLOUT just stares at him, very coolly.*)
>
> Oh, blimey…the worm is contemplating turning, I do
> believe… (*Pause.*)

CLOUT: 'alf the profits. (*Pause.*)

HACKER: Comedian.

> (*CLOUT shrugs his shoulders, goes back in his shovel.*)
>
> You're wasted 'ere. They're looking for you at the
> Palladium.
>
> (*CLOUT digs on.*)
>
> I knew you 'ad something. I knew something 'ad to go on
> in that peculiar 'ead of yours. But a stand-up comic? Never
> dreamed of it.
>
> (*Pause. CLOUT begins unloading turfs.*
>
> *HACKER watches him some time.*)
>
> Under the law of the land, all your ideas are my property.

CLOUT: What land?

HACKER: England, of course.

CLOUT: This ain't England, Mr 'acker.

HACKER: Oh, but it is. Ceded to HM Government in
perpetuity. From the grateful Belgians. Corner of a foreign
field, etcetera. I wouldn't 'esitate to sue, I warn yer.

CLOUT: My 'ead's my 'ead.

HACKER: Look, I pay yer, so I own yer. Put it bluntly 'cos yer
make me.

CLOUT: (*Picking up the wheelbarrow.*) Get more turfs –

HACKER: 'ANG ABOUT.

(*CLOUT stops.*)

Up yer wages.

(*He starts going again.*)

FUCK ME, WHERE IS YOUR LOYALTY!

(*He stops again.*)

Not just to me. Not just to me who 'as provided you with work and wages when work and wages can't be 'ad, but to these dead Englishmen. They died for us. It makes yer blush to 'ave to mention it!

(*CLOUT starts off again.*

HACKER watches him to the edge of the stage.)

'alf the profits in what?

CLOUT: (*Stopping.*) Gallipoli.

HACKER: Never mind the little jobs, eh? Kindly overlooks the bread and butter funerals. Decent of yer. FUCKING 'ELL!

CLOUT: Mr 'acker, look at the papers. From now on there is gonna be a world war every week. This is an expanding business like no other. If you're appointment to 'is 'ighness, you can't miss, 'alf the profits will be 'undred times what you 'ave 'ad –

HACKER: And a million times what you 'ave!

CLOUT: I'm not asking for my name on the factory gates. But if we miss this it could be Peckham for good. (*Pause.*)

HACKER: 'e looks a silly bugger but 'e's cunning as a –

CLOUT: 'OW ABOUT IT?

(*Pause. HACKER smiles, but thinly.*)

HACKER: Alright, what's the idea?

CLOUT: (*Taking a dirty paper from his pocket.*) Appreciate it if you'd sign 'ere, sir.

HACKER: Christ, 'e doesn't miss a trick. (*He takes it, examines it.*) 'ow long's this been 'anging about?

CLOUT: Fair number of years, sir.

HACKER: I can see. Waiting till yer got me in a corner, eh?

CLOUT: Sign there, Mr 'acker…

HACKER: You've 'ad a lawyer on it.

CLOUT: It's proper, sir, down to the stamp.

(*HACKER reads it, then takes a pen and signs it, but as CLOUT goes to take it, holds on to one side.*)

HACKER: This 'ad better be good, ol' son. God in 'eaven, it 'ad. (*Pause.*)

CLOUT: Yer put four in one 'ole. (*Pause.*)

HACKER: Come again.

CLOUT: You 'eard me.

HACKER: Yes, I think 1 did.

CLOUT: It reduces labour by four 'undred per cent.

(*Pause. HACKER is still holding on to his end of the paper.*)

HACKER: Disgraceful. Bleeding disgraceful.

CLOUT: (*Significantly.*) Prince of Wales.

HACKER: Repulsive, unpatriotic, fucking disgrace.

CLOUT: PRINCE – OF – WALES.

(*Long pause. Suddenly, HACKER releases the paper, walks away, turns again.*)

HACKER: If Bride sees it – I DON'T AGREE WITH IT. (*Pause. Then with decision.*) After this is over I will commission a fucking great big sculpture called the 'Agony of War'. For Peckham churchyard. I will 'ave a chapel built for war widows. To make amends.

CLOUT: Least we can do.

HACKER: All right, then. That I swear. Now let's get on with it. Be working nights, of course. I imagine you won't be putting in a claim for time and 'alf?

CLOUT: (*Putting away the contract.*) 'sir.

HACKER: SIR? Bit redundant, ain't it? SIR?

CLOUT: Prefer it, Mr 'acker, if you don't mind.

HACKER: Why should I mind? Grovelling's an 'abit like any other, I suppose.

(*He follows CLOUT, who is pushing a wheelbarrow. MRS TOYNBEE and LALAGE come in.*)

MRS TOYNBEE: They've put Billy in the long shed with the others. In a coffin with a number on. I am suggesting to Hacker he is brought home labelled tools. I originally thought we could manage this ourselves, but not now there are military policemen everywhere. We aren't the only people forced to steal our loved ones from the government.

We loaned our sons for the duration but they are hanging
on to them till Judgement Day.

LALAGE: You're going on a bit…

MRS TOYNBEE: I want him in England!

LALAGE: This is, apparently…

MRS TOYNBEE: England? How can it be? England is an island.

LALAGE: Because it's full of English dead.

MRS TOYNBEE: That doesn't make it England.

LALAGE: Well, what does? This is more England than
Knightsbridge is. (*Pause.*)

MRS TOYNBEE: I don't think you want him brought home.
I don't think you want Billy underneath our tree. (*Pause.*)

LALAGE: No. I don't think I do. (*Pause.*)

MRS TOYNBEE: I see. So I can't rely on you?

LALAGE: I don't think so…

MRS TOYNBEE: You don't think so.

LALAGE: I mean no. (*Pause.*) I think we are creating a new
world now. A new world of equality and justice. This is
1920, isn't it? And the way we treat the dead will show our
intentions about all the rest. They have decided to abolish
all distinctions in the graveyards. The same style for
everyone. I accept it. If we cannot even manage that, what
will happen to the rest of it?

MRS TOYNBEE: You are a socialist.

LALAGE: Is that what it is?

MRS TOYNBEE: Yes.

LALAGE: Probably I am, then.

MRS TOYNBEE: You are for this regulation. This monotonous
equality.

LALAGE: Yes.

MRS TOYNBEE: This greyness. This sameness.

LALAGE: Yes, I am. (*Pause.*) I am. (*Pause.*)

MRS TOYNBEE: You'll note, I'm sure, how this equality has to
be enforced. How they've had to send in the police. To
terrorise us. To arrest and imprison people like me. You'll
notice how this urge for sameness causes misery and grief!

LALAGE: I'm afraid I think you should conform. Of your own
free will.

MRS TOYNBEE: I will not! They do not own my son, I do.
(*Pause.*) I take it you won't hinder me?

LALAGE: They're taking one dead soldier home. To shake their
plumes over in the Abbey.

MRS TOYNBEE: You haven't answered. Will you hinder me?

LALAGE: I don't know!
(*Pause. MRS TOYNBEE stares at her.*)

MRS TOYNBEE: This is your socialism. This. You will have me
taken by the police.

LALAGE: Please, don't be emotional.

MRS TOYNBEE: It is not emotional, it is a fact. Will you see me
taken by the police?

LALAGE: I can't answer.

MRS TOYNBEE: You have answered. (*Pause.*) We are enemies,
then. (*Pause.*) Of course I shall not disclose anything more
to you. That is the price of socialism. Sealed lips. (*She starts
to go, stops, turns.*) I must tell you, I haven't said one quarter
of what I might have said. Not one tenth.

LALAGE: No, of course.
(*MRS TOYNBEE goes out, passing RIDDLE, who is on his way
to work, carrying a spade.*)
You're late again.

RIDDLE: Dead men are very patient. Very good employers on
the whole.

LALAGE: Will you help me?

RIDDLE: I do. Every night.

LALAGE: Tell her it isn't Billy. (*Pause.*) Because it isn't, is it?
Anyone can see that.

RIDDLE: On the contrary, no one can see anything.

LALAGE: Precisely. Disabuse her, please.
(*Pause. He just looks at her.*)
If you love me. (*Pause.*) Or desire me, or what.

RIDDLE: I would forfeit three pounds seventeen and sixpence.

LALAGE: I will make it up to you.

RIDDLE: No. Let her believe. I would not steal her orgasm
from her. It is too divine a thing. (*He starts to move away.*)

LALAGE: Why do you attack me all the time?

RIDDLE: (*Stops.*) Attack you?

LALAGE: Orgasm.

RIDDLE: Did I say orgasm?

LALAGE: God Almighty. I wish I knew what I had done to you.

RIDDLE: (*Significantly.*) Nothing. You've done nothing to me.

LALAGE: I'm sorry I can't do what you expect. I've tried, and I will go on trying.

RIDDLE: You would say that. That's so typical of you. You will try. You will improve. What you will never see, you English women in your laundered lingerie, is that effort never altered anything. For all your trying, I've known better from army whores though I was the ninety-ninth man in the queue. (*Pause.*)

LALAGE: Well, there seems no point in discussing what effort cannot influence, does there? You will have to take us as we are.

RIDDLE: Nothing will ever wake you.

LALAGE: And what will wake you?

RIDDLE: I'm finishing with Europe. I'm finishing with dead continents and dead women. I'm going to a place where there is desire in the hips of the women and a slow look in their eyes, where flesh is flesh and as old as sex itself, where men do not come chattering from books.

LALAGE: Mexico? Peru?

(*He looks at her, full of contempt.*)

RIDDLE: You mimicking, unloved, female thing.

LALAGE: I'm sorry, but that is a lie. However I have disappointed you, out of ignorance or shame, I know that is nonsense and a lie. You have suffered four years of one lie and now, out of pain, you've given yourself to another. The lie of submissive, dark-skinned women. I know it is a nonsense. I know it like I know nothing else. It makes me pity you.

RIDDLE: Well, that ends it, then. I will not lie with a woman who scorns the man.

LALAGE: You see, you will keep on using these phrases like 'to lie with' and 'Woman' and 'Man'. It is meant to put mystery into it but all it does is fuddle things. I would have expected the war to make men desperate for truth, but it's made you bow down.

RIDDLE: Nothing will ever move your womb.

(*She turns away, in frustration and despair.*)

You should be sodomised. It's all you're fit for, jellies, creams and second-rate hotels…

(*He waits to see if he has provoked her, then turns to leave.*)

LALAGE: Marry me.

(*Pause. He stares at her.*)

I will help you. Marry me.

(*He looks at her, blankly, then goes out.*)

SCENE 2

Night. Some hurricane lamps indicate work is still going on. Voices off, calling a dog.

PRINCE / GENTLEMAN: PASSCHENDAELE! HERE, BOY! PASSCHENDAELE!

(*There is a bout of whistling.*)

PRINCE: (*Clattering against some old iron.*) F-F-Fuck! Banged my knee!

GENTLEMAN: (*Entering with a dog's lead.*) PASS-CHEN-DAELE!

PRINCE: (*Hobbling in and sitting.*) F-F-Fuck the dog! (*He rubs his knee.*)

GENTLEMAN: Spaniels cost money.

PRINCE: Get another one.

GENTLEMAN: Silly.

(*He walks up and down whistling.*

The PRINCE OF WALES looks around, takes out a map.)

PRINCE: This must be Hill 60. We've walked f-f-fucking miles. (*He leans back, staring at the night sky.*) The sky was all lit up at night.

GENTLEMAN: Really?

PRINCE: A firework party lasting four years. Green flares for artillery. Red for gas. Starshells trickling through the air… obviously lovely. Lovely as only proper evil can be…

(*Suddenly he dives flat in mock battle.*) GERMAN ATTACK!

GENTLEMAN: (*Crouching unconvincingly.*) Oh, not again…

PRINCE: (*Being a machine gun.*) Rat-tat-tat-tat-tat-tat-tat! You're hit!

GENTLEMAN: Naturally. (*He gracefully lays back.*)

PRINCE: But I'm all right. I stand up, to help you. I'm a captain, you're a private, but I help you – (*He stands.*) THEN I'M HIT TOO!

GENTLEMAN: Same as last time…

PRINCE: (*Collapsing.*) Stretcher-bearers! Help my men!

GENTLEMAN: 'Oh, our beloved captain's dead, who we would have followed to the gates of Hell…'

PRINCE: Where's the f-f-fucking dog? It should be licking me.

GENTLEMAN: Got fed up, I expect. This is the third time tonight, you know…

PRINCE: (*Dying.*) They gather round me –

GENTLEMAN: (*Tugging at a shoe.*) My shoes are soddened…

PRINCE: GATHER ROUND ME.

GENTLEMAN: (*Scrambling over to a suitable pose.*) Sorry.

PRINCE: Gather round me, eyes moist in the star shell's eerie glare… (*They are a tableau for some seconds, then the PRINCE OF WALES sits up.*) I wish they'd let me fight here, George. I think if I'd died national unity would be secure. Sometimes princes have to be sacrificed. I hate seeing England cracked up as she is. We are good people, aren't we?

GENTLEMAN: I wish I could see the dog.

PRINCE: As a king in the making, I feel I should know what's making 'em beef. As soon as we've done the battlefields I intend to do the slums. I will go to them at their cottage doors, and pulling aside the rambling roses I will say tell me what is wrong. Do not be frightened. I am only a king. (*GENTLEMAN walks to the edge of the stage and whistles again.*)
Of course the risk is they won't tell the truth. They will hand me a cup of tea and say everything is lovely. That is their way. They mistake that for loyalty. But I will say, no, that is false loyalty. Give me the facts and I will act on them.

GENTLEMAN: Can't do more than that, can you?

PRINCE: I can't think why no one thought of it before…

(*CLOUT comes in with a wheelbarrow.*)

GENTLEMAN: Excusez-moi, avez-vous vu un petit chien?

CLOUT: Sorry, guv?

GENTLEMAN: Ah. English.

PRINCE: We're looking for a little dog. Answers to the name of Passchendaele.

GENTLEMAN: When it feels like it.

CLOUT: No, sir.

(*He carries on working.*
PRINCE OF WALES watches him.)

PRINCE: Working damn late.

CLOUT: If I could, sir. (*Pause.*)

PRINCE: You are an English workman, aren't you? An ordinary English workman?

(*CLOUT ignores this.*)

So let me ask a simple question. What is wrong?

(*CLOUT lays a turf.*)

Nothing? NOTHING is wrong? (*Pause.*) I don't believe that, because you see I live in London. I have a house there and when I look out of my window the streets are full of people. Rather angry people, falling down, and fellows on horses being rather rough with them.

(*Pause. CLOUT ignores all this.*)

Please help me. I want to be good.

(*CLOUT ignores him.*)

GENTLEMAN: It isn't on, you know. Every flag-waver is an assassin in his darker blood. A proper king knows that. He never stoops.

(*PRINCE OF WALES looks at him, resentfully.*
MRS TOYNBEE appears, clasping a spaniel.)

MRS TOYNBEE: Clout, I'm looking for Mr Hacker.

CLOUT: 'e's laying 'eadstones, Mrs T.

MRS TOYNBEE: Would you mind telling him I'm here?

(*Grudgingly, flinging down his spade, CLOUT goes out. Pause.*)

PRINCE: Excuse me, but I think that m-m-may be my dog.

MRS TOYNBEE: Ah…

PRINCE: Yes, it definitely is m-m-my dog…

MRS TOYNBEE: I heard him whining and I picked him up. I was afraid he'd fall into a shell-hole. What's he called?

PRINCE: P-P-Passchendaele. Out of respect… (*He gazes at her, captivated.*) I w-w-wish I could think of something else to say…

MRS TOYNBEE: Let me give him back to you.

PRINCE: Would you like him?

GENTLEMAN: Can't possibly.

PRINCE: W-w-would you?

GENTLEMAN: YOU CAN'T.

PRINCE: I think it would be very nice to be your d-d-dog…
(*In a sudden rush of embarrassment, he flees.*
The GENTLEMAN looks at MRS TOYNBEE, then hurries after him.
HACKER comes in, muddy.)

HACKER: God, Sylvia, you look wonderful…

MRS TOYNBEE: (*Going to him.*) Shhh.

HACKER: Why shh?

MRS TOYNBEE: Because we've got enemies.

HACKER: Who 'as?

MRS TOYNBEE: You and I.

HACKER: Enemies? I've never 'ad enemies.

MRS TOYNBEE: Well, you have now.

HACKER: Who?

MRS TOYNBEE: Someone who would frustrate a cherished scheme. Why else do you think I'm creeping round here at night?

HACKER: I can't think with your health – (*He goes to stroke her collar.*) CHRIST, IT'S A DOG!

MRS TOYNBEE: Will you listen?

HACKER: Thought it was a fur, sorry.

MRS TOYNBEE: About Billy. About my boy.

HACKER: Yep.

MRS TOYNBEE: About taking him home.

HACKER: Yep.

MRS TOYNBEE: My idea is that we –

HACKER: TAKING 'IM 'OME?

MRS TOYNBEE: Will you be quiet!

307

HACKER: Sorry. (*Pause.*) Taking 'im 'ome? Did we say that? Did we? (*Pause.*) Bugger. I never – I forgot we said that.

MRS TOYNBEE: Are you helping me, or are you not?

HACKER: Sylvia, my love –

MRS TOYNBEE: I am so cold, hold me.

HACKER: (*Holding up his hands.*) Muddy –

MRS TOYNBEE: Hold me!

(*He puts his arms round her.*)

Don't abandon me.

HACKER: Abandon you?

MRS TOYNBEE: I'm sorry that we haven't – haven't –

HACKER: Blankenberghed?

MRS TOYNBEE: Yes.

HACKER: You ain't been well.

MRS TOYNBEE: No. And I shan't be until this is done. (*She separates from him.*) In England we will. After his funeral I promise you.

(*Pause. HACKER is diffident.*)

HACKER: Sylvia… I 'ave never 'ad one like this in my life… (*Pause.*) I wonder if…forgive a bloke for asking… I wonder if…down there…you feel the same as me… (*Pause.*)

MRS TOYNBEE: Yes. I promise you.

HACKER: Thank God. I thought it might be all on my side. (*He turns away, modestly.*) Thank God…

MRS TOYNBEE: I thought we might hide Billy in a tool-box. Does that seem sensible?

HACKER: (*Turning to face her again.*) Yes. I'll arrange it.

MRS TOYNBEE: Thank you. (*She turns to go.*) I pretend to no equality. I put my hand on my heart and thank God for a man.

(*She goes out.*

HACKER watches her.

CLOUT is making up for lost time, heaving a headstone across the stage.)

HACKER: An English funeral, Clout…rooks in the tree tops… the smell of dew… 'er in 'er stiff black dress, aching for me underneath…

CLOUT: SHALL WE JUST GET ON WITH IT!

SCENE 3

*In the pale dawn light, the figure of COLONEL HARD is seen silhouet-
ted. Voices off, and shovels clanging. The SOLDIERS come in.*

RIDDLE: It has occurred to me, these last few mornings, there
is no singing any more. Now this says something.

BASS: It says we're workers again. You don't 'ear workers
singing. Not in England.

RIDDLE: Singing is the slaves' consolation. When you hear it,
kill it.

FLOWERS: Riddle would shut down the music halls.

RIDDLE: Had I the slightest wish to change the world,
Mr Flowers, it would be the first thing I should think of.
(*They are moving offstage when HARD speaks.*)

HARD: Gentlemen.
(*They drift to a standstill.*)
Give me five minutes of your time. The corpses will not
grudge it.
(*They examine him.*)
I have watched you, and read you. I read men like others
read horses or books. And in your strong backs I read
a certain privilege, the privilege of making history. I am
inviting you to write with me what children will pore over
in their history books. What do you say? (*Pause.*)

FLOWERS: (*Sarcastically.*) You're keeping the best part back,
guvnor. Who is it you want to kill?

HARD: The task is Ireland. Screwing the lid down on the
Gaelic beast. We have our own uniform, and the money is
ten shillings a week. (*He walks round them, tapping his stock on
his boot.*) This is not men's work. Give your oath and I will
whisk you away within the week. (*Pause.*)

RIDDLE: Is there singing?

HARD: Singing?

RIDDLE: Yes. Do they sing?

HARD: It is not obligatory.

BASS: I like the money. What's the oath?

HARD: To the Crown.

BASS: I can take or leave the Crown.

HARD: (*Shrugs.*) The Crown's a word, sir.

FLOWERS: I thought you were waiting for the revolution, Bass? The great up'eaval and what not?

BASS: In the meantime I 'ave a family wants to eat.

TROD: I had a sister died in Cork. She said all the girls are named Colleen...

FLOWERS: This man is mentally ill.

HARD: We wouldn't discriminate against him for that.

FLOWERS: (*To TROD.*) You need an 'ospital, son. Not a Black and Tan camp.

HARD: You may not dissuade a volunteer. It is sedition.
   (*Pause. FLOWERS stares at him.*)

FLOWERS: You should not come 'ere, guvnor. Of all places, not 'ere.

HARD: The Empire commands us.

FLOWERS: We 'ave served the Empire. I 'ave two brothers dead for it.

HARD: No amount of sacrifice can be enough. I am a speaker for the Empire. I have had Chinese rebels stand on their benches to cheer me while their wrists bled from the chafing of their chains. I have been kissed on both cheeks by great black mutineers before we hanged them. And do you know why? Because I reminded them of Duty, which is the purest essence the man-animal can extract from himself. Duty, which smoulders as a tiny flame in every drug-blinded Calcutta tramp, and which Empire fans into a blaze that none can stop. All men long to serve. Service to the Empire lifts us from our secret cess.

FLOWERS: It put me in it, mister. Four sucking years of it. I'm not against yer Empire. Good luck to it. I fancy a farm in Africa myself. Black men running about while I sit on my arse. But you 'ave a neck to come 'ere after what we've seen and done. I am 'uman, and I take offence. (*Pause.*)

HARD: There can be no African farm for you. Not without this. What happens in the Irish bog will silence tremors in the Bush. These gentlemen will hold the Empire together if you will not. (*He turns to TROD, taking out a card and a Bible.*) I swear to serve...

TROD: (*Placing a hand on the Bible.*) I swear to serve…

HARD: My King and Country…

TROD: My King and Country…

HARD: To the best of my endeavour…

> (*FLOWERS walks forward to the edge of the stage as BASS waits his turn.*
> *RIDDLE joins him.*)

RIDDLE: Do we disappoint you, Mr Flowers?

FLOWERS: It's not a mistake to make a mistake. It's a crime not to profit by it.

RIDDLE: It's not true that the war was not enjoyed. It was, by some of us. It has got around how terrible it was. Because of the poets. But some of them enjoyed it too. I am against sentiment and pacifism. We must live in the blood.

FLOWERS: Killing Irish, Riddle?

RIDDLE: One day. And making love to their widows the next.

> (*FLOWERS stares at him.*)

You do not understand me, do you?

FLOWERS: No. I do fucking not.

> (*RIDDLE goes back to HARD for the oath, as TROD comes down.*)

TROD: I had a vision, then, as I was speaking. We were in Connemara, in a truck. I saw green fields, and a winding road. I saw us on it, singing, and three men standing behind a hedge. Why were they behind a hedge?

FLOWERS: Pissing, no doubt. Though the Irish aren't usually so modest.

> (*MRS TOYNBEE comes in as RIDDLE finishes the oath. The MEN pick up their shovels and go out.*)

MRS TOYNBEE: Colonel Hard?

HARD: (*Turning.*) Yes, I am Colonel Hard.

MRS TOYNBEE: *Cult of Empire?*

HARD: I am the author of that book.

MRS TOYNBEE: At Tonbridge I asked you a question once. About the place of women.

HARD: Women?

MRS TOYNBEE: Yes. Service, you said.

HARD: Really? I may well have done.

MRS TOYNBEE: Then I bought a copy of your book.

HARD: I am flattered.

MRS TOYNBEE: And you signed it.

HARD: Yes, I do that, after the meetings I hold a stall. (*Pause.*)

MRS TOYNBEE: Lies. (*Pause.*) Your book. (*Pause.*) Lies upon lies.

HARD: I'm sorry you felt that. Empire is a difficult subject.

MRS TOYNBEE: My son read it. He believed you. Now he's dead.

HARD: I'm sorry. We lost a lot of people.

MRS TOYNBEE: Give me my money back. (*He gawps.*) My five shillings. Give it back.

(*He smiles uncomfortably.*
Suddenly, BRIDE bursts in.)

BRIDE: (*To HARD.*) YOU CANNOT TAKE THEM! GIVE THEM BACK!

HARD: Everybody seems to want something from me.

BRIDE: I am desperately short-handed, you have no right to take my men!

HARD: Hire civilians.

BRIDE: The fallen are to be buried by their comrades! It is the usage of war, it's written in the articles, how dare you subvert the articles?

HARD: I hold the King's Commission. I come from London.

BRIDE: Shit on London! London killed them! Piss on it!

MRS TOYNBEE: Mr Bride…

BRIDE: Oh, Abbey, Abbey, Abbey, Abbott, Abbott, Ackroyd, Ackroyd, Ackroyd, Ackroyd –

MRS TOYNBEE: Mr Bride –

BRIDE: I'M ALL RIGHT!

(*She recoils.*
He turns on HARD.)

Release them from their oath.

HARD: The war is over now. It must take second place.

BRIDE: I am an acting colonel! I hold rank!

HARD: (*Moving suavely* away.) Very good luck. (*He stops, feels in his pocket.*) I don't have five shillings. Will three and ninepence do instead?

(*He holds out the money to MRS TOYNBEE.*
She ignores him.

He goes out, passing HACKER *who charges in distraught.*)

HACKER: (*To* BRIDE.) They're quitting! The buggers are quitting at the end of the week!

BRIDE: You said you would finish by the end of the week.

HACKER: I 'ad every intention, but 'ow can I. The buggers are standing about. Once a man's given notice 'e's a burden on yer.

BRIDE: My poor boys… my unfinished cathedral…

HACKER: Clout and I are up to our eyeballs and all we get is backchat and cheek.

BRIDE: How far are you?

HACKER: Nowhere near it.

BRIDE: It is for the fallen, Hacker…!

HACKER: That's all very well, Bride, but they don't shift marble, do they?

BRIDE: (*Decisively.*) I'll help you myself.

HACKER: (*Horrified.*) No call for that.

BRIDE: If things are going badly, we must –

HACKER: (*Blocking his way.*) No, they're not. (*Pause.*) Badly, yes, but there are degrees of badness. This is quite good as badness goes… (*Pause. In desperation.*) You'd only get under our feet. There's eight 'undred cemeteries, ain't there? Give them a look.

BRIDE: (*Drifting away, stops.*) I had a practice in Bermondsey before the war. It was all rickets and TB. The same dirty infants kept on coming back. The smell! Piss and infestation! I had a vision of the perfect world. Trim grass, rose trees, clean homes, square and brilliant white. My silent city. My just society… (*He goes out.*)

HACKER: Bride's mad.

MRS TOYNBEE: Yes. He is.

HACKER: Well, I suppose I 'ad better get back. Threaten the labourers. Oh, look who it is.

(*LALAGE comes in.*)

Good morning, Lalage. I do like the name. I 'ad Clout look it up. It's Greek for wild and awkward isn't it?

LALAGE: I've made up my mind.

HACKER: About what?

LALAGE: If you try getting my brother home. In a toolbox or whatever. I will go running to the police.

(*Long, awful pause. HACKER looks at MRS TOYNBEE.*)

HACKER: Sylvia? What police?

MRS TOYNBEE: (*To HACKER.*) Go back to what you're doing.

HACKER: WHAT POLICE!

MRS TOYNBEE: Tell you later.

LALAGE: Tell him now.

MRS TOYNBEE: (*Turns to HACKER.*) There will be no funeral in England if she can stop it.

LALAGE: I could apologise, but I'm not going to. Once you apologise for something you know to be right, you may as well pack up. I shall have to accept that doing the right thing nearly always upsets people. It's one of the defining characteristics. Nothing that ever changed the world was very welcome. But that's the way of progress. The best of us are spoilsports.

HACKER: You've been talking to Riddle. Riddle's got at you.

LALAGE: Got at me, yes. Talked to me, never. (*She starts to go out, then stops. To HACKER.*) I want you to be certain what the consequences are going to be. If you persist. There are military police here and the penalties are considered rather excessive for this kind of thing. (*She goes out.*)

HACKER: Christ, Sylvia, right now this is something I could do without.

(*CLOUT comes in with his wheelbarrow, drops it noisily to remind HACKER of their tasks.*)

All right, Clout.

MRS TOYNBEE: Are you capitulating to that threat?

HACKER: I don't think so…

MRS TOYNBEE: You don't THINK so?

HACKER: Of course I'm not, I – (*He sees CLOUT is standing impatiently.*) I'm coming, Clout! (*He turns back to MRS TOYNBEE.*) Only I'm buggered if I see a way round – (*CLOUT drops his spade noisily into the empty wheelbarrow.*) Someone wants to make a point.

MRS TOYNBEE: Do this for me. I am yours for this. But not without it.

(*Pause. HACKER looks injured.*)

Does that hurt you?

HACKER: A little bit… I thought you might have wanted me for myself…

MRS TOYNBEE: I promise you I will be all you want. To the limit of my ability.

HACKER: Sounds like athletics.

(*CLOUT is watching, arms folded. She takes HACKER's hand, kisses it.*)

I mean, what sort of kiss is that? Is it pity or respect?

(*She releases it.*)

I wish it was just a bit of common or garden lust. I'm sorry, but I do.

(*She goes out.*

He watches her.)

Ol' son, you could do it to 'er if she was a corpse…

(*He shakes his head, then remembers CLOUT.*)

I'm not pulling my weight, Clout, I admit that. There are things on my mind preventing me from giving my all to this.

(*CLOUT just looks at him.*)

I 'ave to get a body back to England. (*Pause. He looks in despair to his employee.*) Clout, will you 'elp me, please?

(*Pause.*)

CLOUT: (*Coldly.*) Sixty-six and two thirds.

HACKER: What?

CLOUT: PER CENT.

(*Pause. The full import sinks in.*)

HACKER: THIS IS SUPPOSED TO BE A PARTNERSHIP!

(*CLOUT bends, picks up the handles of the barrow.*)

'old it!

(*Pause. CLOUT waits.*)

Give us the fuckin' paper, I'll sign it.

ACT THREE

SCENE 1

The 'Dead March' is played by a military band, offstage. In the middle, on the turf, stands a dais, draped in a Union Jack. Other Union Jacks are massed along the rear. Either side of the dais, the SOLDIERS in crisp uniform. Grouped around, MRS TOYNBEE and LALAGE, BRIDE clasping his ledger, and a BISHOP in ceremonial scarlet. HACKER and CLOUT stand modestly to one side. The Royal GENTLEMAN attends the PRINCE OF WALES. At last the music stops. The BISHOP climbs up.

BISHOP: Why God likes pain. (*Pause.*) Always being asked that one, why God is so very fond of pain. (*Pause.*) Because He is. Wriggle around it as we might, it's inescapable, He must like pain. His own and other people's. He must approve of it. And this is as good an occasion to mention pain as any. Better than most, in fact. Because we are situated in a sea of it. An Atlantic of stilled agony. (*Pause. He examines his fingers a moment.*) Well, I will not apologise for Him. I am always apologising for Him. It's getting a bit much.

GENTLEMAN: (*Standing underneath, arms folded.*) NOT – THE – SPEECH.

BISHOP: It is, in fact, becoming something of an outrage.

GENTLEMAN: WRONG – SPEECH.

BISHOP: This mission – this so-called calling – (*He plucks his robes.*) – which consists in making the vile palatable, and finding symmetry in the hideous, it is becoming an impertinence.

(*The GENTLEMAN begins coughing.*)

Fear not. I do not deny the existence of the person God. I merely ask what sort of character He has.

GENTLEMAN: NO.

BISHOP: I ask you, would you let Him near your child? Because, quite frankly, I would not!

GENTLEMAN: (*Coughing.*) NO. NO. NO.

316

BISHOP: I look around me at His works – (*He waves an arm over the graves.*) And I must answer, let Him touch me not!

GENTLEMAN: FINISH.

BISHOP: However –

GENTLEMAN: (*Declaring publicly.*) THE PRINCE OF WALES!
(*There is a fanfare.*)

BISHOP: I consecrate this cemetery, therefore –

GENTLEMAN: THE PRINCE OF WALES!

BISHOP: All right, I consecrate it!
(*The fanfare sounds again as the BISHOP is bundled down by the GENTLEMAN.*
The GENTLEMAN urges the PRINCE OF WALES to go up with jerks of his head. Reluctantly, he does so.
An awful pause.)

PRINCE: (*Paralysed by shyness.*) I – I – I – (*He stops.*) Our – Our – Our – (*He stops again.*) This is torture to me…
(*He hangs his head.*
Suddenly, MRS TOYNBEE steps forward.)

MRS TOYNBEE: You are very good. Believe me, you are very good.
(*He looks at her. He is charged.*)

PRINCE: I – I – I am the head of what they call the British Establishment.

GENTLEMAN: NO.

PRINCE: The g-g-great British Establishment that sends young soldiers to their deaths.

GENTLEMAN: WRONG SPEECH.

PRINCE: No more of that. No more deaths. I am King Edward and I won't have deaths! Finish with that. Altogether better establishment from now on. Promise.

MRS TOYNBEE: God save the Prince of Wales!

PRINCE: (*Joyously.*) I declare this cemetery open!
(*Clapping, and the SOLDIERS raise their caps three times, with cheers.*
Grinning, the PRINCE OF WALES starts to come off the dais, but is stopped.)

GENTLEMAN: Stay there. You stay there. Christ, what is going on today!
(*He goes back up.*

*The GENTLEMAN takes a slip of paper and gives it to the
PRINCE OF WALES to read.)*

PRINCE: *(Reading.)* It is now my solemn duty, on behalf of King
and Empire, to choose from all our missing the Unknown
Warrior.
*(He clears his throat.
BRIDE steps forward with his ledger.
The GENTLEMAN takes it from him and hands it up to the
PRINCE OF WALES.)*

GENTLEMAN: Book. *(He removes a pin from his lapel, hands this
up.)* Pin. *(He shakes out a white handkerchief.)* Blindfold.
*(He goes behind the PRINCE OF WALES and covers his eyes,
then holds the book for the PRINCE OF WALES to flick through
the pages.
The PRINCE OF WALES stops at a page and jabs with the pin.
The GENTLEMAN looks down.)*
Number 1127161.
(The PRINCE OF WALES starts to descend.)

FLOWERS: 'Shun!
*(The SOLDIERS stamp to attention. As he comes down the
PRINCE OF WALES stops by FLOWERS.)*

PRINCE: I remember you.

FLOWERS: Me, sir?

PRINCE: Why didn't you tell them that I kissed your hand?

FLOWERS: Tell who, sir?

PRINCE: The newspapers. It was a cameo of m-m-modern
history. Like Sir W-W-Walter Raleigh laying down his
cloak.

FLOWERS: Thought we should keep it to ourselves, sir.

PRINCE: It was meant to be symbolical.

FLOWERS: Sym – what, sir?

PRINCE: Don't d-d-damned well keep it to yourself, that's what
symbolical means!

GENTLEMAN: *(Administering the formalities.)* The Contractor,
your Highness – *(He looks at a list.)* MR RONALD HACKER.

HACKER: *(Attempting to bow.)* Pleased to –

PRINCE: Jolly pretty. Lovely. Everything. *(He walks past
HACKER.)* Want to meet the woman.

GENTLEMAN: As you wish. (*He beckons MRS TOYNBEE with a finger, as she comes forward he leans towards her inquiringly.*) Who are you?

MRS TOYNBEE: Sylvia Toynbee.

GENTLEMAN: Mrs or Miss?

MRS TOYNBEE: Mrs.

GENTLEMAN: (*Turning back to the PRINCE OF WALES.*) Your Highness, MRS SYLVIA TOYNBEE!
(*The PRINCE OF WALES shyly takes her hand.*
The GENTLEMAN picks out BRIDE next.)
Next!

PRINCE: Tongue-tied.

MRS TOYNBEE: Like last time.

PRINCE: Yes. Yes. (*With sudden inspiration.*) The dog! The dog!

MRS TOYNBEE: He's very well, thank you.
(*Pause. The PRINCE OF WALES looks down, ashamed.*)

PRINCE: God, I have simply nothing in my head…!
(*The GENTLEMAN coughs, waiting with BRIDE.*)

MRS TOYNBEE: (*Smoothly.*) I am holding a seance here tonight. Would you care to join us?

PRINCE: Yes, oh, yes!
(*She turns away.*)

GENTLEMAN: Your Highness, Chief Graves Commissioner MR HECTOR BRIDE!
(*The PRINCE OF WALES shakes his hand.*
There is a silence.)

PRINCE: Nothing to say. Nothing to say to this man.

GENTLEMAN: (*To BRIDE.*) You may withdraw. (*He steps back.*)

PRINCE: That's it, then, is it?

GENTLEMAN: You must be polite to the officials!

PRINCE: George, she wants to meet me here tonight.

GENTLEMAN: Will you listen! You have got to be decent to officials. Sans them, sans everything! Do you follow me?

PRINCE: I'm sorry, yes. (*He is suddenly cast down.*) Oh fuck, I've ballsed-up everything!

GENTLEMAN: Don't say that.

PRINCE: Yes, I have.

GENTLEMAN: Keep your head up, please.

(*He nods to stage left.*
The band strikes up.
They leave sedately.
After a few bars, the band stops.
The SOLDIERS *break rank, tearing off their caps and belts.*)

BASS: (*To* FLOWERS.) Kissed your 'and? 'e kissed your 'and?

RIDDLE: Never told us, Mr Flowers. That a prince had genuflected to your cunt-crazed paw.

FLOWERS: Five years of my life. I won't be used.

(*He stalks out.*
TROD *and* BASS *hurry out after him.*)

BISHOP: I meant to say that God is merciful to those who perish in a just cause…that's what I meant to say…

RIDDLE: Is there a God? What is a just cause? Did they even perish?

BISHOP: Precisely the objections that occurred to me… (*He goes out.*)

HACKER: Well, Clout, they 'ave the Unknown Warrior.

CLOUT: Sir.

HACKER: Mr Billy Toynbee. In Westminster Abbey before a massive concourse of the nation. Buried among kings and poets. Ramsay MacDonald, Mr Asquith, and assembled upper-class tarts weeping. I feel quite envious.

CLOUT: Unknown, though, Mr 'acker.

HACKER: Yeah, but what a spot! Fuck it, I wouldn't say no to obscurity like that. (*He claps* CLOUT *on the shoulder.*) Your triumph, Clout. Your credit, son.

CLOUT: (*With a yell.*) Don't squeeze me arm, please, Mr 'acker!

HACKER: Why what's the matter with it?

CLOUT: Got fluid on the elbow, copying that number out three 'undred thousand times.

HACKER: Not used to writing, are yer, son? Brute strength's more your forte.

CLOUT: (*Moving off.*) Better get after Bride. Switch these ledgers back…

(*He removes a ledger from his jacket. It is the one* BRIDE *always carries.*)

SCENE 2

Night. Hurricane lamps are burning. HACKER *and* CLOUT *carry on a table, on which are balanced some chairs.*

HACKER: Don't geddit. Sensible woman. Don't geddit. What's she after?

MRS TOYNBEE: (*Carrying a chair.*) We'll have four more chairs and cushions, Mr Clout, please, if you can manage it.
(*He goes out, ill-temperedly.*
HACKER *sets them out.*)
The Bishop is swallowing his theological inhibitions, which will bring us up to eight. Eight is a good number. It is mystical, being a figure formed from two noughts.

HACKER: I must say, Sylvia, I dunno if I go for this.

MRS TOYNBEE: Go for it?

HACKER: Black magic.

MRS TOYNBEE: It's not black magic.

HACKER: Whatever it is, then.

MRS TOYNBEE: It's not the seance you object to, is it? It's the Prince.
(*He shrugs.*)
He is a lonely young man.

HACKER: So am I, Sylvia.

MRS TOYNBEE: You are married.

HACKER: No. I'm not. (*Pause. He recollects.*) Oh, yes, I am…

MRS TOYNBEE: You told me so yourself.

HACKER: All right, I am, I'm married, but I'm lonelier than 'im. You can be lonely in a double bed. You can 'ave a body next to yer and it can be as 'ostile as lead ripped off a prison roof. (*He looks at her, as she plumps a cushion.*) Christ, Sylvia…take my 'and…take it…
(*She looks round quickly, then takes it, across the table.*)

MRS TOYNBEE: You've been drinking.

HACKER: Yep.
(*She withdraws her hand.*)
This new arrangement. 'im being put in Westminster Abbey…it's not the funeral I 'ad 'oped for…

MRS TOYNBEE: We will sneak in. Watch from the back.

HACKER: Promise me you'll wear the dress.

MRS TOYNBEE: I promise.

HACKER: Oh, Christ, my love, my 'ands will be all over it –

MRS TOYNBEE: I HOPE TO GOD YOU ARE NOT DRUNK.

> (*CLOUT comes in, with chairs.*
> *HACKER sinks into a chair, as CLOUT and MRS TOYNBEE*
> *organise them round the table.*
> *BRIDE appears, in coat and scarf.*)
> Good evening, Mr Bride.

BRIDE: They have just taken him. The Unknown Warrior.
They are all unknown except to me!

MRS TOYNBEE: Would you care to take a seat?

BRIDE: This monstrous funeral in obscene London, London
that killed them, one practised parade for dignitaries
to weep! There should be a million! A million wailing
funerals clogging every street, a million caskets lumbered
through the traffic, tumbling and bursting, a million bodies
spilling off of carts in Piccadilly and a howling of relatives
to shake their palaces! (*Pause.*) Instead, it is an exhibition
of their dignity, civilised and ordered as befits a governing
race, an occasion to make Sikhs and Bantus wet-eyed
with respect… (*He looks at HACKER.*) Did I tell you, I'm not
proper in my head?

HACKER: I think you mentioned it.

BRIDE: (*Sitting.*) When he returned the book to me, after
pricking with his pin, all the numbers seemed the same.
Page after page. 1127161.

CLOUT: Not possible.

BRIDE: No. Something's happened in my head…

> (*The BISHOP comes in.*)

BISHOP: Good evening, Mrs Toynbee.

MRS TOYNBEE: I'm very glad you've come.

BISHOP: I brought a half bottle of Black and White. In case it
turns any colder. The spirits have nothing against alcohol,
have they? Might help them a bit.

MRS TOYNBEE: (*Indicating a place.*) Sit there, would you? Lalage
has generously offered to read. It is the fate of sceptics to
record the ecstasies of others.

HACKER: (*As the BISHOP sits.*) Get something in the glass, won't we, yer worship? Liquid spirits is better than none.

BISHOP: I am a clergyman, not a judge. I am a doctor.

HACKER: Doctor, is it? Might need a doctor when we've done with this. If it turns any colder. Look! See yer breath! (*He stands up, breathes out.*)

MRS TOYNBEE: Please, don't persist about the weather.

HACKER: No, I was only saying –

(*He moves up two places to sit next to her.*)

MRS TOYNBEE: (*Indicating his original place.*) Sit there, would you?

HACKER: No cushion on that seat.

MRS TOYNBEE: Does that matter? Take one off another seat.

HACKER: I really mean, it's not next to you. That's what I really mean.

MRS TOYNBEE: No. It isn't.

HACKER: Who's next to you, then?

MRS TOYNBEE: Ah, there's someone coming…

HACKER: If I'm not next to you, who is, then?

MRS TOYNBEE: Would you lay out the cards, please, Bishop?

BISHOP: Willingly.

MRS TOYNBEE: In a circle, reading inwards.

HACKER: (*Persisting.*) Sorry, I'm not getting through, who is, then?

MRS TOYNBEE: (*Looking off.*) It's Lalage…

HACKER: All right. Don't answer.

(*He goes back to his place.*

CLOUT moves to be beside him.)

Not next to me, Clout!

CLOUT: Sorry, Mr 'acker.

HACKER: See enough of you all day.

CLOUT: Sorry.

HACKER: No, I'm sorry. Spooks are getting at me. Sorry, son.

(*He helps himself to the BISHOP's whisky.*)

LALAGE: (*Coming in.*) I can't believe that soldiers who died for one superstition are likely to come flocking to another.

MRS TOYNBEE: All we ask is for you to write. No one wants you to participate.

(*LALAGE sits.*)

HACKER: Look out, Bishop, there's a thing on yer back!

BISHOP: (*Turning.*) What –

HACKER: 's 'all right. Flown off. Looked like a bat with 'airy legs… (*He laughs, drinks.*)

LALAGE: I think it's time we scrapped beliefs, don't you? Made them illegal or something.

BISHOP: This is an entertainment, surely. We wouldn't want to be governed by the supernatural, would we, Mr Bride?

HACKER: (*Acting sudden strangulation.*) Ahhhhrrrr! Something's got me round the neck!

BISHOP: It has as much truth as the Communion. And as little.

HACKER: (*Sinking down, hands to his throat.*) Aghhh… Agh…

LALAGE: Who are we waiting for?

MRS TOYNBEE: The Prince of Wales.

LALAGE: The Prince of Wales?

HACKER: (*On the ground now.*) GET…IT…OFF…

MRS TOYNBEE: He had nothing to do, so I asked him along.

LALAGE: (*Sitting.*) Funny. Princes having empty evenings.

MRS TOYNBEE: He's only human.

HACKER: (*Getting up.*) Only? Nearly human, she means. (*He brushes off his knees, sits again.*) Spirits got me. All right now.

MRS TOYNBEE: Mr Hacker has been drinking.

HACKER: MR Hacker? MR Hacker? As a point of fact I 'ave barely touched it. Clout will bear me out. I 'ave 'ardly touched it, 'ave I, Clout?

BISHOP: You have knocked the cards off.

HACKER: Clout, what 'ave I drunk this evening? I am not a drinking man, am I? This is purely to keep the Belgian damp out of my gizzard.

BISHOP: You have knocked the cards off.

HACKER: Yes, and I will pick 'em up.

(*TROD appears as HACKER bends down.*)

TROD: Excuse me.

(*They look at him.*)

I hear you're planning to establish contact here tonight.

HACKER: ESTABLISH CONTACT? That's good. ESTABLISH CONTACT. I like that.

MRS TOYNBEE: That is correct.

HACKER: Establish contact with what, I wonder? Who would
you want to make contact with? DON'T TELL ME!

MRS TOYNBEE: (*Turning angrily on him.*) Why don't you go
home if you won't take this seriously?

BISHOP: Hear, hear!

(*Pause. HACKER is stunned.*)

HACKER: Me? Is that supposed to be for –

MRS TOYNBEE: Yes. You. (*Pause.*) I'm not sure there is a seat.

TROD: I can find a box.

MRS TOYNBEE: All right. Get a box.

(*He goes out again. Uncomfortable pause.*)

LALAGE: How long do we have to wait?

BISHOP: Royalty are late on principle. I've stood in many
freezing places for a duke or duchess and never got a thank
you. Why don't we start? There is nothing so good for the
soul as the discovery you are dispensable.

BRIDE: We are sitting above men who knew that fact above
all other things. Their souls were near to perfect by that
reckoning...

PRINCE: (*Off.*) COO-EEE!

LALAGE: Would that be him?

HACKER: That's 'im, I know 'is voice, such as it is. Needs a
tannoy to be 'eard across a dinner table.

PRINCE: (*Coming in, followed by the GENTLEMAN.*) Good evening,
Mrs Toynbee... (*He removes his cap. He is wearing matching
cap and plus fours.*)

MRS TOYNBEE: Your Highness...

PRINCE: Brought George. Hope you don't mind. Got to bring
George. George is an equerry.

GENTLEMAN: Good evening, madam, gentlemen.

PRINCE: Want to do away with him, don't I, George? Will do,
in fact. Have a very modern monarchy. Where do I sit?

MRS TOYNBEE: There is a seat here.

HACKER: Next to Sylvia.

PRINCE: (*Sitting, as the GENTLEMAN takes the remaining seat.*)
Thrilled about this. Absolutely.

MRS TOYNBEE: You must believe.

PRINCE: Oh, yes.

MRS TOYNBEE: It's futile if you don't believe.

PRINCE: Believe anything you say.

MRS TOYNBEE: No, it has to be a positive belief.

PRINCE: Yes…

MRS TOYNBEE: Must trust.

PRINCE: W-w-will do, yes.

MRS TOYNBEE: Very well, then, place your fingers on the glass.

HACKER: Trod 'asn't come back yet.

PRINCE: Oh, let's begin! Please let's begin!

MRS TOYNBEE: Place your index fingers on the glass.

HACKER: Clout, I 'ope you're properly manicured for this.

MRS TOYNBEE: (*As they reach out.*) No talking. Everyone to close his eyes, and concentrate every ounce of mental energy upon the glass. Think. Just think. (*Long pause.*)

LALAGE: Nothing.

MRS TOYNBEE: Shh. (*Pause.*)

HACKER: Christ, my arm. (*Pause.*)

BRIDE: They will not speak to us. They will not demean themselves.

MRS TOYNBEE: Is there a spirit present?

PRINCE: Must be. This is Passchendaele!

BRIDE: They are present but they will not speak to us.

HACKER: Is it just me? My arm's like a –
(*Suddenly MRS TOYNBEE lets out a strange little cry.*)
What?
(*She shudders, breathing deep.*)
Sylvia.

PRINCE: I feel it!

HACKER: (*Eyes wide open.*) What? FEEL WHAT?

MRS TOYNBEE: Oh…oh…!

PRINCE: Oh, yes, I feel it!

LALAGE: The glass is perfectly stationary.

HACKER: (*On his feet now.*) FEEL WHAT EXACTLY?

PRINCE: OH!
(*He suddenly leaves the table, wanders a little way, clasping his face.*
The GENTLEMAN rises.)

MRS TOYNBEE: (*Opening her eyes.*) My God…

HACKER: What in Christ's name is all this?

MRS TOYNBEE: (*Going to the PRINCE OF WALES.*) It's all right… it's perfectly all right. This does happen. This is a phenomenon known as the surge.

HACKER: (*To the GENTLEMAN.*) Shouldn't you be seeing to 'im? Mr Equerry?

GENTLEMAN: (*Ineffectually.*) I think… I…

HACKER: Seeing as 'e's so 'orribly affected?

GENTLEMAN: I think… I…

HACKER: Seeing as being so near to Mrs Toynbee 'as spiritually buggered 'im?

MRS TOYNBEE: Would everybody just keep quiet?

HACKER: (*Helping himself.*) Whisky for you, Bishop? Doctor, or whatever. Keep the evil out of yer?

BISHOP: (*Taking it.*) I had no feeling. I had no feeling at all.

HACKER: No, well you wouldn't 'ave done. Nor did Clout 'ere. Nor anybody else, I think. But then look where we are sitting.

BISHOP: Too far from the source of –

HACKER: Much too far from the source, I'd say.

PRINCE: (*Returning to his seat.*) Extraordinary. Q-q-quite extraordinary.

LALAGE: It's awfully dull down here.

HACKER: 'ear, 'ear!

MRS TOYNBEE: Yes, well, perhaps you aren't good at giving yourself, dear.

LALAGE: That must be it.

PRINCE: Try again, shall we?

BRIDE: They will not speak with us. What can they tell us we could ever understand?

MRS TOYNBEE: Mr Bride, all over the world mothers and widows are seeking contact with their loved ones. They are doing this from Texas to the Urals.

BRIDE: We mock them with our curiosity.

MRS TOYNBEE: It is not curiosity! I have lost my son.

BRIDE: Lost, yes. There is no compromise with lost.

HACKER: Might I suggest we all change seats? Shuffle round a bit? Give the spirits a bit of variety?

MRS TOYNBEE: We are all talking too much. Close your eyes and –

HACKER: (*Jokingly.*) Clout, you bugger, you're asleep!

(*TROD comes in, holding an ammunition box.*)

TROD: You've started.

BRIDE: Here is a soldier. Here is a man who has seen the very bottom of the earth. If they will not talk to their brother, they will not talk to anyone.

(*He shifts along.*

TROD puts his box between BRIDE and the BISHOP.)

MRS TOYNBEE: (*To TROD.*) Will you ask, then? Ask for a spirit?

TROD: If you desire me…

PRINCE: We do desire you. I m-m-must tell you, I have not enjoyed an evening more in my whole life.

HACKER: I dread to contemplate your evenings, Mr Wales.

GENTLEMAN: He is not to be titled Mr Wales.

HACKER: Mr Prince, then, is it?

GENTLEMAN: It is nothing, or your Highness.

HACKER: Nothing or your Highness?

GENTLEMAN: I mean, no title, or –

PRINCE: Teddy.

GENTLEMAN: Yes.

MRS TOYNBEE: Can we get on?

TROD: (*Closing his eyes.*) Contemplate the dead. They are with us. Welcome them into your thoughts…

PRINCE: It's moving! Already, it's moving!

BRIDE: (*Appalled.*) THEY ALL WANT TO GET THROUGH!

MRS TOYNBEE: Somebody read!

BRIDE: OH, GOD!

LALAGE: (*Reading as the glass darts about.*) FRITZ IMMELMANN…

BRIDE: German!

LALAGE: WUR-TEM-BURG … REG-IMENT…

BRIDE: OH, GOD!

LALAGE: COR… PORAL… AGE… 19…

TROD: Have you a message for us, Corporal Immelmann?

LALAGE: Yes… SYL-VIA…

MRS TOYNBEE: Oh, God, it's the man who murdered my son! I'm going to faint… Teddy!

(*The* PRINCE OF WALES *puts an arm round her.*)

HACKER: Bloody 'ell...!

LALAGE: WOULD... LIKE... TO... KISS... YOUR... ARSE.

(*The glass stops.*)

HACKER: (*Getting up.*) Trod, you dirty little bleeder!

BRIDE: Sit down! Will you sit down!

PRINCE: Bit thick. Bit thick. I think...

HACKER: (*To* TROD, *who is shuddering in his seat.*) Murky young
    devil.

BRIDE: They revile us! We have offended them!

LALAGE: Perhaps we could break off now?

HACKER: Why not? My fingers are like ice. But then, I keep
    'em to myself, yer see.

(*Suddenly the glass shoots away again.*)

    I'm not on it!

PRINCE: Shut your eyes!

TROD: Read! Read!

LALAGE: BRIDE... HECTOR... BRIDE...

BRIDE: I hear you! I hear you!

LALAGE: WAIT-ING... FOR... YOU... COME... COME... Keeps
    saying come...

(*Suddenly the glass flies off the table.*)

HACKER: Woke you up, Clout!

LALAGE: Oh, the glass is broken...

PRINCE: (*Disappointed.*) No message for me, then...

HACKER: Not impressed by titles, are they? Probably
    Bolshevik spirits, fruit.

(BRIDE *gets up, and unnoticed, drifts out.*)

BISHOP: (*Getting up.*) I think we should call it a night, don't
    you?

LALAGE: (*Tying up her scarf.*) A silly ending to a silly day.

HACKER: Sylvia. I would like a word with you. In private.
    Please.

MRS TOYNBEE: Would somebody collect the cards?

HACKER: Sylvia, please?

(*There is a pistol shot.*
Everyone freezes.
Then there comes a terrible dejected moan.)

LALAGE: Somebody!

    (*No one moves, all horror-struck.*)

    Isn't anyone going to look?

    (*As no one moves, she hurries off.*)

PRINCE: I'm sorry, I – I never look at people who are hurt…

    (*MRS TOYNBEE hurries off after LALAGE.*)

    The war cripples… I could never visit them…

TROD: (*Still seated, gathering the cards.*) No more for tonight, I take it…

HACKER: (*Staggered.*) Christ, someone's dead!

    (*TROD just carries on.*)

    You khaki bloody maniacs. What 'ave you been up to out 'ere? Don't come 'ome. We don't want you.

    (*The WOMEN enter, supporting BRIDE between them. His head is draped in LALAGE's scarf.*)

    Oh, Christ…

MRS TOYNBEE: He seems to have missed. And got his eye.

HACKER: Oh, Bride, poor bloody Bride.

    (*They help him to a chair.*)

    Poor bloody Bride.

MRS TOYNBEE: It isn't helping, saying that.

HACKER: I 'ave to say it.

GENTLEMAN: Not exactly helping though, is it?

HACKER: IT'S 'ELPING ME!

LALAGE: Somebody's got to go for help. (*She looks at the GENTLEMAN.*) Will you?

GENTLEMAN: I am an Equerry.

LALAGE: All right, you are an Equerry!

GENTLEMAN: I'm not permitted to –

PRINCE: George has got to stay with me.

BISHOP: I'll go. (*He moves off, stops.*) If someone else went in the opposite direction –

LALAGE: Mr Hacker –

HACKER: Trod, you go.

LALAGE: (*Puzzled.*) Why don't you?

HACKER: 'e knows it round 'ere. It's 'is battlefield.

    (*TROD doesn't move.*)

LALAGE: (*Exasperated.*) I'll go.

HACKER: No need for that.

LALAGE: Evidently there is.

(*She goes out, left, the* BISHOP *right.*)

MRS TOYNBEE: (*To* HACKER.) Go with her, please.

HACKER: I'd rather not.

MRS TOYNBEE: WHY EVER WON'T YOU HELP THIS MAN!

HACKER: Why me? Why don't they go?

(*He indicates the* PRINCE OF WALES *and the* GENTLEMAN.)

If I've gotta go, why not them? Why can they stay 'ere and not me?

(*Pause. She looks at him.*)

All right!

(*He goes out, followed by* CLOUT.

The GENTLEMAN *sits down again.*

TROD *holds the cards.*)

TROD: My friend did that. The night before we broke their line. He didn't even say goodbye to me. He said if ever he went I was to expect him to appear to me, in the body of a sheep. (*Pause.*) When we got into their line I got lost. In the Hindenburg line. I was completely lost. I went down all these concrete steps. There was electric light on. It smelt damp. Down and down, I went, past all these sausages and pairs of boots. Millions of sausages. Millions of boots. I walked for half an hour, underground. Then I saw a mattress, and I fell asleep. When I woke up I was being nuzzled by a sheep. They kept animals down there, for fresh meat. (*Pause, then he buttons up his greatcoat. Turns to go. He looks at* MRS TOYNBEE *a moment.*) Your white widow's arse…

(*Pause. Then he goes out.*)

PRINCE: I wish I had been in the war. Then I might have said that. If you haven't been in the war, you cannot get away with that… (*He looks at* MRS TOYNBEE.) The number of times I have wanted to speak crudely to a woman… the crude things that have lingered on my lips… (*Pause.*) I w-w-would like you to be my mistress, please.

MRS TOYNBEE: There are times I don't think one discusses that sort of thing.

PRINCE: Such as?

MRS TOYNBEE: Such as Mr Bride is very ill…

PRINCE: It m-m-makes me more impatient. Can you
    understand that?

MRS TOYNBEE: Yes.

PRINCE: I have twelve castles. Say which one you want.

MRS TOYNBEE: I don't want a castle.

PRINCE: No, no. S-s-sorry. Some people do, though.

MRS TOYNBEE: Not me.

PRINCE: No.

    (*The* GENTLEMAN *lights a cigarette.*)

MRS TOYNBEE: (*Looking at* BRIDE.) I do think we should –

PRINCE: Can we settle this! (*Pause.*) S-s-sorry…

    (*She turns, looks at him for some time.*)

MRS TOYNBEE: All right. Yes.

PRINCE: Swear you love me.

MRS TOYNBEE: I said yes.

PRINCE: Say you wanted me from the day we met.

MRS TOYNBEE: Really, you're a little bit too forward.

PRINCE: GOT TO! GOT TO!

    (*She looks coolly at him.*)

MRS TOYNBEE: You are very childish, and very weak… I don't
    think you will make much of a king.

PRINCE: Poor old England. Rotten luck. (*Pause, then with
    desperation.*) I WANT TO F-F-F- (*He shuts his eyes in despair.*)
    – FUCK YOUR CUNT!
    (*He turns away, ashamed.
    MRS TOYNBEE goes to him, takes his hands.*)

MRS TOYNBEE: Don't be afraid, I desire you…
    (*She releases them, just as* HACKER *appears from the
    darkness.*)
    (*To* HACKER.) Have you found someone?
    (*Pause. He just looks at her.*)
    You never went.

HACKER: Why is it, I wonder, in this world, muck comes
    up tops? Why is it that the narky, dirty little corners
    of yer character are the places the truth chooses for its
    nest? When you look in the mirror of a bedtime and say,
    Hacker, you 'ave so much in you that I blush to recognise,

and the mirror says, yes, but without it you would be the fool of the universe… (*Pause.*) I didn't get to any 'ouse. Nor a telephone. I went a 'undred yards, and doubled back. I felt filth lying there behind them 'eadstones. Then I heard yer, and the 'ole bleeding world was the same filth. (*Pause.*)

PRINCE: If you will lie around eavesdropping –

HACKER: Shuddup.

PRINCE: No, I shan't shut up –

HACKER: SHUDDUP! (*He looks at him, for the first time.*) You thing. Pick a castle. Jesus Christ.

PRINCE: If you love someone you want to give them all you have. I happen to have Cornwall.

HACKER: Shut up. You will 'ave me in prison.

GENTLEMAN: Do bear that in mind. *Lèse majesté* and so on.

HACKER: Majesty? 'im? I would serve twenty years in Dartmoor before I took my 'at off to it. To think I bust my back, getting this finished, for you to mince in…

GENTLEMAN: This will be reported.

HACKER: Let it!

GENTLEMAN: Lose your contract, I'm afraid…

HACKER: RIDDANCE TO IT! (*Pause.*) England…what I would not 'ave done for that place once… (*Pause.*) No. Be honest, Hacker. Don't exaggerate. With Bride there, in that condition, must be honest, 'ard as it is. England, what I would not 'ave done for it on condition I wasn't out of pocket. You people turn patriots into spivs. (*He turns to GENTLEMAN.*) Is that sedition? Stick it down. (*He looks at MRS TOYNBEE.*) And for you…to think I would 'ave given two arms for a sniff of your knicker… (*Pause.*) And to be 'onest – as Bride is 'ere – I STILL WOULD! All the tricks I worked for you, and I could still treasure one of your muff 'airs in a tin!

MRS TOYNBEE: I promised I'd make love to you. If you insist on it, I'll stand by that.

(*Pause. HACKER is winded.*)

HACKER: (*Sarcastically.*) Well, there is honour for yer. There is cricket as ever was. She tips a fuck to me like dropping a porter 'alf a crown. (*Pause.*) I don't believe you 'ave a body. You 'ave a ready-reckoner bound in skin.

MRS TOYNBEE: We live as we must, don't we!

HACKER: I'm sorry, but I can't stand 'ere and not 'it back. I am no bloody gentleman, all 'andshakes and treachery. Give a bloke 'is dignity!

PRINCE: My fault. All this.

GENTLEMAN: Nonsense.

PRINCE: Mine entirely.

GENTLEMAN: (*Turning to him.*) Nothing can be your fault. It says so in the constitution.

PRINCE: IT IS MY FAULT!

(*The GENTLEMAN shrugs, turns back.*)

MRS TOYNBEE: (*To PRINCE OF WALES.*) I think it would be better if you went.

PRINCE: Never.

MRS TOYNBEE: Please. I'm asking you.

(*Pause. Then the PRINCE OF WALES kisses her hand and starts to leave. He turns to HACKER.*)

PRINCE: I don't think you should turn on England because of me…it's the hereditary system…spewed up me.

(*He goes out, followed by the GENTLEMAN.*
HACKER has not taken his eyes off MRS TOYNBEE.)

HACKER: If I was a gent, Mrs, I couldn't bring myself to do this. But they don't polish us in Peckham. I want you to know what hurt is, just like me. (*Eyes fixed firmly on MRS TOYNBEE.*) Billy ain't the corpse rattling on the royal train. So there. Under the drapes, behind the colour party's back, there lies the trunk of some obscure Kraut. Your boy never did show up. And never will.

MRS TOYNBEE: I fully understand your bitterness. I've hurt you and I suppose we shall always have to live with this dismal passion for revenge. You want to hurt me where I'll bleed the most. But there was a disc around his neck (*She takes it from her bosom.*) I wear it here.

HACKER: (*Appalled at her innocence.*) Alright, you have a disc! THEY JUST GOT 'OLD OF SOME OL' DISC! (*Pause.*)

MRS TOYNBEE: I am eternally grateful to you. In spite of everything.

HACKER: GRATEFUL? I 'AVE MADE A BERK OF YOU! (*He shakes his head in amazement.*) You people…yer gobs are clamped so tight on the tits of privilege, yer can't stop sucking even when the dugs are dry…

MRS TOYNBEE: That was my son. I knew it, the moment I knelt down to him. I knew it in my womb.

(*She goes out, watched by HACKER.*)

SCENE 3

Bright early morning. HACKER is discovered. He has not moved. CLOUT with two suitcases and HACKER's hat and coat.

CLOUT: Mr 'acker, we are going to miss the boat.

HACKER: Coming, Clout.

(*SOLDIERS enter whistling 'When Irish Eyes'. They cross the back of the stage.*
CLOUT assists HACKER into his hat and coat.)

RIDDLE: (*Stopping.*) Scuttling back to London with the profits, gentlemen?

HACKER: Well, at least we leave something behind us, don't we? Something to feast your eyes on. More than you lot did.

CLOUT: Mr 'acker!

HACKER: Coming!

(*CLOUT leaves.*)

I hear they've blown a lorry load of Tans to buggery. Enjoy your trip.

(*Exit RIDDLE whistling 'When Irish Eyes'.*
HACKER's gaze falls on MRS TOYNBEE's chair. Surreptitiously, with a glance over his shoulder, he examines the chair, then picking it up, he kisses the seat.)

Fuck it. I have the moral fibre of a rat…

(*He exits.*)